THE
CLAPHAM SECT

THE
CLAPHAM SECT

How Wilberforce's Circle
Transformed Britain

Stephen Tomkins

Copyright © 2010 Stephen Tomkins
This edition copyright © 2010 Lion Hudson
The author asserts the moral right
to be identified as the author of this work

A Lion Book
an imprint of
Lion Hudson plc
Wilkinson House, Jordan Hill Road,
Oxford OX2 8DR, England
www.lionhudson.com
ISBN 978 0 7459 5306 9

Distributed by:
UK: Marston Book Services, PO Box 269, Abingdon, Oxon, OX14 4YN
USA: Trafalgar Square Publishing, 814 N. Franklin Street, Chicago, IL 60610
USA Christian Market: Kregel Publications, PO Box 2607, Grand Rapids, MI 49501
First edition 2010
10 9 8 7 6 5 4 3 2 1 0

The text paper used in this book has been made from wood
independently certified as having come from sustainable forests.

A catalogue record for this book is available
from the British Library
Typeset in 10/12 Italian Garamond BT

Contents

Dramatis Personae: The Clapham Sect and Significant Supporters

First Generation

John BERRIDGE – vicar of Everton; friend of John Thornton

William BULL – Independent minister of Newport Pagnell; friend of John Thornton

William Legge, Lord DARTMOUTH – supporter of George Whitefield, John Newton, and Henry Venn

Selina Hastings, Lady HUNTINGDON – supporter of George Whitefield and Henry Venn

Martin MADAN – chaplain of the Lock Hospital, influential on John Thornton's conversion

John NEWTON – curate of Olney, rector of St Mary Woolnoth; paid and published by John Thornton

Thomas SCOTT – curate of Olney, chaplain of the Lock Hospital, rector of Aston Sandford; converted by Henry Venn and John Newton; favourite preacher of the Clapham sect; Church Missionary Society (CMS) secretary and tutor

John THORNTON – son of Robert, husband of Lucy, father of Henry; forefather of the Clapham sect

Lucy THORNTON – wife of John, mother of Henry

Eling VENN – wife of Henry, mother of John

Henry VENN – husband of Eling, father of John; curate of Clapham, rector of Huddersfield and Yelling

Elizabeth WILBERFORCE – mother of William and Sarah

Hannah WILBERFORCE, *née* Thornton – sister of John, aunt of William Wilberforce

Second Generation

Jean BABINGTON, *née* MACAULAY – sister of Zachary, wife of Thomas, mother of Tom

Thomas BABINGTON – husband of Jean, father of Tom; owner of Rothley Temple; abolitionist; MP

Thomas Fowell BUXTON – father of Priscilla; Wilberforce's chosen successor; abolitionist; MP

John CLARKSON – Thomas's brother; naval lieutenant; governor of Sierra Leone

Thomas CLARKSON – John's brother; founding member of Abolition Society, director of Sierra Leone Society and African Institution

William DAWES – astronomer and engineer at Botany Bay; governor of Sierra Leone

Edward ELIOT – Pitt's brother-in-law; lived in Broomfield on Thornton's estate; founding member of Bettering Society; MP

Mary GISBORNE, *née* BABINGTON – sister of Thomas, wife of Thomas

Thomas GISBORNE – husband of Mary; poet and moral philosopher

Charles GRANT – father of Charles and Robert; chairman of the East India Company; MP; lived in Glenelg on Thornton's estate

Selina MACAULAY, *née* MILLS – wife of Zachary, mother of Tom; pupil, employee, and friend of the More sisters

Zachary MACAULAY – husband of Selina, father of Tom, brother of Jean Babington; governor of Sierra Leone; editor of *Christian Observer* and *Anti-Slavery Reporter*; merchant

Selina MILLS – see MACAULAY

Hannah MORE – sister of Patty; founder and manager of schools; writer

Martha (Patty) MORE – sister of Hannah; founder and manager of schools

Granville SHARP – chairman of Abolition Society, founder of Province of Freedom, director of Sierra Leone Society and African Institution

James STEPHEN – husband of Nancy, then Sarah, father of George and James; abolitionist lawyer and writer; MP

Nancy (Anna) STEPHEN – first wife of James, mother of George and James

Sarah STEPHEN – see WILBERFORCE

Marianne SYKES – see THORNTON

John Shore, Lord TEIGNMOUTH – governor-general of British India; president of Bible Society

William Perronet THOMPSON – governor of Sierra Leone; general; MP

Henry THORNTON – son of John and Lucy, brother of Robert and Samuel, husband of Marianne, father of Marianne and Henry;

banker and economist; owner of Battersea Rise; chairman of Sierra Leone Company; MP

Marianne THORNTON, *née* SYKES – wife of Henry, mother of Marianne and Henry

Robert THORNTON – brother of Henry; MP

Samuel THORNTON – brother of Henry; MP

John VENN – son of Henry and Eling, father of Henry and Jane; rector of Little Dunham and Clapham; founding member of CMS

Kitty VENN, *née* KING – wife of John, mother of Henry and Jane

Barbara WILBERFORCE *née* SPOONER – wife of William, mother of William, Samuel, Robert and Henry

William WILBERFORCE – son of Elizabeth, nephew of Hannah, brother of Sarah, father of William, Samuel, Robert, and Henry; abolitionist, etc., etc.; MP

Sarah WILBERFORCE, later CLARKE, then STEPHEN – sister of William, second wife of James Stephen, stepmother of George and James

Third Generation

Thomas Gisborne (Tom) BABINGTON – son of Thomas and Jean; business partner of Zachary Macaulay

Priscilla BUXTON – daughter of Thomas; abolitionist

Charles GRANT – son of Charles, brother of Robert; Baron Glenelg; MP and Secretary of State for the Colonies

Robert GRANT – son of Charles, brother of Charles; MP; governor of Bombay

Thomas Babington (Tom) MACAULAY– son of Zachary and Selina; historian; poet; MP

George STEPHEN – son of James and Nancy, brother of James; solicitor; founder of Agency Committee

James STEPHEN – son of James and Nancy, brother of George, husband of Jane, *née* Venn; counsel to the Colonial Office, later Under-Secretary

Henry THORNTON – son of Henry and Marianne, brother of Marianne

Marianne THORNTON – daughter of Henry and Marianne, sister of Henry

Henry VENN – son of John and Kitty, brother of Jane; minister; secretary of CMS

Jane VENN, later STEPHEN – daughter of John and Kitty, sister of Henry, wife of James

William WILBERFORCE – son of William and Barbara; dairyman and debtor

Introduction

Before breakfast one morning in 1844, Sir James Stephen, the Under-Secretary of State for the Colonies and one of the more influential people in the British Empire, started dictating an article for the *Edinburgh Review* about his celebrated father and father-in-law and their circle. He thought he remembered one of their more outspoken opponents, Sydney Smith, mocking them in the *Review* as "the Clapham sect" and repeatedly referred to this in his article. In fact what Smith had called them was "the Clapham church" and "the patent Christians of Clapham", but Stephen had to get to the office and had no time to check. The editor was struck by the snappy phrase and used it as the title of the piece. And so, by misquotation and editorial headlining, the Clapham sect was created.

This leaves us with several questions about the Clapham sect: what, if anything, that name means; whether there was any such thing; when it existed, and where; and whom it involved. It was certainly not a sect in any modern sense of the word – all of its members were devoted sons and daughters of the Church of England. It was not an organization at all: the people we are talking about had an insatiable passion for forming societies and committees, but the Clapham sect was not one of them. Had they not been named by Stephen, it is unlikely that they would be remembered as anything more concrete than the various friends of William Wilberforce. What Stephen meant by "sect" was simply a group of friends who shared a particular religious outlook, in this case evangelical Anglican activism, but even then not all the people he lists as members of the circle were evangelicals, or even Anglicans. As for the "Clapham" part, half of the people Stephen lists never lived in the village or anywhere near it. Those who did overlapped for a relatively short period in which only some of the work for which they were famous was completed.

It is, in other words, not a perfect name. And yet there is a real and important entity behind it, however hard to pinpoint. There was, in the late eighteenth and early nineteenth centuries, a network of friends and families in England, with William Wilberforce as its centre of gravity, powerfully bound together by shared moral and spiritual values, by religious mission and social activism, by love for each other, and by marriage. Their greatest and most celebrated achievement was the abolition of the slave trade and then slavery itself throughout the British Empire and beyond. They were founders of the British colony of Sierra Leone, of schools, and of Christian missions, some of which continue today. A number were MPs and used their influence in Parliament to promote causes from prison reform to the protection of Sunday, and from peace to censorship. They tried to reform the Church of England, and achieved the moral transformation of Britain. They were pioneers of Victorianism and of Christian colonialism. They privately gave away extraordinary amounts of money to people in need.

All this was their faith. Their one overriding concern was to serve God, in their daily lives and their national and international campaigns. But to say this is emphatically not to say – as has been emphatically said, not least by Ford K. Brown in his seminal *Fathers of the Victorians* – that promoting evangelical Christianity was their one great cause to which all else was subservient.[1] Their campaigns were driven by two irreducibly separate religious motives: one, to promote true religion and save souls; the other, to make life better for people and to make the world a better place. Neither was merely the means to the other; both were essential; both were, as they understood it, the work of God.

The story of the Clapham sect is one of very public achievements, reaching across continents and far beyond their own lifetimes. But it is also a family saga. These were people for whom family and friendship were of the utmost importance: they lived in each other's spare rooms, married each other's brothers and sisters, prayed together, worked together, dreamed and schemed together, consoled each other, and criticized each other with ruthless honesty. Simply to tell the story of their work would be to miss a whole dimension of it.

The concept of the Clapham sect is perhaps too vague for any very emphatic delineation of who was in and who out, but I would include the following people and their families in a rough order of importance: William Wilberforce, Henry Thornton, Zachary Macaulay, James Stephen, Hannah More, John Venn, Thomas Fowell Buxton, Thomas Babington, Thomas Gisborne, Edward Eliot, Charles Grant, and Lord Teignmouth. Two people who are often listed that I would not include as members of the group are Granville Sharp and Thomas Clarkson. They played very important roles in the Clapham sect's most important campaigns, the fight against slavery and the founding of the Sierra Leone colony, but they were collaborators and not spiritual brothers, and for that reason they are part of the story but not part of the Clapham sect. Conversely, some of the generation of their parents, and of their children, were so intimately involved with them as to beg inclusion as virtual first and third generations of the Clapham sect. These include respectively John Thornton, Henry Venn, and John Newton; Marianne Thornton, Thomas Babington Macaulay, and George Stephen.

In any book like this, the sea of names makes great demands on the memory and patience of the reader. This particular one, covering three generations of the same families, in an age where parents tended to give their Christian names as well as surnames to their children, makes greater demands than most. Six generations of James Stephens get a mention. The Clapham sect added to this confusion by naming their children after each other as well as themselves: Thomas Gisborne Babington, Hannah More Macaulay, Thomas Babington Macaulay. For this reason, I have included a basic dramatis personae on page 7.

I wrote a biography of Wilberforce a few years ago, and this book of course overlaps with it considerably, but I have tried to repeat myself as little as possible for the sake of anyone who may have read the earlier book, while including everything necessary for those who have not yet had that pleasure. The story of the Clapham sect deserves to be told for their own sake, but it cannot be disentangled from that of Wilberforce.

I cannot thank James Stephen for the name. There are long sections of the book where it seems quite absurd, referring to a small group of friends who have almost nothing to do with Clapham. We are stuck with it though. They are sometimes called "the Saints", but in their own day at least the nickname was only applied to them as a group in Parliament and so does not fit those who were not MPs, and anyway is as vague as "the Clapham sect" is over-specific. That, for better or worse, is what they are called. What they actually were is a longer story.

PART ONE

FATHERS AND MOTHERS

The Thorntons

John Thornton was said to be the richest businessman in England. When he died in 1790, he left treasures on earth amounting to £600,000, according to his obituary in the *Gentleman's Magazine*, the equivalent of £45 million today, and his only equal in Europe was Henry Hope, the "merchant prince" of Amsterdam.

The figure is all the more remarkable considering that Thornton gave away £3,000 a year for fifty years of his life. He bought debtors out of prison and provided food and blankets for the poor in winter. He supported struggling ministers and missionaries and gave away tens of thousands of Bibles. For Thornton material generosity went hand in hand with spiritual outreach, the two great obligations of his life. He was not a powerful man, nor was he a preacher, but instead he spent thousands buying the rights to parishes so that he could appoint true "gospel ministers", and make his own contribution to "the rising tide of true religion", considering this a better harvest than mere money deserved. He lived a life of quite eccentric simplicity for a rich man, economizing so that he would have more to give to his mission. He never missed the chance to make a profit, but was equally determined that his wealth should benefit other people, materially and spiritually, and above all that it should save souls, throughout Britain and the world.

He was the Clapham sect in embryo.

Conversion

John was born in an old stone house beside Clapham Common, on 1 April 1720, his father having moved there from Hull where the Thorntons were a major trading family. Clapham was a wealthy village amid marshy grazing land four miles from Westminster Bridge on the road to Epsom, its roads often impassable in winter and a haunt of bandits. It was popular with successful London merchants, accessible to the City but distant enough to be a country retreat. Samuel Pepys had lived there, as had the Bishop of Exeter.

The Thornton family had made their fortune in Russian trade, importing timber, pig iron, flax, yarn, fur, spice, and wax from the Baltic, selling in return cloth, metals, herring, glassware, and cutlery. John's grandfather had a trading house in Hull, which in 1732 passed to their cousins the Wilberforces, another leading family of Russia merchants – it was the birthplace of William Wilberforce and is now the Wilberforce House museum. John's father Robert was a director of the Bank of England as well as a merchant, though John himself was never interested in banking. Otherwise though, he went about his father's business, often overseas, going to Riga for two years at the age of twenty-one. In time he became a member, then consul, then assistant of the Russia Company. According to his son Henry's memoir, he did not by then want to become a governor of the Company because he had become serious about religion and objected to the unsavoury toasts and songs he would have had to hear at their public dinners. John inherited partnerships in factories near Hull, and in 1755 he joined Benjamin Pead in opening an oil mill in London containing Britain's first major soap works, an industry slowly being learned from the Dutch. He owned shares in the Bank of England, the East India Company, and the South Sea Company, and made £13,000 from insuring New York companies.

There was no very remarkable amount of religion or charity in John's upbringing, but around the age of thirty he fell for Lucy Watson, a popular woman in her thirties from Hull. It was one of the many marriages that interwove the great merchant families of the city, Lucy being the heiress of Alderman Samuel Watson, a sometime partner of the Thorntons and Wilberforces. At first Lucy refused John on the grounds of religious differences, but he persisted and finally married her, "after many years of ineffectual endeavour" as Henry put it, on 28 November 1753.[1]

One religious difference that had obstructed their marriage was that the Watsons were Dissenters and the Thorntons belonged to the Church of England – although in later life John had vastly more sympathy for Dissenters than most in his own church and often went to their services. The other problem was that John simply did not yet take God seriously enough for Lucy. She was a spiritual woman, very active in providing for the poor in the area. Every new year she wrote a pious review of the year, "that my heart may be suitably affected with the blessings I have received, humbled under a sense of my ingratitude for them, and stirred up to more active services". Henry tells us she did not think John "a sufficiently religious character" yet, and a few years into their marriage she was writing to him about his laxness in "the duty of secret prayer".[2]

John became an evangelical Christian in the first year of their marriage, according to his friend Henry Venn, the evangelical curate of Clapham church.[3] Before then, John had been arrogantly resolute to win Lucy around to his own conventional Anglicanism according to their son's report: his opinions were "crude", his way of arguing for them "harsh", and in the end it was he who shifted. From then on, John more and more exhibited the spirituality of his wife. During that first year of marriage Lucy was dangerously ill for some months, and if this drove John into a period of spiritual searching, he would have been following a common pattern.

Lucy clearly had a hand in John's religious development. The credit for his conversion is usually shared between Martin Madan, the 28-year-old chaplain of the Lock Hospital at Hyde Park Corner, the first venereal disease clinic, and Henry Venn of Clapham, but if a sermon or buttonholing from such preachers provided a turning point in his spiritual life, the sustained example and exhortations of his sweetheart, then wife – however reluctant he was to learn from her – were clearly important too.

The Evangelical Revival

The evangelical revival was about fifteen years old in Britain by this point – twenty in North America. It was already a diverse, many-headed movement, but what all its preachers had in common is that they believed the mass of church-goers were Christians in name only. They insisted, on the one hand, that they must turn from their sin, be born again with "a new nature", embrace "vital Christianity" and lead radically holy lives. And on the other hand – paradoxically, but equally passionately – they insisted that no human can possibly be holy enough to satisfy God: it is only Christ's self-sacrifice on the cross that can satisfy God, and we are saved simply by "trusting in his blood". Any hope of heaven through merely being good is damnable nonsense, they said: we are saved by faith alone.

This message was thoroughly controversial in itself for British society, but it was made more outrageous by being preached not just from pulpits but in fields and market squares, bowling-greens, and brickyards, to crowds of thousands. It looked dangerously subversive. The great crowd-pullers were John Wesley and George Whitefield, who had both been ordained in the Church of England, but had no parishes and generally found themselves unwelcome in other men's churches, so simply toured the country preaching wherever they could gather hearers. The meetings were often set upon by mobs – and the preachers and their followers were then blamed for the disorder. Wesley organized his converts into a network of local societies for preaching, worship, and pastoring, which looked suspiciously like a new sect of Dissenters, although he insisted that they stay in the established church. Whitefield offended respectable tastes with his histrionic preaching – even Thornton lamented his many "wildnesses" – while Wesley's preaching had been known to provoke wailing, convulsions, and all kinds of charismatic phenomena. It was all horrifically reminiscent of the religious fanatics who a hundred years before had killed the King and dismantled the state.

Meanwhile, there were others who agreed with the evangelical message but did not see the need to spread it in such a contentious way. A small but growing number of evangelical ministers had parishes and other posts in the Church of England. There was no completely clear division between these regular ministers and the itinerant preachers, especially at first – Venn, though a parish incumbent, often left Clapham for outdoor preaching tours, though he is said (questionably) by his more conservative son to have repented later – but in retrospect we tend to call the regular ministers and their followers "evangelical Anglicans" and the others "Methodists". The word "Methodist" had no such precise meaning at the time, and the other term was not in existence, but "Methodist" being a term of abuse eventually became attached to the more disreputable group.

Evangelicalism had a passion that no other British religion of the time shared. The two great outward channels of that passion, as exemplified by Thornton, were evangelism and social action, saving souls and bodies. The logic of the first is obvious: nominal Christians stood on the brink of eternal hellfire, and no effort could be spared to turn them back. Not all could be preachers, but all had a part to play.

The logic of evangelical social action is less obvious. In many ways evangelicalism was extremely other-worldly: the body is for a moment, the soul forever, so believers were expected to rejoice when loved ones went to heaven, and to despise earthly reputation and pleasure. And yet many were zealously committed to social action from the start, founding schools, orphanages, and medical dispensaries. In part, this was precisely because they believed in holding their earthly wealth lightly and so were willing to share it. In another part, it was because evangelicals were creatures of the Enlightenment and so believed that God gave us a world to be improved, not just conserved. But evangelical social action was above all

– paradoxically – an outworking of the belief that we are saved by faith in Christ's sacrifice and not by our own deeds. This belief meant that costly mercy is God's most important attribute, and so gratefully forwarding it is essential to being his child. It meant that believers had passed from infinite darkness to perfect light, and so should be able to point to an observable change in the world as a result. And it meant that, though it is easy to become a child of God, it is impossible to be a good enough person – there is always some good that remains to be done.

It was certainly not true that evangelicals saw helping people materially as a mere back door to saving their souls. As John Thornton's son Henry said of his father's giving, "a part was subservient to the cause of the Gospel", but "a large part of this sum was to those who had no other claim on his *funds* than that of compassion".[4]

Philanthropy: Sailors and Magdalens

John Thornton's earliest known charity work began in 1756, as a founder member of the Marine Society. This somewhat equivocal philanthropy was the brainchild of his fellow Russia Company merchant Jonas Hanway, devout Christian, travel writer and the first man in London to carry an umbrella. The idea, set out in the society's advertisement, was for "stout lads" to be "handsomely clothed and provided with bedding", and put "on board his Majesty's ships, with a view to learn the duty of a seaman". In other words, it was a scheme to provide more sailors for the Seven Years' War. The society provided over 10,000 recruits, and its provision of new clothes is said to have reduced typhus. A million people died in the course of the war, which made Britain the greatest colonial power in the world. "What a year of slaughter has this been," reflected Lucy Thornton in 1757. "Why is my happy lot in England, rather than America, India or Germany? Why does our selves, our houses, our substance escape the victor's fury, but because our good God delights in and over us?" Another benefit of having God on their side was that John was destined to make large profits from lending to the government to finance the war, and from handling government payments to Russia. He was now "very rich", reported the politician James West, "in great credit and esteem, and of as much weight in the City as any one man I know".[5]

In 1758, Thornton and Hanway became founder members of the Magdalen Society, led by another Russia merchant, Robert Dingley, to give prostitutes a new start. They bought a house in London where over a hundred could live at once, paid for treatment at the Lock Hospital, provided clothes, taught the illiterate girls to read, helped them find new work, and gave them some money toward a new life. By 1765, 683 girls had come to the house, and 308 had found jobs or been reconciled to their families.

Thornton supported the evangelical mission to England by letting Whitefield preach from his house. More directly, he paid to have Bibles printed and used Russia Company ships to send them abroad. Later he extended this enterprise, sending free Bibles and other religious books to the Caribbean and Australia, as well as around Britain, at a cost of £2,000 a year according to the *Gentleman's Magazine*. In November 1779, he helped found what became the Naval and Military Bible Society, to give pocket Bibles to soldiers and sailors in the American War of Independence, on the suggestion of one of his alms distributors. By the time of Trafalgar, twenty-six years later, the society had handed out 43,000 Bibles. It continues today as the Naval, Military, and Air Force Bible Society.

Lucy's records of the early years of their marriage mention arduous journeys and long illnesses. At the age of thirty-four, she noted in herself the "loss of teeth, alteration of shape, some grey hairs, a faded complexion, a feebler memory, drowsiness and many other infirmities". Meditating on the prospect of death, she considered how she would live in the memory of relatives; "but in a few years even this imaginary living is also over, and perhaps it will never be known but upon old parchment or in a register that Lucy Thornton ever lived. Vain world farewell, then, my home is not here." To leave something to the future, she resolved at new year 1758: "to make the cultivating my children's minds a great part of my employment, and [I] would reckon no time better spent".[6]

John and Lucy's youngest child, Henry, who would gather the Clapham sect, was born in 1760. They now had four surviving children: Samuel was seven, Jane five and Robert one. Lucy persuaded John, against his inclination, to have the house extended and redecorated, and enlarge the grounds until they were nearly two miles round, with deer in a paddock. "Mrs Thornton…" Wilberforce recalled, "had somewhat of a turn for the splendid in all particulars."

American Friends: Mohegan Missionary and Slave Poet

Coming at the dawn of the colonial era, the evangelicals were from the start enthusiastic about mission overseas, as well as to "the heathen of England". Wesley had started his career as a missionary to Native North Americans. Thornton became involved in the same mission in 1766, after the Mohegan convert Samson Occom visited him on a fundraising tour of Britain. Occom was collecting for Moore Charity School in Lebanon, New

Hampshire, where Native American children were taught Christianity, farming, and ancient Greek and Hebrew. He stayed at Thornton's, finding him "the right sort of Christian and a very charitable man".[7] Each was impressed by the other, and Thornton gave Occom £100, promising to use his influence in the cause. Occom met George III who gave him £200, and he made a wide enough impact to be lampooned on the London stage. He collected £12,026 from 2,000 givers, which was kept in trust with Thornton as the treasurer, and the Earl of Dartmouth – one of a handful of evangelical peers – as president.

Soon trouble came though. The school was run by Eleazar Wheelock, a Congregationalist minister, and the year after Occom returned from his fundraising tour Wheelock turned the mission school into a college for white boys. He had taught thirty-five Native American boys and ten girls, plus a number of white boys, expecting all of them on graduating to spread Christianity and white culture among the indigenous people. "I have taken much pains to purge the Indian out of him," he said of Occom, "but after all a little of it will sometimes appear."[8] Wheelock never repeated the success he had had with the fervent Occom, his first pupil, so he decided to divert his energies into teaching white boys who could then go among the Native North Americans as evangelists. His college charter was granted by the state governor on 13 December 1769, and, perhaps trying to placate the English trustees of the charity school, he named it Dartmouth College, after Lord Dartmouth, the president of the board. This is the same Dartmouth College that is today an Ivy League university.

The board, who had not been consulted, were dismayed. Thornton spoke for them all when he told Wheelock, "I am afraid the step you have taken to get a charter will prove the ruin of your school to all valuable purposes... As soon as it takes place I shall be very ready to relinquish any further say in the affair."[9] He told him a parable of a paper kite which in its pride wants to fly free like an eagle and so falls into the sea.

Wheelock assured the trustees that the college would do nothing without their approval, Thornton ensured that the funds raised by Occom were not used for the college but only for teaching natives, while also promising to give Wheelock money for the college personally, and they remained on good terms. Thornton sent Wheelock a carriage, offered to pay for his house, and was his main provider for years, spending on him, all in all, a thousand pounds.

Thornton also made peace when Wheelock and Occom fell out soon after Occom's return from Britain. Wheelock accused Occom of becoming haughty and rude after his experience of celebrity in England, of taking overpayment, and of drunkenness. Occom claimed that after using him to raise funds, Wheelock had abandoned him to grinding poverty and debt, with ten children and constant visitors to look after. Thornton took Occom's side and repeatedly wrote to Wheelock on his behalf, sending Occom £50 of his own money to help him pay his debts, and arranging a £50 salary from the trust.

Another unexpected friend and protégé of Thornton's in New England was the slave poet Phillis Wheatley. She was owned as a domestic servant by the evangelical Susannah Wheatley of Boston, whose husband was Thornton's American agent. Just seven years after coming to Boston from Gambia, Phillis was writing English poetry, and she published *Poems on Various Subjects* seven years later, in 1773, an unprecedented achievement for a slave, causing a sensation on both sides of the Atlantic. She published it in London, on a visit where she stayed with the Thorntons, enjoying long discussions with the teenagers Robert and Henry. John had already been sending her spiritual letters, and they kept up their correspondence when she returned home. "She is a blessed girl," he told John Newton.

When Susannah died, Phillis told Thornton that she was free but had lost her best friend. He offered to be her new mentor, and asked her to join a missionary expedition to Africa. She declined: westernized and unable to speak the language, she said, "how like a barbarian should I look to the natives".[10] Unprovided for either by the Wheatley family or by Thornton, she married a freed slave who ended up in debtors' prison. She returned into service and was buried in an unmarked grave in 1784.

Debt Relief

Thornton's failure to help Wheatley is all the more marked by the fact that he was a founder member and vice-president of the Society for the Discharge and Relief of Persons Imprisoned for Small Debts, established in February 1772. He considered it unjust and unreasonable that someone could be gaoled simply for running up a couple of pounds' debt, especially when this only made it harder to repay. So the society raised funds to buy debtors' freedom. In the first eleven years, they freed 7,743 debtors, each owing less than £10, plus wives and children locked up with them – their records count 26,707 people affected altogether. They paid out a total of more than £17,000 in that time, an average debt of about £2 4s. Thornton personally gave £109 a year to the fund. In 1829, Joseph Hume MP told Parliament that the Small Debt Society had bought the release of 43,399 debtors in the previous year.

The society lobbied, without success, for a change in the debt laws, which, they argued, "are enormous, absurd, irrational, and injurious to the state, the debtor and the creditor, enriching only pettifoggers, bailiffs, and jailers, who generally are the worst, meanest, and most detestable of men". Their giving came with sermonizing. In a foretaste of Victorian charity, which owed so much to the Clapham sect, each freed man was given a tract telling him, "it is your duty to be THANKFUL". "You cannot fail to offer up your fervent and constant prayers for the humane imparters of [this charity], and to show yourself worthy of their pity, and their bounty." Readers were told to decide whether it was wickedness or foolishness that had got them into trouble, and either way to amend. They were urged to sobriety, industry, honesty, and charity, and to make the gospel "your study, your delight, and your practice".[11]

Thornton helped establish two evangelical colleges in Britain. In 1768, he contributed £1,000 to the Countess of Huntingdon's Trefeca College in Breconshire, for the training of Methodist ministers. Then, in 1782, he put up most of the money for a Dissenting Academy, the Newport Pagnell Evangelical Institution for the Education of Young Men for the Christian Ministry, proposed by John Newton, and run by their friend the Independent minister William Bull. From 1787, Thornton paid all expenses of the academy himself, continuing to do so through a legacy for twenty-four years after his death.

John Newton

Probably Thornton's greatest passion was getting diligent, upright, evangelical ministers into parishes. He used whatever influence he had to recommend people, but increasingly found that his reputation as a "Methodist" did them more harm than good. "I am a speckled bird," as he put it, "and so well known as such that too oft my interference has been a bar." So instead he simply bought up advowsons (the right to appoint the minister of a given parish) himself, accumulating eleven altogether, from Yorkshire to Cornwall. "If you hear of any advowsons or presentations to be sold in useful spots," he told one contact, "with incumbents above fifty or sixty [years old], I should be glad to lay out a few thousands that way. I don't care how small if there are many hearers."[12] He also toured the country himself to find promising parishes.

The most influential of these appointments was John Newton, whom Thornton brought from Olney in Buckinghamshire to St Mary Woolnoth in London. Newton had a colourful past. After following his austere father's footsteps into the merchant navy, he was press-ganged into the Royal

Navy, deserted and was recaptured. Swinging between piety (brought on by brushes with death) and proselytizing antichristianity, he took up the slave trade, but ended up as a virtual slave himself on Plantain Island, off Sierra Leone, where he survived on wild roots, was stoned (literally), and taught himself geometry. He was converted in 1748 by reading Thomas à Kempis and by further narrow escapes from death – and then became a slave ship captain, continuing until 1753 when he had to take an onshore post after having a fit. In 1750, aged twenty-four, he married Mary Catlett, with whom he had been in love for seven years. He tried to enter the church, but was turned down, not having been to university. For nine years, he preached excitingly autobiographical sermons to Dissenting congregations, until a minister asked him to set down his story in a series of letters. These came into the hands of Lord Dartmouth, who persuaded a bishop to ordain him in 1764, and bought the curacy at Olney for him.

It paid very little money, but John told Mary, "By one means or other the Lord will give us comfortable provision which I cannot, dare not doubt."[13] The means was John Thornton. After reading his autobiography in 1764, Thornton wrote to him with a deal, which Newton readily accepted: "Be hospitable and keep open house for such as are worthy of entertainment. Help the poor and needy. I will statedly allow you £200 a year, and readily send you whatever you have occasion to draw for more." Thornton paid him throughout his years at Olney, and Newton wrote to him every fortnight with his news and reflections. Newton told William Bull that he had spent £2,000 of Thornton's money on the poor in fifteen years, much of it going to lacemakers hit by unemployment. Newton also suggested further ways in which Thornton might help people – money for a struggling Baptist minister, doctor's fees for a young man with tongue cancer, intervention for a man condemned to death. Mary Newton ran a free medical dispensary, for which Thornton provided the medicines. He gave £200 a year to Newton's close friend the (so far unpublished) poet William Cowper to allow him to stay in Olney, and helped finance the publication of his *Iliad* and *Odyssey*. Thornton suggested the pair of them produce a hymn-book, *Olney Hymns*, which he financed, publishing for the first time such works as "Glorious Things Of Thee Are Spoken", "O! For A Closer Walk With God" and "Amazing Grace". He had other books of Newton's printed including *Omicron Letters*.

In 1777, Thornton wrote offering Newton a living in Hull, which he would have accepted, he later told Hannah More, but someone forgot to post the letter. Instead Thornton brought him to London in 1780, giving him a better income and a larger audience, and he increasingly found himself the most influential evangelical parish minister in Britain. Newton called Thornton his best friend, saying, "It was a pleasure to me if I only saw him passing by." Speaking for his wife, Newton said, "She revered and regarded him, I believe, more than she did any person upon earth, and she had reason."[14]

Beyond the numbers of those who were touched by Thornton's philanthropy and mission during his lifetime, several things about his lasting influence are clear. First, it was his religion that Henry Thornton and Wilberforce and friends practised in the Clapham sect. The activism, the giving, the society-founding, the mission at home and abroad, the commitment to evangelizing the church itself: these were learned from John Thornton. Secondly, like few others of his generation he gave them the model for a lay middle-class evangelicalism, showing them that they did not need to give up secular trades and positions and become preachers of the gospel in order to advance the cause, but could be as influential and more where they were. Thirdly, by the later years of his life there were an estimated forty to fifty evangelical clergy in the Church of England, including ten of his own appointments, others he helped to get in place, and still others he supported financially, allowing them to take small livings that would otherwise have been inadequate. So, on the one hand, a significant part of the foothold that the movement had in the church was due to him, but, on the other hand, set against the 13,500 clergy in the church as a whole, the foothold was thin and precarious. The evangelical gospel had gained ground since the 1740s, and was no longer seen by the educated classes as a terrifying force to be fought with physical violence, having tended to feed, educate, and placate the poor rather than inspire them to rebellion. But it was still utterly peripheral to British religion, a fringe if no longer a lunatic one. Thornton had achieved everything that could be expected of a man with no power or position beyond that of mere money, but the next generation found themselves in a position to take his campaign onto a totally new scale and into the heart of the political nation.

In *Fathers of the Victorians*, Ford K. Brown wrote off the first generation of evangelical mission as a colossal well-meaning failure, despite the scores of thousands of converts, because they wasted their energy preaching to "miner, orange-girl or cobbler" when the ruling classes would have provided much more useful converts. This judgment was based on the groundless assumption that what the evangelicals really wanted – or perhaps should have wanted – was not to save individual souls but the moral and ecclesiastical reform of the nation. This assumption is unfair either way, but, questions of failure and folly aside, Brown was absolutely right in pointing out an enormous difference between the Clapham sect and their predecessors in the means they used for promoting the gospel and human happiness.

Holy Trinity, Clapham

One more contribution of John Thornton's deserves mention, which is the building of Holy Trinity Church, Clapham, in 1775. A trust, of which Thornton was treasurer, got an Act of Parliament passed in 1774 giving permission for the existing church to be replaced, and the new Holy Trinity was opened in 1776. It was large and plain, to suit evangelical sensibilities; "an ugly, square, comfortable building…" according to a Victorian critic, "built in an age when church architecture had reached its lowest depth". The pews and galleries were made from imported oak, "so that all British oak might be saved for the building of ships".[15]

"I expect when it is finished to put in a rector," Thornton told Newton, "and then the tables will be turned."[16] In fact, the existing rector, Sir James Stonhouse, stayed for the rest of Thornton's life, and it was Thornton's sons who appointed his replacement, bringing back the Venn family, in the person of Henry's son John.

The Venns

Henry Venn was the new 29-year-old curate of Holy Trinity, Clapham, when he played his part in John Thornton's conversion. The respectable Venn family claimed an unbroken line of clergy going back to the reformation, an upbringing which hardly inclined Henry toward evangelicalism: his father Richard, as the rector of St Antholin's, was the first minister in London to forbid George Whitefield to preach in his church. (Charles Wesley once managed to preach there in the rector's absence, after denying he was a Methodist.) Henry himself as a child so bullied an older boy on his street for being the son of a Dissenting minister that the boy was scared to leave home; and he told a Dissenting visitor to the rectory, "I will not come near you; for you are an Arian." Henry was a driven child. He once felt so jealous of his elder brother being praised for his Latin, it was said, that he had a fit. At the age of eight, picking up on the unpopularity of Walpole's 1733 excise bill, he spent the whole day of the debate walking the streets crying "No excise" until he lost his voice.

He was ordained on 17 June 1747 while still a student at Jesus College, Cambridge, combining his studies with a curacy at the village of Barton. He was one of the best cricketers at Cambridge, but a week before his ordination, after playing for Surrey against All England, he gave his bat to the first comer, believing cricket to be unsuitable for a conscientious man of the cloth. "I am to be ordained on Sunday," he explained; "and I will never have it said of me 'Well struck, parson.'" Despite his life of rigorous self-denial, he was said to be a friendly young man of high spirits and a great storyteller.[1]

On graduation he served at St Matthew's, Friday Street, in London in the summer and West Horsley in Surrey in the winter. He was a popular minister, and attendance at communion rose fivefold in his time at West Horsley, though (perhaps not unconnected) he was less popular with other clergy.

Like John Wesley, Venn read William Law's *A Serious Call to a Devout and Holy Life* and came away with a powerful sense of his sinfulness and need for God. Like Wesley he fought to live up to this standard of holiness, keeping a journal of his hourly successes and failures, and eventually turned to the evangelical idea of justification by faith, seizing it as a liberating relief. Henry's son John tells us that his conversion was not the result of being persuaded by anyone, because he knew no other evangelicals, but simply came from his own reading of the Bible. From his letters though, it is clear that he had read and been moved by Wesley's writings, so it seems unlikely that they had no influence on him. The fact is that John Venn was at pains to make his father's memory as respectable as possible, passing in complete silence over his very extensive collaboration with Methodist leaders such as George Whitefield. The mission of the Clapham sect depended on wooing a dubious ruling class, and any connection to such controversial characters as Wesley or Whitefield seemed to John to call for less than complete frankness.

Clapham and Touring with Whitefield

Shortly after his conversion in 1754, Henry Venn came to Clapham as curate to the absentee rector Sir James Stonhouse, who lived on his family estate in Berkshire. Venn was rather anxious about preaching his new evangelical message in such a well-heeled and respectable neighbourhood, "where many London merchants", he said, "having acquired fortunes, chose their country seats, desiring in general, only to enjoy themselves". Would he have the courage to tell the grand people he lived among and depended upon that they were mere lost sinners? He wrote a starstruck letter to Wesley saying he had found his writings "to be as thunder to my drowsy soul" and "begging you would send me a *personal* charge, to take heed to feed the flock committed to me", suggesting a biblical text that Wesley might use, and how he expected him to interpret it. No reply from Wesley survives.[2]

Venn overcame his awe of those wealthy parishioners, and found that, as he had suspected, "the doctrine of the Gospel preached with zeal and boldness was very offensive" to them.[3] He was a hard worker, preaching weekly in three London churches as well as twice a week in Clapham. One of these churches was St Antholin's, where he preached the message his late father had stopped Whitefield preaching. And yet, whatever part he played in John Thornton's conversion, it seemed at the time an isolated and not especially significant exception to a general sterility, and he had to go further afield before he saw fruits from his work.

Venn attended Wesley's annual conference for Methodist preachers and his fellow ministers in 1756, but afterwards became closer to Whitefield. After a serious illness, he stopped repeating old sermons and started preaching extempore – he is said to be the first English parish minister to do so. That year Whitefield started visiting Clapham to share Venn's pulpit and to preach at John Thornton's house, and in September 1757 Venn joined Whitefield and others in a preaching tour of the west country, where they were guests of the Earl of Dartmouth in Cheltenham and the Countess of Huntingdon in Bristol.

The evangelical revival appealed across all the rigid class barriers of eighteenth-century Britain. The morality of evangelicalism was famously well suited to the rising middle class: sobriety, hard work, thrift, charity, and (paradoxically, considering the indecorum of the religion itself) respectability. But the evangelists also had a huge response from even the poorest and roughest working communities, such as the miners of Bristol, the Welsh valleys, Newcastle, and Cornwall. And the movement had two very influential leaders among the aristocracy in the shape of the Earl of Dartmouth and the Countess of Huntingdon.

Dartmouth opened his house in Cheltenham for public sermons after his chaplain Downing was banned from preaching in the parish church, and Venn, Madan, and Whitefield came to contribute. Venn reports a sermon of Whitefield's to a vast crowd in the parish churchyard:

> *His words seemed to cut like a sword upon several in the congregation, so that whilst he was speaking they could no longer contain, but burst out in the most bitter piercing cries. At this juncture Mr Whitefield made an awful pause of a few seconds – then burst into a flood of tears. During this short interval, Mr Madan and myself stood up, and requested the people as much as possible to restrain themselves from making any noise.*[4]

Afterwards, Venn and Madan went around talking to listeners about what they had heard.

Whitefield was thrilled by Venn's preaching: "The worthy Venn is valiant for the truth – a son of thunder," he told Lady Huntingdon. "He labours abundantly, and his ministry has been owned of the Lord in the conversion of sinners. Thanks be to God for such an instrument as this to strengthen our hands!" Huntingdon herself, one of the spikier characters of the evangelical movement, was more critical when she heard him ("My dear friend, no longer let false doctrine disgrace your pulpit"), but then plain speaking was one of the evangelicals' most important values. "When we lose our plainness, there ends the Christian." Their letters to each other are often full of criticism, which, as in this case, usually received hearty thanks.[5]

Venn made this preaching excursion as a newly wed, having married Eling Bishop, the daughter of a Suffolk rector, on 10 May 1757. Eling's father died when she was thirteen and left them poor, despite having had four livings. She had the kind of upbringing that evangelicals considered more Anglican than Christian, but it was shaken by a book she read to prepare for her first communion on her twenty-first birthday. Shocked by how serious the occasion was, she had a nightmare about trying to reach the body of Jesus floating on flood waters, only to be told, "It is the body of Jesus, but not for you." She woke screaming and was oppressed by the dream for years. After her mother died, Eling worked as a dressmaker in Teddington, where Henry met her eight years later.

The following summer, 1758, Venn took part in more aristocratic evangelistic meetings, in the Countess of Huntingdon's London house. Venn, Madan, and William Romaine, the only evangelical parish clergyman in London as yet, led prayers and preached there regularly, taking over from Whitefield – whose converts there had included George Lyttelton, the future Chancellor of the Exchequer. This prompted Horace Walpole to warn a friend: "If you ever think of returning to England, as I hope it will be long first, you must prepare yourself with Methodism, I really believe that by that time it will be necessary; this sect increases as fast as almost ever any religious nonsense did."[6] Evangelicals saw these "spiritual routs" ("rout" meaning a "riotous assembly") as an exciting campaign for a more godly ruling class who would lead the nation back to the Lord. The first generation did not overlook the value of appealing to the influential when they had the chance.

At home in Clapham, Venn's congregation was far from enthusiastic about his teachings. One woman asked Eling "to repress the disgusting earnestness of her husband". He was a good man, she said, but too extreme, and his sermons alarmed people, which was folly when he was financially dependent on their friendship. Eling replied that her husband was only dependent on one friend: "for the Master Mr Venn serves is too great and too good ever to see him or his real losers for faithfulness in his own service".[7]

It was not the kind of reassurance that the villagers were after. The friction and fruitlessness continued – doubly disheartening for Henry and Eling, considering how well he was received elsewhere in the country.

They already had a baby girl, Eling, and then John was born, and they were counting the farthings. If they were not to be real losers something needed to change. Henry mentioned the problem to Lord Dartmouth, who found him a new curacy at Huddersfield in Yorkshire.

And so in 1759, "grieved at the obstinate rejection of the gospel during five years by almost all the rich (and there were but few poor in the place)", Venn says, "I accepted a living unexpectedly offered to me by my very affectionate friend, the Earl of Dartmouth."[8] He shook the dust off his shoes and left Clapham.

Darkest Huddersfield

Huddersfield was a rapidly growing industrial town of 5,000 people, the first industrial parish to have an evangelical rector and, along with Samuel Walker's Truro, one of only two large evangelical parishes in the country. Venn was building on the achievements of Wesley, who had visited and founded a Methodist society two years before, saying: "A wilder people I never saw in England. The men, women and children filled the streets and seemed just ready to devour us."[9]

Venn was immediately popular, drawing crowds from around the region, so that at one early service he reckoned his congregation exceeded 3,000, "and the power of the Lord was present". And yet he was miserable there. He had expected a drop in income to be balanced by the lower cost of living, but in fact his income was worse than halved, leaving him dependent on the donations of distant friends. "Unbelief, pride, and selfishness conquered me entirely," he recalled, and he decided to return to London while his midweek preaching posts in the City were still open to him. It was Eling, reluctant though she had been to go to Huddersfield, who persuaded Henry to stay and fulfil his duty.

Their sacrifice proved worthwhile, because, as Henry told John Newton, 900 people were converted by his preaching there. Their daughter Eling reminisced about the constant stream of wool workers coming to the door: "I remember the look of many of them to this day, with channels upon their black cheeks, where tears were running. 'Oh, Sir!' they would begin at once to say with eagerness, 'I have never slept since last Thursday night. Oh Sir, your sermon.' ... This would happen three or four times in the morning."[10]

Venn kept up his alfresco preaching in the surrounding countryside – "that dreadful wilderness beyond Huddersfield", in the words of a Methodist preacher – and visited Dissenting churches in the area. Wesley said of him, "I think, he is exactly as regular as he ought to be," and that, like himelf, Venn observed "every punctilio of order, except where the salvation of souls is at stake".[11] He started children's meetings in the church, like Newton at Olney. On Sundays "Venn people" patrolled the streets of the town to keep people quiet and send them to church.

Almost every major figure of the evangelical movement, from Lord Dartmouth to John Wesley, visited Huddersfield to witness Venn's famous success. He exchanged visits with Thornton and preached at Lady Huntingdon's house. He rather fell out with Wesley though. Venn had become vehemently Calvinist, following Eling's lead. The dispute between Calvinism and Arminianism was the great fault-line in evangelicalism, the former teaching that God decided who will be saved and who damned beforehand, the latter upholding free will. The Calvinist Whitefield was divided from the Arminian Wesley, sometimes violently. In crossing the line, Venn was joining Thornton, Newton, and most evangelical Anglicans of that generation. The succeeding generation, with remarkable unanimity, abandoned the doctrine.

More troubling to Henry Venn, Wesley's preachers were still visiting Huddersfield to preach there – "not in opposition to Mr. Venn (whom they love, esteem, and constantly attend)", Wesley insisted, "but to supply what they do not find in his preaching". Venn protested, so in 1761 Wesley agreed to limit their preaching visits to one a month, and the following year reluctantly suspended them altogether, but in 1765 they started coming back. "Mr. Venn's curate," reported one of them, "took the pains to go from house to house to entreat the people not to come to hear us, but he lost his bad labour." As late as 1789, Venn was complaining that the 86-year-old Wesley was "ever indefatigable in suggesting prejudices against me".[12]

Venn became well known for his 1763 book *The Complete Duty of Man*, a systematic exposition of evangelical theology and life, challenging the less evangelical classic *The Whole Duty of Man*. He formed the Society for Clergy in the North, for beleaguered evangelical ministers to meet and encourage each other, which became the Elland Society and gave money for the education of evangelical ordinands.

In 1767, when John was eight, Eling died after suffering several months' illness and religious doubts: the devil "was suffered to pour in upon her soul the most blasphemous suggestions", as Henry put it. Her spirit recovered, and her last words were, "Oh the joy, the delight!" "All circumstances considered," recalled Henry, "few have been called to bear a heavier cross than I was by her death." Nevertheless, within a year he was in love with his new maid Ann Hudson, whom he called Priscilla or

Priscy, and proposed to her. She turned him down, and married his curate John Riland instead on Venn's recommendation. The couple lived in the rectory with him, and she looked after his children. He always wrote to her as "my beloved Priscy", and when in July 1771 he married Katherine Smith, he told Priscy: "There is but one I could have preferred."[13]

"The Archdeacon of Yelling"

In 1771, his own consumption persuaded Venn to leave Huddersfield for the quieter parish of Yelling in Huntingdonshire, twelve miles from Cambridge, where he stayed until his death eighteen years later. "The shattered state of my health," he told Lady Huntingdon, "occasioned by my unpardonable length and loudness in speaking, has reduced me to a state which incapacitates me for the charge of so large a parish."[14] In his last weeks in Huddersfield, John Venn says, the church was so packed people were turned away at the door.

At Yelling, Henry became a mentor for students and young clergy at Cambridge, most famously Charles Simeon. The itinerant evangelical clergyman John Berridge reported to Thornton that Venn's daughter Jane "visits all the sick in the parish, makes up their medicines, delights in the work, and would make a good parson's wife". Henry still preached in unorthodox places. Berridge (who was threatened with ejection and gaol by the Bishop of Ely for preaching outside his parish) told John Thornton in 1774: "I have been recruiting for Mr Venn at Godmanchester… I hope he also will consecrate a few barns, and preach a little in his neighbourhood, to fill up his fold at Yelling." Sure enough Venn told Lady Huntingdon, "I have had several congregations in barns and other places."[15] He also preached in farmers' houses and Dissenting chapels.

And a decade later, when Henry Venn was sixty and his son John twenty-five, he was still at it. Henry, Berridge told Thornton, "is doubtless become a vagabond preacher as well as myself, a right gospel hawker and pedlar… Through mercy he is grown as scandalous as I could wish him." After preaching successfully in Bluntisham, "he promised to preach there once a fortnight in some barn at his return". Berridge talked of this as a relatively recent development for which he took credit himself, so Venn may perhaps have put field preaching behind him for a while. Berridge also complained that Venn, the "Archdeacon of Yelling", would not let his protégé Charles Simeon do the same thing in the same place.[16]

Even so, John Venn's statement on the subject clearly does not deserve to be taken at face value as it generally has been. He said:

Influenced by the hope of doing good, my father, in certain instances,
preached in unconsecrated places. But having acknowledged this, it
becomes my pleasing duty to state, that... when he afterwards considered
it in its distant bearings and connections, he lamented that he had given
way to it, and restrained several other persons from such acts by the most
cogent arguments!"[17]

This statement tells us more about the demands of respectability on John
than about his father. Devoted as John was to his father, he found the
reality of Henry's religion incompatible with the rebranded evangelicalism
of the Clapham sect.

Henry Thornton

Henry Thornton was remarkably critical of his father John. At the age of forty-four, he wrote a little book of "recollections" on his life and upbringing for the benefit of his children, and set alongside the affection of his own daughter Marianne's memoir of her father, or the love and reverence with which the Venns and Wilberforces wrote about their parents, his negativity toward John is striking.

John, his son judged, was "not a man of much prudence", and, having had little education himself, he failed to oversee his children's. He was negligent both professionally and as a father, the latter being a fault he managed to combine with over-strictness. He even lacked a decent religious education, and, though he meant well, did not "sufficiently [acquaint] himself with morality". His Christianity, though in many ways worthy of emulation, was also seriously deficient. "He was naturally rough, vehement, and eager, and his religion, especially at the first, was tinctured with the faults of his temper."[1]

Henry's bitterest complaint was that his father's Calvinism was so strong he took little interest in the children's spiritual training, leaving their predestined conversion up to God. Such laissez-faire religion sounds unlikely from a man so busy about Christian mission, and yet John's letters show the same principle at work. Phillis Wheatley wrote to him on behalf of her dying mistress, saying that her son was coming to England and asking John to "advise and counsel him … be a spiritual father to him". John completely refused: "It is a settled point with me that none can touch the heart to purpose but God."[2]

Like many philanthropists' children, Henry felt that home life lost out to grand schemes. His "being occupied rather with the care of Christian churches in general than with his own particular family afforded us none of that advantage which his presence ought to have supplied". Henry thanked God, he told his own children, that he himself had learned from this mistake. And yet, Henry also suffered from John's exceedingly strict religious rules. "I learnt to expect so little liberty and indulgence when young that a small degree of it continued long to content me."[3]

Henry thought better of his mother Lucy, though he still had complaints, the main one being that for all her piety she had a taste for "the vain and giddy world" of high society and did not understand its dangers. She took the children to balls, parties, and the "hurtful and ensnaring" opera, with their "scenes of vanity and dissipation". They mixed "with people of little or no religion", "the gayest of the gay, the loitering, the trifling, the silly, the vain and the useless part of the world".[4] The children enjoyed their flattery and learned their ways. Essentially, Henry felt, it was again his father's fault: John knew the dangers and would never have subjected himself to them, but he stayed at home with his books or travelled on his missions, letting Lucy take the children to the seaside, or to such fashionable resorts as Harrogate and Tunbridge Wells.

A Strict and Peculiar Upbringing

Mrs Walker, the head nurse of the household, taught Henry to say his prayers, and instilled in him a terror of the judgment of God. Then from the age of five to thirteen he went to a boarding school on Wandsworth Common, coming home on Sundays. Henry remembered being "remarkably enslaved by the fear of man and under the influence of false shame, vain, averse to religion and a stranger to self-denial".[5] But his overriding memory was being embarrassed by his parents. John insisted on using "several vulgar words and phrases", while Lucy treated Henry, her favourite son, like a child. Worse was their religious oddity. Henry had been taught to follow but not understand their evangelical regime. Unable to explain it to his friends, he behaved like other boys during the week, and lived the evangelical life with his family on Sundays, "a habit of mind... which it has cost much pains and labour to remove". He had never, he realized sadly, felt a great deal of love for his parents. School had come between them, but, more than that, he felt they had simply not troubled to engage his affections.[6]

In 1775, John Thornton took the family to Paris. He had planned to spend most of the visit in tranquil solitude, and resented the fact that they claimed his attention. They visited a banking acquaintance, saw Queen Marie Antoinette in the court, and spoke to a monk at Chartreuse who had eaten no meat for over forty years. "I met with no serious people abroad," John told Newton, while Henry recalled, "I easily discerned the religion both of the monks and of the laity to be little else than superstition."[7] The English in general tended to hate Catholicism as a foreign religion intent on overturning their way of life, but evangelicals had their own reasons for reviling it: true religion being a matter of the heart and life, any religion based on ritual was a charade, a carcase; and for evangelicals the Bible was God's last word, "the whole and sole rule of their faith" in Wesley's words, making the authority that Catholics ascribed to the Pope and church tradition idolatrous.

On their return, Lucy arranged for the boys to visit the English court and see George III. When she refused to buy them new clothes for the occasion, the man who took them was so embarrassed he abandoned them in the drawing-room, to be stared at for an hour, "mortified and ashamed".

John selected his sons' next school by piling them into his coach and driving around until they found one. The master, according to Henry, taught a bit of every subject without having mastered any, while the boys were shockingly immoral. Henry was eighteen when he completed his education, in 1778, and the only subject he had any real knowledge of, he later realized, was religion. Even there his mind was starting to fill with questions, which he wanted to put to his father, although he knew he would not be able to answer them.

John's ability to give Henry a place in the world was hampered by his unworldly seclusion, but there was at least his business. In 1778, he found Henry a job at the counting-house of his cousin Godfrey Thornton, who in 1793 would become the governor of the Bank of England. The job was little more than delivering paperwork and weighing hemp, but at least it broadened Henry's horizons. Then in 1780, he started work at John's own business at 6 King's Arms Yard, Coleman Street, in the City of London. The most remarkable of Henry's complaints about his father, considering his reputation and his fortune, is that he was a rotten businessman: "There is a proverb," stated Henry, "which says 'Jack of all trades never thrives'. This proverb was verified in my father's case... He made... occasional and sometimes large speculations in any article which happened to take his fancy." While Henry was working there, he reckoned, John lost perhaps £3,000 in wheat, a hundred more through bad bookkeeping, and a lot of money in tobacco and in various goods to be sold on in the Caribbean – though John did make a hearty profit through lending to the government for the American War of Independence. John only went into the office twice a week. "My father did not pursue business with sufficient constancy of attention to make it answer."[8] It is not easy to reconcile this with other accounts of John's success, though Henry was only working for John's personal business, not one of his larger partnerships. It seems that John's haphazard approach made a net profit through large gains and losses, and the fastidious Henry was appalled at his lack of method. Perhaps by the age of forty-five John had made his fortune and started to take it easy, though clearly Henry was more focused on his father's faults than other observers. Whichever way, Henry once again felt humiliated with disappointment in his father's legacy to him.

Parliament

In 1782, Lucy had the idea that Henry, aged twenty-two and unscathed by education or experience, should become an MP, representing the 20,000 people of Hull (or the 1,200 who had a vote). Such an early start was not especially unusual at the time. Henry's cousin William Wilberforce had become one of the two MPs for Hull in 1780, aged twenty-one, and now the death of the other caused a by-election. Lucy loved the idea of Henry representing her birthplace, where they still had friends and family, and so, between mother, father, and son, it was decided. "Nothing could be more rash than this project, nor more sudden than the determination which was taken. I was little more than 21 years of age. I had as yet scarcely received any education. I was without political friends or acquaintance. I was uncommonly ignorant of the world."[9]

Henry went up to Hull on his own. He introduced himself to the great men of the city and was well received, but quickly found the business of canvassing hugely expensive, not least because he was expected, as in other constituencies, to pay each man who voted for him – two guineas in the case of Hull. It was far beyond his means, he had no idea whether his father was planning to foot the bill, and the bribery seemed grossly immoral. He gave up and came home, once again indignant that John had neither accompanied nor advised him, nor funded the scheme.

In later years, though, he thanked God for the misadventure, because it was then he met the girl who would become his wife. Marianne Sykes was fourteen, and lived in West Ella, near Hull. She was from another charitable evangelical Yorkshire family with a fortune built on trade, though the Sykes family's imports were from Sweden and they had roots in the Yorkshire gentry. Marianne was vivacious, studious, pious, and playful. A portrait from this time shows her fashionably dressed in a turban, holding a spaniel. Her mother told the story of the arbour Marianne's grandfather made for her, how her greatest joy was to decorate it with woodbine and jasmine, and how one day she refused to go in it because thoughts of it had distracted her from her prayers. Henry was immediately taken with Marianne – "she was reckoned a very sensible young woman" – but he was not one to leap into anything without due consideration, and it was fourteen years before they married.[10]

The Thornton family did not give up the idea of Henry's entering Parliament, and that autumn of 1782, on the death of one of the MPs for Southwark – a constituency where there was no vote buying – Henry stood again. This time some local backing and a proper campaign were arranged, and now John gave him the benefit of his advice: it was unworthy to approach voters, he said, so Henry should ride around the borough letting anyone who wished to talk approach him. Once again Henry found his father's advice worthless. He stood as an independent candidate, in which he was taking something of a moral stand. Although there were no formal political parties as we know them today, most MPs in the eighteenth century were in the pay of senior politicians. Their campaigns were driven by powerful political machines, their expenses were met, they could expect lucrative appointments, and in return they would vote in the House of Commons as told. Thornton, like Wilberforce, was determined to be independent, to vote according to his conscience, to be of use to the public, and so he funded the election himself. He gained the support of Hester Thrale, the woman of letters, who introduced him to Dr Johnson. The reputation of the Thornton family for trade, religion, and charity made him popular and he won by 978 votes to 588.

After the election, Henry was thrilled to meet William Pitt at a dinner party, who was already Chancellor of the Exchequer at the age of twenty-three and a close friend of Wilberforce. Like Wilberforce, Thornton thought highly of Pitt and generally supported his policies without throwing himself unreservedly into his party. He also met the writer Fanny Burney at a party at Thrale's, who found his manners affected and complained that he "was pleased to follow me about with a sort of hard and unmeaning curiosity, very disagreeable to me, and to himself very much like nothing".[11]

Henry's brothers both became MPs shortly after him. Robert took Bridgwater in Somerset in 1783, and later represented Colchester from 1790 to 1817. Samuel made up for Henry's false start by representing Hull continuously for twenty-two years from 1784, and then the county of Surrey.

Backsliding and Banking

As he made these first steps into the world, Henry's attachment to his parents' evangelicalism was slipping. His theological questions continued to perplex him, and were amplified by the religious hypocrisy of his new acquaintances, which disgusted him and made him feel – despite what one might think was the compelling example of his father's sincerity and commitment – that religion was humbug. The Thornton faith still had a powerful grasp over him, and, to spare their feelings as much as anything, he steered clear of bad company. In fact he avoided company altogether, being naturally insular, and having been taught that the mass of humankind was wicked and damned. Nevertheless, looking back in later life, he saw himself drifting toward "a sort of infidelity".

The great break from Thornton family life came when, shortly after his success in Southwark, Henry made a lucrative career change from trade to banking. Bitterly concluding there was nothing to be gained from the family business, he joined Down & Free (thereafter Down, Thornton, & Free), at 1 Bartholomew Lane, just by the Bank of England. John told him that bankers were a bad influence, and Lucy said that it would be a step down in society. "I did not however," he said, "greatly respect their judgment," and he went into it with £6,000 capital from his father.

Henry found he had a genius for the business, and before long turned the bank from a small concern making less than £1,500 a year into one of the largest banks in England. The economic historian Sir John Clapham considered Henry Thornton perhaps the most able banker of his time. The source of this success lay in the correspondent agreements Down, Thornton, & Free made with the rapidly growing numbers of small country banks. (Between 1750 and 1793, the number of banks outside London increased by a factor of nearly forty.) Also, Henry reckoned that the Thornton name, with its "reputation for wealth", attracted lucrative accounts, and he gradually brought to the bank many of the family's rich mercantile associates. "When I look back to the early days of the house…," he insisted, in a dispute with his partner Peter Free in the last year of his life, "it is impossible not to be struck with the magnitude of that share which I and my connections had in first building it up."[12] The bank's innovation in paying interest on current accounts also seems to have helped draw new custom, while the fact that, being an MP, Thornton could send and receive post for free meant a considerable saving for a bank with such far-flung custom. Thornton listed the personal qualities that made him the banker he was, for the sake of those of his children who might follow in his footsteps: "A little good common sense, regular attendance, a spirit of liberality and kindness not degenerating into profusion and servility, together with an exact integrity, are the chief points to be regarded." Being closely acquainted with customers was not necessary, since "many of them may be very unfit to be friends".[13]

Throughout the 1780s, Thornton was a timid MP who made little impression on the House of Commons. From 1782 to 1790 he made nine reported speeches on four different subjects, all financial. Eager though he was to be a good public servant, he was shocked to find what "a very slight knowledge both of men and things" he had, and ashamed by how hard he found it to follow debates. He found himself puffed up by flatterers and then utterly dejected when his speeches were ignored. Nature and nurture combined to make him aloof, and he made few friends in Westminster. He joined committees looking at smuggling and the accounts of the East India Company, but even there he was too shy and slow to be of any use: "I was a very silent and inefficient member." He suffered from a weak constitution and was repeatedly ill.

Slowly, however, he learned. He took notes on speeches, he read history, law, and politics, and over the years in Parliament the political life taught itself to him. He grew in confidence and competence, and even his insular religious upbringing proved beneficial, as he later saw it, instilling in him a rare degree of integrity and a sense of duty, and keeping him independent of party politics.

At the same time, the faith that had been such a central part of his upbringing, without ever really being his own, seized hold of him and made him determined to change the world – though he in turn would have to remake that faith too. Both of these changes, political and religious, Thornton ascribed above all to one person. In 1785, Thornton became reacquainted with the cousin he had known briefly as a child, one who was happy to share his greater experience of the world with him for his education, and whose own new-found faith and sense of mission would inspire Thornton in a way that his parents had failed to do, and reintroduce him to their religion: William Wilberforce.

William Wilberforce

William Wilberforce was doubly related to the Thorntons. His grandmother Sarah Wilberforce was Robert Thornton's sister. More significantly, John Thornton had a half-sister, Hannah Thornton, who married another William Wilberforce (the son of Sarah Wilberforce), and so Hannah and William were young William's uncle and aunt. It was Hannah who first taught her nephew evangelical Christianity. She was part of John Thornton's circle, a close friend of Newton and Bull, and a follower of Whitefield.

In 1769, at the age of ten, William Wilberforce was sent to live with Hannah and William in Wimbledon in Surrey. His father had died, so his mother sent him there from Hull, leaving her with his sister Sarah. Despite the terrible wrench, William was very happy in his new family. They were kind and caring, and he "loved them as parents". His religious upbringing until now had been what he later called "practical Christianity" – prayers, church, being good, but none of what evangelicals considered the true essence of religion. Hannah taught him her own faith, and he took to it eagerly. He was instructed by Newton, and John Thornton once gave him a very large gift of money telling him to use some of it to help the poor. He became friends with Henry Thornton, who was a year younger than him.

After two years of this, William's mother discovered her son was being turned into a Methodist and came down in fury to bring him home. Both William and his aunt were heartbroken, but his mother set about winning him back to respectable moderate Christianity, with balls, card parties, and the theatre. "I might almost say," he recalled, "that no pious parent ever laboured more to impress a beloved child with sentiments of piety, than they did to give me a taste for the world and its diversions." And soon enough he was "as thoughtless as the rest".[1]

William's reconversion lasted through school and Cambridge. He was a bright student with an independent fortune – not only from his father but from Hannah's husband William who died childless in 1777, leaving him the house in Wimbledon – and university tutors assured him he had little reason to study very hard. Consequently, like Henry Thornton, he spent the rest of his life regretting and resenting lazy habits of mind. He was a popular student thanks to his witty conversation, his gift of mimicry, his celebrated singing, and his Yorkshire pies.

Parliament
Graduating in 1779, Wilberforce decided on a life in politics. He moved to London and prepared to stand for Hull in the forthcoming election, two years before Thornton's abortive attempt. He wined and dined Hull merchants, and attended Parliament where he became a close friend of William Pitt, who had been in his year at Cambridge but had not mixed with him, taking his education rather more seriously.

The election was called in September 1780. Wilberforce had no scruples about paying the two guineas to voters, but he insisted on standing independently, which cost him £9,000. Being from a local trading dynasty did not usually endear a candidate to the voters of Hull, but he was a compelling speaker and gained 1,126 votes, the exact total of the other two candidates combined.

Wilberforce's four years as MP for Hull were fairly quiet. He worked on parliamentary committees but made no great name for himself. He joined all the gentleman's clubs where dukes and statesmen gambled phenomenal amounts, and drank quite remarkably too, though Wilberforce was far more moderate. (Thornton refused to join any.) Hannah and her circle followed his progress from a distance, sadly. Newton told Cowper: "The strongest and most promising [religious convictions] I ever met with were in the case of Mr Wilberforce when he was a boy. But they now seem entirely worn off, not a trace left behind, except a deportment comparatively decent and moral in a young man of a large fortune."[2] Still they prayed for him constantly.

Wilberforce's house in Wimbledon was a favourite retreat for his Westminster friends, especially Pitt, who, fifteen months into his political career, was now Chancellor of the Exchequer. They went there to dine, race, fish, and walk in the country. "Hundreds of times," recalled Wilberforce, "I have roused Pitt out of bed in the morning and conversed with him while he was dressing. In fact I was at this time the depository of his most confidential thoughts."[3]

Pitt, gaining the King's favour, became Prime Minister in 1783, but it was a very weak government, so he needed a general election to strengthen his position. Wilberforce made a major contribution to his victory, winning over the leading men of Yorkshire at a meeting in York Castle yard in March 1784. A small man standing on a table, addressing people who had been standing in the freezing wind, rain, and hail for hours, in the heartland of the opposition, Wilberforce gave an incredible performance in defence of Pitt's talent and integrity, the first notice that he would be one of the great speakers in the age of eloquence. Such was the impact on his audience, that Wilberforce ended up standing in the election as a candidate for the county of Yorkshire, one of the most prestigious and hard-fought constituencies in the country. Wilberforce and his running mate snatched it from the local nobility with the help of £19,000 in donations, three-quarters of which they returned unspent. After this triumph, Wilberforce was widely expected to join Pitt's government, and perhaps be raised to the House of Lords, but instead he formed a group of forty independent MPs who pledged to take neither "place, pension, nor peerage" – though within a few years all but Wilberforce and one other had succumbed.

Conversion

In fact, rather than launching him into a political life of power and wealth, this election of 1784 indirectly sent Wilberforce in a radical new direction. While celebrating victory with his new constituents, he ran into Isaac Milner, who had taught him at Hull Grammar School, though just nine years his senior, and the pair arranged a holiday in France with Wilberforce's mother and sister. Milner was a mathematician and a pioneering chemist, who permanently damaged his health with a poisonous gas unleashed in a chemistry experiment. As a student, his performance in his finals had been so spectacular that the examiners' book set him down as "incomparable", leaving a blank line to separate him from the rest of his year. By 1784, he was a fellow of Queens' College, Cambridge, the first Jacksonian professorship of natural philosophy, a fellow of the Royal Society, a computer for the board of longitude, and the rector of St Botolph's.

Before they set off, while Wilberforce and Milner talked, the name of James Stillingfleet came up. Stillingfleet was the evangelical rector of Hotham in Yorkshire, a friend of Henry Venn and John Thornton, and Wilberforce repeated the respectable consensus that he "carries things too far". "Not a bit too far," said Milner and fervently defended him. Wilberforce was dismayed to realize that he would be stuck in a carriage for weeks with a "Methodist", a throwback to the religion of his aunt

Hannah's circle which he now despised, but it was too late to back out. As it turned out, Wilberforce was enthralled by their religious discussions – though Milner had to ask him to tone down his robust parliamentary debating style – and he was relieved to find that Milner's evangelicalism had surprisingly little effect on his social life. The parson took part in balls and card parties throughout their holiday, even on Sundays, and never offered to read prayers.

Milner persuaded Wilberforce that on the return journey they should read a book they found in Nice, *The Rise and Progress of Religion in the Soul* by Philip Doddridge, a Dissenting minister and hymn-writer whom Lucy Thornton fondly remembered from her younger days. Wilberforce was profoundly disturbed by the book. Doddridge argued that the Bible demands holiness and seriousness from all Christians, and that anyone who does not live to serve God with every moment is a Christian in name only, bound for hell. Again Wilberforce recognized, with a shudder, the religion of Hannah Wilberforce, the Thorntons, and John Newton – and yet if it was also the religion of the Bible, then where did that leave him, who followed the religion demanded by respectable society instead of that demanded by God?

Returning to the continent in 1785, Wilberforce studied the Greek New Testament with Milner *en route* to Italy and Switzerland, until his mother and sister complained about their unsociability. By the time he was home in Wimbledon for the autumn, Wilberforce was convinced, totally and miserably, that the evangelicalism from which his mother had reclaimed him fourteen years previously was true Christianity, and that his life would have to change completely.

Wilberforce shut himself up in his house, avoided friends and business, and devoted himself to prayer, study and self-examination. "For many months," he said, "I was in a state of deepest depression." He was not used to such concentration, and felt guilty about how much his mind wandered. He was cutting himself off from all the pleasures of his social life, and trying to live by a strict new moral code. He was learning to see himself as a sinner, instead of a principled, popular young man, and to see his littlest failings as damnable sins. More profoundly troubling than all was the thought that God expected an account of what use he had put his life to, with all its power and privilege, and the answer was none. Then alongside all this was the thought of the anger and mockery of his friends and the wider world, perhaps the ruin of his career, when he came out of the Methodist closet.

Reconnecting with Clapham

Wilberforce made the announcement in a letter to friends in November. Pitt assured him of his continued friendship, but said it would do him good to get out more. Wilberforce needed a different confidant, and so it was that on 7 December 1785 he called at St Mary Woolnoth to see John Newton. He had to walk around the square a couple of times before he found the courage to knock. Newton was overjoyed with Wilberforce's news, saying he had always hoped and prayed daily for him. He advised him to make no sudden changes, but reacquaint himself with his aunt Hannah and the Thorntons. Lucy had died earlier that year, but Wilberforce ate with Hannah and John in Clapham later that week. He did not tell them about his conversion yet – though Thornton had already heard rumours that he was observing the sabbath – but he was mightily impressed by Thornton's faith, not least by its jolliness. "How unaffectedly happy he is," he said "– oh that I were like him."[4]

Wilberforce met with Newton often and attended St Mary's. He found him wise, comforting and encouraging, and was struck by what a happy man Newton seemed as well, for all his religion, and he was impressed by the "tears of joy" he shed over the news of his niece's death.

When Wilberforce finally let Newton tell Hannah and John about his conversion, John wrote with congratulations and counsel: "My dear sir, you may easier conceive than I can express the satisfaction I had from a few minutes converse with Mr Newton yesterday afternoon. As in nature, so in grace, what comes very quickly forward, rarely abides long." He advised against attending too many different churches, and offered him a room at Clapham. This gave Wilberforce a country retreat half the distance from Westminster of Wimbledon, and so allowed him to sell his Wimbledon villa as an unnecessary extravagance. Clapham became his main home beyond his Westminster lodgings. Thornton told him, "Young men and old have different habits, and I shall leave you therefore to keep your own hours, and take care that you are not interrupted."[5]

Finding this religious network of family and friends to attach himself to was invaluable for Wilberforce in these vulnerable early years of his new faith. It gave him the support of like-minded believers with the same standards of behaviour. It gave him the example, especially from John Thornton, of Christianity as activism – giving, organizing, campaigning for a better world – not just a matter of personal spirituality. It convinced him that "vital Christianity" need not be gloomy, but despite all its strictures ought to make life more, not less, enjoyable.

At least one of Wilberforce's new friends pressed him to give up the godless world of politics, and perhaps enter the church. He seriously considered it, but like many converts of the period was finally persuaded to stay put. Evangelicalism was after all about serving God in everyday life, not just in church but in the workplace, whether as a banker or a cobbler.

Two people convinced Wilberforce not to leave Parliament. One was John Newton. Despite his deep distaste for the political life ("From poison and politics, good Lord deliver me"), he believed that it was Wilberforce's divine calling. He told him, "It is hoped and believed that the Lord has raised you up for the good of his church, and for the good of the nation."[6]

Thomas Scott

Wilberforce's other adviser was Thomas Scott, who had recently taken on Martin Madan's old job as minister at the Lock Hospital chapel, which, on Newton's recommendation, Wilberforce made his regular church. Scott had gone into the church at twenty-five, in 1772, to escape the life of an agricultural labourer, a sceptic looking for a comfortable life, "a rebel and blasphemer", in his own words, "an irreverent trifler with his majesty". His autobiography *The Force of Truth* is an account of his long, unsuccessful struggle to evade evangelical conversion, which started in 1775 with his attempts to put right the "enthusiastical delusions" of the curate of a neighbouring parish, John Newton of Olney. Newton replied with friendship and refused to argue, leaving Scott to pursue a course of private reading, which over two years convinced him that Newton's gospel was true. Henry Venn's *Essay on the Prophecy of Zacharias* then persuaded Scott to come out, with its heart-stopping condemnation of those who fawn on Christ in their closet, but "consult the world, how far they will allow you to obey his plain commands, without saying you are a Methodist".[7]

Scott took over Olney when Newton moved to London, and then became chaplain at the Lock in 1785. He was a celebrated Bible commentator, publishing his notes on the whole Bible in weekly instalments from 1788 to 1792, and then working them into several six-volume editions. As for his preaching, Wilberforce and others remarked on his appalling style – "the worst voice, the most northern accent, and very plain manners", as Hannah More said – and the fact that the content was so good and so powerful "that this did not matter.[8] He was one of those preachers who, as *The Times* said, "found a sure way to the hearts of their hearers without appealing to their senses or their taste".

The Beginning of the Clapham Sect

Wilberforce took two people along with him to Scott's church, and this is when the nucleus of the Clapham sect formed. One was Edward Eliot, an MP from Cornish gentry, a close friend of Pitt and Wilberforce. The three of them had been part of Goostree's, a small gentleman's club founded by Pitt, had visited the French court together in 1783, and had spent idyllic free days in Wimbledon rowing, fishing, eating peas and strawberries, arguing and laughing uproariously. Eliot served in Pitt's treasury, and when he married Pitt's sister Harriot in 1785, Pitt's wedding present was to make Eliot the King's Remembrancer on £1,500 a year. While Eliot did not object to the nepotism, his first act was to cut his income by stopping his sworn-clerks buying their places.

In 1786 Harriot Eliot died in childbirth. Wilberforce predicted that, utterly in love and without the consolation of faith, Edward Eliot would be shattered with grief, and so he was. What Wilberforce did not predict was that grief turned Eliot to God. Before his bereavement, he later recalled, "I was little more than an infidel, but it pleased God to sanctify his visitation and gradually to draw me by it to a better mind."[9] And as with Wilberforce, his conversion meant committing himself to both private devotion and public action.

The third of their church-going party was Henry Thornton. Renewing their childhood friendship, Thornton found Wilberforce an inspiration. He lapped up his experience of political and social life, learning from him constantly. Even spiritually, Thornton followed in his cousin's footsteps. Thornton had never left the faith that Wilberforce and Eliot were turning to, but it had become stale and too familiar, continued more for his father's sake than his own, and it had never captured him in the way it had his friends. Now though, he was infected by Wilberforce's spirituality and by his determination to change the world for good. The example of his father seems to have come to him eventually via his cousin. Thornton and Wilberforce found Scott such a compelling preacher that after hearing him in the morning with Eliot at Hyde Park Corner, they often walked four miles to hear him preach in the afternoon at St Mildred's, Bread Street.

And so Scott and Newton persuaded Wilberforce to stay in politics and use his influence there. It cannot have been hard. The impulse to retire from public life for the sake of spiritual purity was perfectly real for Wilberforce, but it would have denied what was at the very heart of his evangelical conversion. Much as he taught himself to be grieved by his personal sins, they were pretty piddling, "humanly speaking": sarcasm, pride, working on Sunday. What struck him more deeply was the sense of half a life frittered away, along with all the wealth and influence that God had invested in him, "the most valuable years of life wasted and opportunities lost, which can never be recovered".[10] Wilberforce was driven for the rest of his life by the urge to put this right and have something to show for his influence in the world. And to do so he needed to maintain that influence.

There is a theory that for some people in this period evangelical conversion was a way of dealing with the psychological burden of new wealth: money brought unaccustomed leisure time, which led to introspection, guilt at undeserved fortune, and a crisis of identity, all of which were expiated by seeing oneself as a sinner, accepting God's forgiveness, and channelling that new fortune and position into doing good. It does at least fit the pattern of Wilberforce's life rather well. But, whatever the explanation, this was a trio of friends determined to use their wealth and influence to change their society.

Britain's problems, as they saw it, were the same threefold problems John Thornton had tried to address in his own way – material, moral, and spiritual – but on an utterly different scale. They took his campaign from the personal level to the national, turning it from the mission of a holy outsider to the business of government. Like John, they wanted to see poverty and suffering alleviated, moral life improved, and religion reformed and revived. Like him, they would give vast amounts of their own money, and support individual ministers, schools, and societies. But they could also hope to mobilize the political nation.

PART TWO

BROTHERS
AND SISTERS

Schooling

Returning to the faith and works of his father, Henry Thornton was not interested in merely duplicating them. "He was on the whole a great character," said Henry, but with many faults; and he believed he could learn as much from John's mistakes as from anything else. John had been "too much separated from the world" and had "abstained from all public places", so he lacked influence. His generosity was not well enough researched, so for example when it came to placing good ministers in the livings he bought, "in some and perhaps in not a very few of the persons whom he patronized he was deceived". Above all, his religion and his religious circle were far too rough-edged and irregular to commend themselves to polite society:

> *He preferred the bold, the strong, the harsh irregular and occasionally half-antinomian preacher to the correct, the cautious, the polite and the anticalvinistic divine however truly evangelical. He therefore rendered the bishops too much his enemies and while he was doing much good to thousands and perhaps tens of thousands of the common people to whom he both sent preachers and distributed books innumerable, he made little progress with the rich; he sometimes repelled rather than attracted them.*[1]

Henry had no intention of being another rich, pious, scandalous hermit. The content of the gospel was scandalous enough; evangelical manners ought to woo and mollify potential allies, not shock or offend them further. As an MP, and as a friend of Wilberforce, he had a chance to win the sympathy and co-operation of the most influential people in Britain, and they would need to be assured that evangelicalism was a force for order and propriety – though without ever compromising what was genuinely offensive to respectable tastes in the word of God. It was a hard balancing act.

Wilberforce felt a similar ambivalence. He was returning to the faith that his aunt Hannah had taught him, and yet it was not the same faith. Hers, he felt, like her brother John's, had been too unaccommodating and uncouth, a faith that would never have allowed his "being connected with political men and becoming useful in life. If I had staid with my uncle I should probably have been a bigoted despised methodist."[2] Now once again he had renounced friendship with the world, but this time he was going to have to maintain a good working relationship with it.

Evangelicals had always held the court of public opinion in contempt. "Let the world deride or pity/I will glory in thy name," as Newton said. The new generation in many ways accepted the same principle. Henry Thornton said: "As for *reputation* you must know I hate the word... Pleasing God and pleasing men are not only different things, but opposite things most commonly."[3] Being a true believer would always attract the disdain and opposition of a godless world, and the obligation to shun things that normal people thought harmless – such as opera, hunting, and Sunday meetings – was non-negotiable, whomever it offended.

And yet if they were going to evangelize the Church of England and Christianize the nation, they were going to have to woo the ruling classes. And while John Thornton had shunned wealthy society to avoid bad company, and was happy enough to be shunned in turn as a religious enthusiast, the younger generation were persuaded to court it, immerse themselves in it, adopting its ways and manners as far as they were not actually sinful. They had to be in the places where power was exercised, as friends, and the powerful had to trust their religion as safe and sensible. While the likes of Henry Venn had been willing to preach in barns if necessary to get the gospel to the masses, Wilberforce and Henry Thornton had to plane down such rough edges if it was ever going to become the religion of the establishment.

Sunday Schools

The first cause that Wilberforce and Thornton got involved with, before Eliot's conversion, was Sunday schools. The first Sunday schools had been springing up around Britain since the 1760s, to teach working-class children how to read and behave, and were coming faster than ever since Robert Raikes, a Gloucestershire printer, had written in the *Gentlemen's Magazine* about his own school.

The Society for the Support and Encouragement of Sunday Schools, of which Wilberforce and Thornton were founder members, was an interdenominational group led by William Fox, a Baptist merchant, in 1785. This was another of Clapham's balancing acts – they were demonstratively devoted sons and daughters of the Church of England, but keen to acknowledge and work with evangelical Dissenters. The society did not set up or run schools, but it gave books and money to those who did, and publicized their work. In the first twenty years, it sent out 50,000 New Testaments, 200,000 spelling books, and £4,100 in grants. It was a good match for the threefold aims of the Clapham sect, hoping to make pupils better Christians, better citizens, and better off.

The Sunday School Society was the first of a number of educational projects they supported. It revived the trend among middle-class philanthropists earlier in the century of starting charity schools for the poor, but unlike their predecessors the Sunday schools were phenomenally successful, because they were wanted by the families they were aimed at. It is estimated that by 1851 three-quarters of working-class children aged five to fifteen were enrolled. There was a new and ever-increasing thirst for literacy among working people, provoked not least by the evangelical revival, and Sunday schools allowed children to learn their letters without losing their earnings. It helped that discipline was less harsh than at weekday schools and that children were often given prizes of clothes and books.

In the long run, the majority of Sunday schools were organized, staffed, and funded by working people. The Sunday school society only supported a small proportion of them directly. Its greater contribution was the respectability it gave to the movement. Many in the political class had reservations about the wisdom and safety of teaching working people to read and write, so the make-up of the society was reassuring. It was chaired by no less a figure than the Marquis of Salisbury, and its directors included: Thomas Raikes, brother of Robert and a director of the Bank of England; Barclay and Coutts, the great bankers; W. M. Pitt, cousin of the Prime Minister; as well as Henry Thornton as treasurer, his two brothers, and his father, and Wilberforce. John Newton raised funds for the society by preaching charity sermons, the eighteenth-century equivalent of benefit concerts.

How far the wealthy philanthropists who organized or supported Sunday schools wanted to give new opportunities to ordinary people (which the schools certainly did) and how far they wanted to keep them in their place is not entirely straightforward. The rector of Limehouse assured readers that the schools were "confessedly instituted with a view to the amendment of the heart, rather than the improvement of the head".[4] Sarah Trimmer, the Sunday school pioneer, sold the idea to her wealthy female readers saying that the schools would make servants less selfish, mercenary, disloyal, dishonest, and wasteful, giving them "a proper sense of the duties of their station". But Fox, the founder of the society, saw their purpose as more mixed: "to diffuse the light of knowledge – to bring men cheerfully to submit to their stations, to obey the laws of God and their country – to make that useful part of the community, the country poor, happy". And then Jonas Hanway, John Thornton's collaborator, appealed to thoroughly altruistic motives: backers would "drive *Misery*, with her ragged wings and shrivelled countenance, swift before them". In general, it is fair to say that aiming to improve the lives of working people – financially on the one hand and morally on the other – and making society better for themselves, were combined in the motives of Sunday school enthusiasts, in varying degrees. The idea of Sunday schools imposing middle-class values should not be overstated, though: Thomas Noble, who founded one in Yorkshire in 1787 "in hopes that it will put a stop to so much vice that is committed every Sabbath Day", was a blacksmith, which was not unusual. The schools were as successful as they were because funders, teachers, and parents wanted such similar things from them.[5]

Besides working for the society, the Clapham sect also privately supported numerous Sunday schools. Thomas Babington taught the school in his own parish in Leicestershire, Hannah and Patty More ran several, and Wilberforce paid ten guineas a year to Dorothy Wordsworth for hers in Norfolk.

Botany Bay
In 1786, the Thorntons and Wilberforce set about providing a chaplain for the first Australian settlers, a more *ad hoc* mission, but the start of one of their greatest ambitions, the Christianizing of British colonialism. Sixteen years after James Cook's landing there, and three years after losing the war with America where British convicts had previously been shipped, the government was preparing for the first convict ships to sail to Botany Bay to start the penal colony. The fleet carried 600 male and 250 female prisoners, plus 200 soldiers and their families, including Lt William Dawes who would later be the Clapham sect's governor in Sierra Leone.

When Wilberforce and Henry Thornton discovered that the plans did not include any provision of a Christian minister for the thousand settlers, they pressed Pitt to appoint one, and he agreed, if they could find a suitable man in time. The Thornton network found Richard Johnson, an evangelical minister in Hampshire, who travelled with his wife Mary, whom he married in between accepting the post and sailing. In October John Thornton introduced Johnson to his prospective parishioners on board the ship at Woolwich, and gave him a personal copy of Cruden's *Concordance*. Johnson also went with a supply of 1,200 Bibles and parts of the Bible and 1,387 other spiritual books, immortalizing him in Australian history as, in Tom Keneally's words, an "irrelevant and unworldly ninny". Henry Venn excitedly reported the occasion to his daughter Jane: "To be the means of sending the Gospel to the other side of the globe – what a favour!" Newton wrote to Wilberforce, "To you, as the instrument, we owe the pleasing prospect of an opening for the propagation of the gospel in the southern hemisphere. Who can tell what important consequences may depend upon Mr Johnson's going to New Holland?"[6]

The Proclamation

By 1786, Wilberforce was planning his own campaign, ambitious and controversial, and arguably as important to him as the abolition of the slave trade. He wanted to found a society, with the highest backing possible, to improve the morality of British life, through the courts, local government, censorship, legislation, prison reform, by every means possible.

His inspiration was a book by Joseph Woodward, *The History of the Society for the Reformation of Manners in 1692*. Woodward argued that, while it was traditional for new monarchs to make a formal demand for higher moral standards, William III's proclamation had had a real impact because he also authorized the founding of local societies to bring offenders to court.

Wilberforce wanted George III to make a new proclamation against vice, and sanction a national reform society consisting of lords and bishops. Opening doors that John Thornton could never have got near, Wilberforce persuaded the Queen and the Archbishop of Canterbury to propose his scheme to the King, who duly issued a proclamation on 1 June 1787, denouncing the moral decay of modern times, and calling for the laws against drunkenness, gaming, profanity, and disorderly behaviour to be better enforced. Wilberforce then toured the country proposing his reform society to lords and bishops, and got an enthusiastic response. It was the kind of experience to justify Clapham's new breed of evangelicalism.

The Proclamation Society
The Society for Carrying into Effect his Majesty's Proclamation against Vice and Immorality (also known as the Proclamation Society) was established in November 1787, aiming "to check the rapid progress of impiety and licentiousness, to promote a spirit of decency and good order, and enforce a stricter execution of the laws against vice and immorality".[1]

The committee would prosecute law-breakers and close down illegal venues, encouraging local magistrates and clergy to do the same. They had in their sights the printing and sale of pornography and blasphemy, drunkenness, swearing, sabbath-breaking, gambling, prostitution, and any threat to decency or order. Beyond that, they wanted to get new laws passed, and to reform prisons to make them places of improvement rather than mere squalor and corruption. The committee was chaired by the Earl of Montagu, and consisted of eighteen lords, twenty bishops, and thirteen slightly more ordinary members. At one point or another all the Thornton brothers and Edward Eliot were members.

Reactions to the Proclamation Society were mixed, though the King's involvement muted criticism. Horace Walpole reported that the King's proclamation had been "no more minded in town than St Swithin's Day", while the celebrated radical lawyer Thomas Erskine privately considered the society a "promoter of ignorance and destroyer of knowledge".

And yet there was huge support for the society, across quite a broad spectrum. It was not just an evangelical movement, but was embraced by their High Church enemies too. The anti-evangelical Bishop of Lincoln, George Pretyman (a friend of Pitt), was a founder member, while the chairman, the Earl of Montagu, was sufficiently distant from the faith of his friend Wilberforce to tell him off for saying grace. The *Anti-Jacobin Review*, which in coming years vehemently opposed most evangelical schemes, supported the cause of moral regeneration ardently. By making this his first major campaign, Wilberforce won the support of a powerful coalition.

The fact is that Wilberforce was appealing to a widespread mood of moral alarm in Britain. Walpole, despite his scepticism about the proclamation, had lamented that England had become "a gaming, robbing, wrangling, railing nation, without principles, genius, character, or allies; the overgrown shadow of what it was".[2] The country was going through unprecedented change. The population was suddenly growing at a rate of 10 per cent per decade (in the six decades before 1741 the rate had averaged less than 1 per cent), and the growth was concentrated in industrial towns, where traditional social structures and ways of life were dissolving. Hence respecting Sunday was not just an evangelical concern: weeks before the King's proclamation, the grand juries of Middlesex and London had called on magistrates to take action against sabbath-breaking, vagrancy, prostitution, and "that general spirit of dissipation and extravagance, which so particularly distinguishes the present times".[3] The *Anti-Jacobin* wanted fines for profaning the sabbath to be increased twelvefold. It has been perhaps somewhat ungenerously argued that as Sunday was workers' one day off, enforcing the sabbath was an efficient means of keeping them quiet. The Proclamation Society's concern with seditious, obscene, and blasphemous books also reflects more widespread anxiety about the rapid growth of printing and its disruptive results.

In its first few years, the society secured convictions against the publishers of *Fanny Hill*, among others, and of a pair of shopkeepers who sold "the most shocking prints" to Westminster schoolboys, hoping that tough prison sentences would deter others. It produced a thorough report on conditions in prisons, criticizing those that were dirty, or overcrowded, or lacked windows, fresh air, or medical care; where women were mixed with men, and young debtors with hardened felons; where prisoners were allowed to buy liquor or coffee; and where gaolers practised extortion.

The most intense effort came from William Hey, the evangelical mayor of Leeds, senior surgeon of Leeds Infirmary, and a syphilis specialist. While London members of the society went for high-publicity exemplary punishments, Hey tried to enforce all laws against all offenders. One person was arrested for saying "Damn my eyes and limbs", and Hey's constables were successfully prosecuted for false arrest. Wilberforce had to bail him out of this and further suits, and retaliations to his campaign culminated in his horse being stabbed and his wife nearly killed.

The society published reports on its work in 1800 and 1801. It recorded punishments for purveyors of obscenity and blasphemy, but admitted these had not proved a lasting deterrent. The society had taken action against "places of public entertainment" which "naturally become the resort of the licentious and abandoned of both sexes". It had got new laws passed on licensing and vagrancy. It took advice on combatting prostitution, but found that "this subject abounds with practical difficulties". As for the sabbath, the society had devoted a great deal of time to it, but found that existing laws were far too weak, and they had failed to get new ones passed.

Results

The Proclamation Society seems to have had rather limited success, considering the power and positions of its members. The report for 1800 boasts only one practical result, a conviction for obscenity, and urges readers "it should ever be borne in mind in estimating the utility and services of a society... that the benefits rendered by it are often far greater than they may at first sight appear".[4] The society had some success improving prison conditions, but gave this up as too expensive, and failed completely to regulate prostitution, leaving members to give money to hospitals and reformatories for the women instead.

How benign the cause was in the first place is another matter. Prison reform and managing prostitution both seem to have been needed. In 1793 Patrick Colquhoun reckoned that there were 50,000 prostitutes in London, one in ten of the female population, which is doubtless an exaggeration, but as the London magistrate of police he conjectured from experience. The London Female Penitentiary put the average age of prostitutes at sixteen. A brothel in Spitalfields specialized in the under-fourteens, and it was reported that London had 400 pimps working with eleven- to fourteen-year-olds. Prisons, the society's own report reveals, were dirty, crowded, corrupt, and brutalizing. But censorship, from political and religious tracts to swearing in public, was a thoroughly questionable goal in the first place, as was limiting the entertainments of working people on their one day of rest, apparently motivated by propertied fear of the working class as much as anything. On balance, the ineffectiveness of the Proclamation Society was probably one of its redeeming features. The moral reformation of Britain was one of the Clapham sect's more morally equivocal undertakings, leading to oppression and harsh restrictions; but it is a recurring feature of their story that, for all their philanthropy, they embraced and promoted some of the most repressive politics of their day. And yet there was a humanitarian dimension to the society as well, as Wilberforce saw it as a move away from the death penalty: "The barbarous custom of hanging has been tried too long… The most effectual way to prevent greater crimes is by punishing the smaller."[5] In later years, Buxton campaigned against capital punishment.

The most serious criticism levelled at the society is double standards. Public criticism at the time was silenced by its royal commission and patrician committee, but after the society was superseded in the same work by the middle-class Vice Society such immunity was lost, and much of the criticism that followed applied equally to both. Detractors pointed out that drunkenness, gambling, and profaning the sabbath were every bit as popular among the aristocracy and gentry as among working people, but "instead of acting boldly and openly towards all ranks of life, your society confine themselves solely to the prosecution (or reformation if they please) of those ranks which they are most likely to overawe and terrify", in the words of one anonymous author. Surely Sunday trading, for example, was more excusable for the poor, but the society's lenience was all shown to the rich. Sydney Smith called it the "society for suppressing the vices of persons whose income does not exceed £500 per annum".[6]

The fact is that the Clapham sect was in a difficult and not wholly defensible position. They were trying to win the support of the ruling classes for their reforms, support that was easily enough granted for suppressing the vices of the poor, but was less unanimous when it came to restricting their own pleasures. On the other hand, it was generally understood that the fashions and habits of the upper classes were copied by "the imitating multitude", a trickle-down theory of behaviour. The gentry had an "all-pervading influence"; "to them the inferior ranks look up, with such a degree of deference, as makes them proud of becoming their imitators". Clapham agreed that "the increased profligacy of the *common people*" followed from "the increased dissoluteness of their superiors". So it was essential to win over the great. Get them praying more and gambling less, and the multitude would follow.[7]

And so the Proclamation Society presents the less than admirable profile of a campaign that directed its moral armoury at the less well off and powerful sections of society, not because they thought such people more deserving or a more effective means of reform, but because they were easier targets, whose resentment did not matter. Viewed as a PR exercise for evangelicalism, it may have been successful; as an exercise in morality it must surely have been counter-productive.

This point was not entirely lost on them. It was clear to the Clapham sect that, if moral regeneration was going to embrace the whole nation, such a society was not enough and other means were called for. So while they were getting working people fined or locked up, the reformers appealed to the conscience and responsibility of the upper classes. This was above all the job of the writer who became an integral part of the Clapham sect despite living in the west country, Hannah More.

Hannah More

She and Wilberforce met for the first time in 1786. Fifteen years older than him and his friends, More was from a family of fallen gentry. Her father Jacob was a well-educated man who had expected to become a rector and inherit a Suffolk manor house; instead he ended up teaching reading and writing in a charity school outside Bristol for £15 a year. Jacob and his wife Mary had five daughters, and with no one else to pass his learning on to, he taught them maths and Latin. Hannah, the fourth in age, did so well he was alarmed by what he was unleashing and stopped, and then continued on and off. "I, a girl," she said, "was educated at random." The experience left her with complicated feelings about women's roles. As a child she wrote plays and essays and hid them in the broom cupboard. She repeatedly urged women to keep to their natural stations, leaving culture, public life, and business to men ("Taste, elegance, and talents may be ours/But learning suits not our less vigorous powers"),[8] though she made a fortune as a playwright, novelist, poet, and essayist, and established and managed eleven schools.

Like other girls of their class and financial position, the More sisters had to teach, so the eldest, Mary, went to school in Bristol, returning at weekends to teach her sisters. They set up their own school for girls in 1758, and it was remarkably successful. In 1762 they moved to a schoolhouse in Clifton to accommodate sixty girls, and they made enough money for the family to move house. Hannah completed her education at the school and started teaching there. At eighteen she wrote a play for the children, *In Search of Happiness*, then at twenty-two she left to marry the uncle of two of them, William Turner, a wealthy 42-year-old. However, Turner kept postponing the wedding for six years until she was unmarriageable. When she finally broke off the engagement, he gave her a £200 a year pension for the rest of her life.

In Search of Happiness was published in 1773, and More visited London to meet the 57-year-old David Garrick, superstar actor and manager of Drury Lane theatre. He declined to stage any of her plays, but they became close friends for the last five years of his life. She idolized him, and he mentored her and introduced her into literary society, including Dr Johnson's circle. Johnson called More "the most skilled versificatrix in the English language". She published poems, plays, and *Essays on Various Subjects Principally Designed for Young Women*, humbly recommending quiet subjugation. She had great success with the play *Percy*, but after Garrick's death she gave up playwriting and lived for a while with his widow Eva.

More had long had a seam of evangelical sensibility in her nature – Garrick used to send her out of the room so she did not have to hear music on a Sunday. For years one of her closest confidants and mentors had been the physician turned minister James Stonhouse (not to be confused with his cousin of the same name, the rector of Clapham), who had been converted to religious seriousness, like Wilberforce, by reading Doddridge.

But, as she mourned Garrick, More was given Newton's *Cardiphonia*, a collection of religious letters, and saw in it a spiritual experience beyond anything she had known, as well as admiring his rational piety. She started exchanging letters with him herself, and got to know Thomas Scott too. Her writings became increasingly religious, *Sacred Dramas* in 1782 being

Bible stories rewritten in the form of plays, which saved readers from over-excitement by, for instance, having Goliath killed offstage. Her publisher complained that she was now "too good a Christian for an author".

Increasingly disillusioned with London high society and looking for a decisive change in her life, More visited the evangelicals Elizabeth Bouverie and Sir Charles and Lady Margaret Middleton, who lived together in Teston, in Kent. Charles was the Comptroller of the Navy and an MP, and would become a founder member of the Proclamation Society and president of the Sunday School Society. What impressed More was their combination of rural solitude and holiness. "Such an enchanting country," she said, "such books! such nightingales! such roses! Then within doors such goodness, such charity, such piety! ... I hope it is catching." Perhaps it was. In March 1785, just after her fortieth birthday, while Wilberforce was contemplating what he had been reading with Milner, she had a house called Cowslip Green built for herself and her sisters in a secluded corner of Somerset, beyond the reach of post and newspapers, and retired there to find a new spiritual life.

While the house was being extended, More had an experience which deepened her retreat, and illustrates the ambiguity of some of Clapham's philanthropy. Ann Yearsley was a destitute farmer's wife living with her family in a nearby stable. More set her up selling milk, but then discovered that she wrote poems, and got them published. The milkmaid poet was the literary sensation of the season, and More put the profits into a trust fund, spending the interest herself on Yearsley and the children. She refused to give Yearsley direct access to the money or even a copy of the deed, telling her fellow trustee Elizabeth Montagu, "I hear she wears very fine gauze bonnets, long lappets, gold pins etc. Is such a woman to be trusted with the poor children's money?" Yearsley accused More of defrauding her of her rights, taking control of her income, without security, so she could only ever receive it as a gift from her, a gift which More's death or bankruptcy might destroy. The desire to benefit the lower orders without letting them take control of their own lives is a repeated theme in the story of the Clapham sect. More eventually resigned the trust to a friend of Yearsley's. To More's mind, Yearsley was ungrateful and insubordinate, and she felt herself publicly humiliated. The affair, she later told Henry Thornton, was "the most effectual blow to her love of reputation".[9]

More continued coming to London for a while, visiting Newton and borrowing pocketfuls of sermons, and hearing Scott preach. Perhaps it was through these connections that sometime in the summer of 1786 she met Wilberforce for the first time. She struck him as "a most excellent woman", while she said he had "the zeal of an apostle". Her biographer Anne Stott says, "She was not in love with him in a conventional sense, but, next to Patty [her sister], he came to mean more to her than any other individual."[10]

Hannah More could never have the political leverage of Wilberforce and his friends, nor did she want it. Instead she had the pen. Even that kind of public influence, in the hand of a woman, was something she and Wilberforce both felt ambivalent about. On the one hand, it challenged propriety and might encourage others in a lack of respect for the divinely ordained order of society. On the other hand, it worked.

The Proclamation Society admitted no women as members until 1800, so More's first contribution to the moral campaign was to publish, in March 1788, *Thoughts on the Importance of the Manners of the Great to General Society*. Considering the lives of the dissolute to be as impervious to satire as the law, her tactic was to ask the good to be better. She called on religious readers to live in the utmost strictness, shunning even such frivolities as walking in the park after church, both out of devotion to the Lord and so that the lower orders would learn by example rules they would never accept otherwise. The book was loved and hated enough to go through seven editions in three months, the third selling out in four hours. The Bishop of London, Beilby Porteus, a good friend of hers and a leading light of the Proclamation Society who caused a riot by stopping a ballet at midnight on Saturday, told More, "It is a most delicious morsel, and I almost envy you the good it will do." Horace Walpole, another good friend though of a very different stripe, protested against its "monstrously severe doctrines". The "little sly book", as she called it, was anonymous – in the hope, she told Patty, that "it may be ascribed to some better person; and because I fear I do not live as I write". It was widely thought to be by Wilberforce until Lord Elgin heard him saying how good it was. *The Monthly Review*, while unsympathetic to its aims, admitted "the work was sought with a degree of avidity, and it became fashionable to peruse it, or to appear to have perused it". Those influenced included the Queen: "When her majesty came to the passage which censured the practice of ladies sending on Sundays for a hair-dresser," More was told, "she exclaimed, 'This I am sure is Hannah More; she is in the right, and I will never send for one again.'"[11]

Wilberforce had imagined the campaign for moral reform being waged in the courts and Parliament; More took it into the field of ideas, and immediately had greater success. In fact this is also where the Proclamation Society had their greatest impact in the courts and Parliament, because their efforts there made moral concern an issue for lively discussion. The reports and debates, and above all the symbolism of the King leading his lords and bishops out to battle, however ineffectually, against immoral lifestyles, did more to encourage a rising tone of moral earnestness in fashionable society than any of their practical successes did to encourage obedience.

The Slave Trade

A history book was all it had taken to persuade Wilberforce to start the Proclamation Society. The abolition of the slave trade and then slavery itself, the greatest achievement of the Clapham sect and their most all-consuming labour, seems to have taken rather more persuasion. Three different groups have been credited with persuading him – the Middleton family, Pitt, and Granville Sharp's abolition group – which may indicate that he took a lot of convincing, or simply that there was stiff competition for the credit.

The campaign against the slave trade had already begun, in the 1770s, not with evangelicals but with the Quakers of North America and Britain. Their belief that every person has the light of God gave them a controversial commitment to equality, making slavery uniquely abhorrent to them. They published exposés, petitioned Parliament, and formed anti-slavery societies. John Wesley reproduced their protests in his pamphlet *Thoughts on Slavery*. Meanwhile Porteus, then the Bishop of Chester, condemned the Church of England's own slave-holdings in Barbados in 1783.

Early Campaigners: Sharp, Clarkson, Ramsay
Another pioneer of the movement and one of its most remarkable characters was Granville Sharp, who was closely involved with the Clapham sect without ever being included in its social network. He was the son of the Archdeacon of Northumberland but the twelfth of fourteen children, and as there was little money for his education he was apprenticed to a Quaker linen draper, then a Presbyterian one. While apprenticed he got into two religious debates that turned on his opponents' reading of the Bible in the original languages and, not being the kind of person to let lack of teaching or time hold back his education, he taught himself Greek and Hebrew to argue with them. Finding his master had a claim

to a barony, he volunteered to argue the case, and won it. Completing his apprenticeship, he escaped drapery and became a clerk in the Ordnance Office, and in his spare time published a stream of tracts on the Bible, music-teaching, and politics.

Sharp's first involvement with slavery came in 1765 at the age of thirty, when he found his brother, a London doctor, treating Jonathan Strong, a slave who had been beaten and left for dead by his master. Strong recovered but was reclaimed by his master, and appealed to the Sharps, who forced his release. The owner sued them for taking his property, and Sharp was stunned to hear from his lawyers that the law was clearly on the owner's side. His response was to spend two years reading law to defend the case himself, which he eventually got dismissed.

In 1772 an American slave called James Somerset escaped from his master in London, was recaptured, and enlisted Sharp's help. Sharp spent five months arguing before Baron (later the Earl of) Mansfield, the Lord Chief Justice, that slavery was illegal on the British mainland, being an infringement of universal freedoms that could only be overridden by an explicit law, and never had been, and Sharp achieved the astounding feat of forcing Mansfield to concede, against his will, that once a slave set foot in Britain he or she was free.

The most passionately driven opponent of the slave trade was Thomas Clarkson, who at Cambridge won the Latin essay competition on slavery in 1785, set by the vice-chancellor Peter Peckard, who had been won over by the writings of Sharp and the Quakers. Clarkson graduated and was ordained but put his church career on hold. He got his essay published by the Quaker James Phillips and then devoted his time to gathering information about the slave trade.

Phillips also published the firsthand revelation of plantation conditions by the evangelical minister James Ramsay. Back in 1759, the year Wilberforce was born, Ramsay had been a 26-year-old surgeon's mate on HMS *Arundel*, which, captained by Charles Middleton, guarded British trading ships in the West Indies. They met a slave ship ravaged by dysentery, and Ramsay alone agreed to board and treat them. He was horrified to find the hold crammed full of dying captives, covered in blood and excrement. Leaving the navy after a leg injury, he spent fourteen years as a parish minister in St Kitts, where he faced violent opposition from plantation managers for preaching to the slaves and condemning their mistreatment. He returned to England, exhausted and disillusioned, in 1781, and Sir Charles got him appointed as his local rector in Teston, Kent, also employing him as a private secretary. Lady Middleton encouraged

Ramsay to publish his revelations about conditions on the ships and in the plantations in 1784. Plantation managers responded by accusing him of being a negligent yet haranguing priest, a money-grubbing pluralist, a slave-owner who abused his slaves, whose tales of child prostitution came from personal experience. They sent him packages of Caribbean rock in the hope, as recipients had to pay postage, of bankrupting him.

Wilberforce's Calling

It was Lady Middleton in 1786 who first got Wilberforce involved, according to the account of Christian Ignatius Latrobe, a Moravian missionary. Latrobe was at the Middletons' home with Ramsay, he recalled thirty years later, when Lady Middleton asked her husband to bring a motion against the trade. Sir Charles declined – he had been an MP for two years and making speeches was not something he wanted to rush into – but he said he would support the motion if someone else could be found. They decided Wilberforce was the ideal candidate – Ramsay had met him and found him interested in his stories. So Sir Charles wrote to Wilberforce, who replied "that he felt the great importance of the subject, and thought himself unequal to the task allotted to him, but yet would not positively decline it".

Wilberforce's sons in their biography, while repeating this story, add that Wilberforce had been interested in the subject since childhood and been gathering information, until the Prime Minister himself brought the issue to a head. In 1787, Wilberforce discussed abolition with Pitt and his cousin and minister William Grenville. Pitt asked: "Why don't you give notice of a motion on the subject of the slave trade? You have already taken great pains to collect evidence, and are therefore fully entitled to the credit which doing so will ensure you. Do not lose time, or the ground may be occupied by another."[1]

Clarkson has a third version of Wilberforce's calling. The Quakers organized a campaigning group, which included Clarkson, Ramsay, Sharp, and Olaudah Equiano, a former slave who had bought his freedom. Early in 1787, Clarkson took a copy of his own book to every sympathetic MP in London, and so met Wilberforce for the first time, finding him passionate but not well informed about the trade, and with no apparent plans to take the matter to Parliament. Wilberforce arranged meetings for the two of them with Ramsay, Middleton, and other MPs. The campaign group of Quakers and others decided to ask Wilberforce to bring an abolition bill in Parliament, and sent Clarkson to ask him, but when it came to it, he says, "I had a feeling within me for which I could not account, and which seemed to hinder me from proceeding. And I actually went away without informing him of my errand." So instead the group arranged a dinner party at the house of Bennet Langton, another friend of Dr Johnson and a member of the Proclamation Society, in May 1787, where Clarkson talked to guests about the horrors of the trade and then Langton put the job to him. Wilberforce replied "that he had no objection to bringing forward the measure in Parliament, when he was better prepared for it, and provided no better person could be found".

On the strength of this result, Clarkson's group formed the Society for Effecting the Abolition of the Slave Trade on 22 May 1787, with Sharp as president, and a committee of nine Quakers including James Phillips, plus Clarkson and one other Anglican – an infinitely humbler assemblage than Wilberforce's Proclamation Society committee, which is perhaps one reason why he did not join it himself until 1791. That summer Clarkson toured the country gathering evidence from the slave ports and drumming up popular support for abolition, while Wilberforce toured palaces and mansions recruiting the upper classes to the Proclamation Society. For a while the campaigns of these two societies ran in tandem for Wilberforce, who said, "God Almighty has set before me two great objects, the suppression of the slave trade and the reformation of manners."

It has been repeatedly claimed, most influentially by Ford K. Brown, that abolition was a means to an end for the Clapham sect, that it was not about humanitarianism but about promoting the cause of evangelicalism. Abolition, Brown said, was "no end in itself" for Wilberforce, but one part of "the great evangelical cause, the reform of the nation". It was designed to inspire "large numbers of moral and earnest men and women to share in an emotional and spiritual undertaking identified with Evangelical leadership", a PR exercise to gain the moral leadership of Britain, which could then be channelled into more important causes. This interpretation has to be utterly rejected. In their private letters and diaries, the Clapham sect only ever talk of abolition as an end in itself that means everything to them. There was little in the way of a popular campaign when Wilberforce took up the cause, and the Clapham sect continued with it for years after popular support had collapsed. As we shall see they even sacrificed other, "more important" campaigns to it.[2]

The abolitionists made a tactical decision to confine themselves to the abolition of the slave trade, and until that was accomplished to avoid even talking about the abolition of slavery itself. They unanimously wanted both abolitions, but while their present campaign attacked the trading rights of slavers, ending slavery would be an assault on the most sacred right in British law – property. The slave trade was quite enough to be getting on with, without being drawn into fighting both battles at once. Only the idealist Granville Sharp dissented from this tactic, saying that, while he accepted it as the policy of his committee, he personally "thought (and shall ever think) it my duty to expose the monstrous impiety and cruelty…not only of the slave trade, but of slavery itself".[3]

Bringing Abolition to Parliament

In the winter of 1787–88, Wilberforce helped Clarkson interview witnesses in London for information to bring to Parliament, and got him access to Custom House records. He constantly consulted Ramsay too, and had discussions with Middleton. The committee commissioned Josiah Wedgwood, an ardent abolitionist, to design the famous engraving "expressive of an African in chains in a supplicating posture", with the slogan "Am I Not a Man and a Brother?" Ottobah Cugoano became the first former slave to publish his memoirs and arguments against the slave trade. Hannah More rushed out *Slavery: A Poem* before the debate in Parliament, and persuaded Sheridan to stage the slave tragedy *Oroonoko* at Drury Lane. Newton lent his pen to the cause with *Thoughts Upon the African Slave Trade*, which not only offered firsthand accounts of the injury the trade did to Africans, but argued that it did immense damage to Britain too, corrupting and brutalizing those who took part, and killing one in five, through storm, disease, liquor, venereal infection, and slave insurrection. Newton's was an invaluable contribution, appealing as it did to British self-interest rather than morality. It was, however, in the forty years since his conversion and the thirty-six since he abandoned the slave trade – a period peppered with unsparing accounts of his wicked life and repeated sermons on Britain's national sins – his first ever recorded condemnation of the slave trade. Wesley was unusual in the first generation of evangelicals for speaking out against slavery. Whitefield, after initial reservations, used slave labour in Georgia, and Thornton in his dealings with Phillis Wheatley and her family never questioned their right to own her. Even Newton, for all his experience and participation, only seems to have had his conscience pricked by the public campaign.

Pitt's government discussed with France the possibility of a bilateral abolition of the slave trade. This would have dealt a powerful pre-emptive blow to one of the strongest arguments against abolition, that if the British abandoned their share of the trade, the French would simply take the slaves, and the profits, instead. Unfortunately, the French rejected Pitt's suggestion. He and Wilberforce agreed that an official report on the trade would reinforce the case in Parliament, and so Pitt belatedly arranged a Privy Council committee, with the help of Bishop Porteus, to examine witnesses for both sides of the argument.

Wilberforce's motion was scheduled for 2 February 1788, and he and Pitt and the Abolition Committee were thoroughly confident of success. "I trust there is little reason," said Wilberforce, "to doubt of the motion for the abolition of this horrid traffic in flesh and blood being carried in Parliament." The slave trade would be outlawed by the summer.

But then Wilberforce fell violently ill. His doctors prescribed opium and the waters of Bath, but gave him only two weeks to live. Pitt promised he would take over the abolition motion after his friend's death, but with the Privy Council report still to come, it would have to wait until the following year.

In the meantime, the nationwide campaign gathered ever greater momentum. Encouraged by Clarkson and the London committee, petitions rained down on Parliament, over a hundred arriving by the end of May. Clarkson, Ramsay, and others published new books. Cowper published abolitionist verses and one, *The Negro's Complaint*, was set to music as a campaign anthem. Wedgwood's "Am I Not a Man and a Brother?" appeared everywhere, on medallions, snuff boxes, brooches, cufflinks, posters, and in magazines.

While waiting, the MP Sir William Dolben, a founder member of the Proclamation Society, after inspecting a slaver moored on the Thames, brought a bill to reduce overcrowding. And now the shocked abolitionists got their first glimpse of the strength of the opposition. Dolben's bill was obviously a far less serious measure than abolition, and yet Pitt only got it through the Commons by threatening immediate total abolition if it failed, and then through the Lords, on the third attempt, by two votes, after threatening to dissolve his government. Over twenty years, it reduced deaths in the middle passage (the second leg of the slavers' triangular voyage from England to Africa, to the Caribbean, and back home) by a quarter.

Wilberforce slowly recovered from his illness. He spent the summer convalescing at Lake Windermere with his mother and sister. Sarah had, as John Thornton put it, "caught some of the fire" of his religion, but found it hard to balance it with the duties of living with their stubbornly unregenerate mother. William complained to Newton about how busy Windermere had become, and to his own journal about his "indolence". The evangelicals of Wilberforce's circle found peaceful rural seclusion essential to their spiritual lives, so it is ironic how many of them spent their lives in London – a compromise between private spirituality and public service to God. Conversely, they believed in relentless busyness in the sense that every moment that was not put to spiritual or material profit was a sinful waste. From new year 1789, Wilberforce kept a journal logging how much time he spent per day on parliamentary business, on spiritual pursuits, on necessities like eating and dressing, and how much was "squandered". Thornton's diary agonized over how long he stayed in bed of a morning.

By January 1789, Wilberforce was well enough to return to gathering facts and working through the arguments for the abolition debate. He brought Eliot into his deliberations, as well as Clarkson and Ramsay, and visited John Wesley. He also briefly met for the first time the man who was to be a leading figure in the Clapham sect, James Stephen. Stephen was a barrister in St Kitts who secretly hated slavery, currently in London on a short visit. He was able to give Wilberforce yet more ammunition for his campaign, and when he returned he kept up the supply. Stephen also investigated the accusations against Ramsay, finding them entirely fictitious.

Many people of Stephen's class in the Caribbean had little experience of the realities of plantation slavery, but Stephen had seen the truth while still on his way out to St Kitts in 1783. Stopping at Barbados, he dined with men discussing a forthcoming murder trial where the accused were four slaves, but the guests were pretty sure a certain white man was guilty. Stephen watched the trial, which involved no jury, defence counsel, or formal charge, and the only evidence was the implausible testimony of a terrified girl whom the chairman threatened with death if she concealed anything that told against the slaves. They were sentenced to death by burning, but the owner of two of them gained their release by supplying a convincing alibi. Despite the fact that this destroyed the only evidence against all four, the other two were burned. Stephen thus came to St Kitts with an implacable hatred of slavery, which grew the more he discovered of it.

The First Debate

The motion against the slave trade was clearly going to take a lot more work than originally thought. Books and magazine articles opposing abolition insisted that reports of the brutality of the slave trade and plantation life had been grossly exaggerated, that they were better than the conditions English workers lived in, while life in Africa was so violent, squalid, and poverty-stricken that slaves were delighted to leave it for the plantations. "Can [Europe] give up, with indifference, those millions whom she might save from brutal tyrants," said one, "and place in a state of servitude comparatively happy?"[4] And above all the trade was a matter of international competition, so if the British gave up their share it would simply be taken over by their traditional enemies, the French.

After a relapse in his health, Wilberforce retired to the Bouverie/Middleton house in Teston throughout April 1788, taking Ramsay and Clarkson, and working full time on abolition. "They are up *slaving* till two o'clock every morning," Hannah More told her sister. Even on Easter Sunday the defender of the sabbath spent three and a half hours on the work, and he refused to visit the dangerously ill Milner in Cambridge. Lady Middleton summoned More to come and join the discussion for a day. In early May she reported to her sister Patty: "Mr Wilberforce and his myrmidons are still shut up at Mrs Bouverie's, at Teston, to write; I tell them I hope Teston will be the Runnymede of the negroes, and that the great charter of African liberty will be there completed."[5]

Wilberforce brought his motion to abolish the slave trade on 12 May 1789, to rapturous praise. Porteus called it "one of the ablest and most eloquent speeches that was ever heard in that or any other place... It was a glorious night for this country." Wilberforce set out the evidence of the horrors of the slave trade, concluding: "So much misery condensed in so little room, is more than the human imagination has ever before conceived." To those who insisted that, pleasant or not, it was essential to the imperial economy, he argued that the cheap slave trade led to a staggeringly high death rate among slaves on the islands, from abuse, excessive work, paltry food, and poor living conditions, so that if the trade were abolished, owners would just have to spend the same money on improving the conditions on the plantations enough to let the slaves stay alive and reproduce.[6]

To those who said the trade was vital to Britain's naval predominance, the "nursery for seamen", he cited Clarkson's and Newton's evidence that it was their grave: "more sailors die in one year in the slave trade, than die in two years in all our other trade put together", and captains often abandoned large numbers of sailors in the Caribbean to avoid paying their wages. As for the fear that the trade would merely be taken up by France, he argued that wrongdoers could not wait until everyone else stopped before they reformed, but should lead by example. Throughout, Wilberforce was careful not to point the finger at those in Parliament who profited from the trade: they were pursuing a lawful business, he said, and "we are all to blame", as a nation and as a Parliament, for making it lawful.

He offered his hearers a vision of a new kind of empire, not built on slavery and diffusing bloodshed, but built on commerce and diffusing civilization. He finished with a challenge: "Sir, the nature and all the circumstances of this trade are now laid open to us; we can no longer plead ignorance, we cannot evade it, it is now an object placed before us; we cannot pass it; we may spurn it, we may kick it out of our way, but we cannot turn aside so as to avoid seeing it."[7]

Wilberforce faced a barrage of counter-arguments, but what won the day was procrastination. Alderman Nathaniel Newnham suggested that before they vote the House should have the benefit of interviewing witnesses for themselves. Despite the wealth of evidence on both sides in the Privy Council report – "the thickest folio I ever saw!" More said – MPs seized the opportunity of having a parliamentary enquiry which would postpone the decision for another year. Rather than force the issue and lose the vote immediately, Wilberforce acquiesced.

It would mean another year's work for Wilberforce and his collaborators, finding and interviewing and cross-examining witnesses, presenting evidence, working through documents, and preparing for another parliamentary motion. And this time it would be without Ramsay. After suffering so long from the stress of the campaign against him, he died in July 1789. "Ramsay is dead," boasted the MP Crisp Molyneux, one of his leading antagonists, to his son – "I have killed him."[8] Wilberforce was going to need new collaborators to fill the gap he left.

Mendip Schools

With the campaign against the slave trade turning into a more long-standing commitment than they had envisaged, Clapham turned their attention back to an issue closer to home: schooling the English poor. When Parliament broke up in July 1789, and after a refreshing visit to Teston, Wilberforce returned to take the Bath waters with his sister, his mother, and his fellow invalid Thornton. William and Sarah went on from Bath to stay with Hannah and Patty More for the first time at Cowslip Green where they were retiring from teaching, and Patty insisted that William visit Cheddar Gorge. He talked to locals and was shocked by their extreme poverty and religious deprivation. Their nearest minister was a curate nine miles away, and there was no cottage industry. Wilberforce gave them some money and returned to Cowslip Green saying: "Miss Hannah More, something must be done for Cheddar."

He, Hannah, and Patty talked late into the night and decided to establish free Christian schools. "If you will be at the trouble, I will be at the expense," said Wilberforce, at which words, says Patty, "something, commonly called an impulse, crossed my heart, that told me it was God's work, and it would do". Stott argues that Patty's account exaggerates Wilberforce's role in the idea, as it must have taken more than one conversation to inspire such a huge project, and it was Hannah's practice to "fend off accusations of presumption by asserting that she had been pressed into action by some prestigious male".[1] Whatever its origins, the "trouble" was indeed the More sisters'.

As Wilberforce and Thornton went to Buxton on Dr Hey's advice for a change of waters, More wrote to Wilberforce with a plan of action: she wanted to start a Sunday school to teach Bible reading, psalm-singing, and the catechism, and a weekday school to teach the children reading, sewing, knitting, and spinning and where they would do paid work.

Wilberforce replied with £40 as a starter, insisting that she "call on me for money without reserve", adding, "I have a rich banker in London, Mr. H. Thornton, whom I cannot oblige so much as by drawing on him for purposes like these."[2]

Cheddar School

Hannah and Patty visited Cheddar in September to put their plans to the farmers who effectively ruled the village. The first and richest begged them not to give his workers religion as "it was the worst thing in the world for the poor, for it made them lazy and useless". But, after the sisters flattered his wine and assured him they would not be asking him for money, he agreed not to stand in their way. Another family they visited said they had heard of Sunday schools and approved – "their apples would be safer if the children were confined". "Miss Wilberforce would have been shocked," Hannah told William,

> had she seen the petty tyrants whose insolence I stroked and tamed, the
> ugly children I praised, the pointers and spaniels I caressed, the cider I
> commended, and the wine I drank, and the brandy I might have drunk;
> and after these irresistible flatteries, I enquired of each if he could
> recommend me to a house; and said that I had a little plan which I hoped
> would secure their orchards from being robbed, their rabbits from being
> shot, and their game from being stolen, and which might lower the Poor
> Rates.[3]

She quickly learned the art of influencing the influential, and before they left Cheddar a farmer's wife had given them a schoolhouse.

Wilberforce sent books for the school, and suggested they ask John Wesley, now eighty-six, to supply one of his preachers as a teacher. In fact, the sisters chose Sarah Baber, a widowed charity schoolteacher, and her daughter. They summoned all the mothers of the parish to announce their plans, and were taken aback by their reaction. Hannah told Wilberforce:

> A great many refused to send their children unless we would pay them
> for it; and not a few refused, because they were not sure of my intentions,
> being apprehensive that at the end of seven years, if they attended so long,
> I should acquire a power over them, and send them beyond sea. I must
> have heard this myself in order to believe that so much ignorance existed
> out of Africa.

"Not a ray of light appeared in the mind of any single one," said Patty.[4]

The school opened on 25 October 1789, with 120 children. The spinning school struggled, but the Sunday school was an immediate success. The children learned quickly, and their parents were so impressed that in 1790 Baber was able to start a second Sunday school for a group of adults which rapidly grew from four to sixty, teaching "the very elements of Christianity". This was controversial: a religious meeting for adults outside the church looked enough like a Wesleyan Methodist society for them to suffer broken windows at first. The teachers visited the sick with medicine and money – to conceal the spiritual motive of their visits, More explained to Wilberforce – slowly gaining permission to read and pray with their hosts, filling the gap left by the vicar.

With the Cheddar school established, Patty and Hannah looked for nearby places to repeat the experiment. They selected Shipham and Rowberrow, a pair of mining villages a few miles north, where Patty found "the people savage, and depraved almost even beyond Cheddar, brutal in their natures, and ferocious in their manners".[5]

They found that a 21-year-old dairy maid, Patience Seward, had started her own Sunday school, buying books and prizes of gingerbread for her thirty pupils out of her meagre wages. Finding she could read and write well and knew the Bible, the sisters appointed her and her half-sister Flower to teach the girls, along with two men for the boys. They had the support of the evangelical curate of Shipham, while the rector, who had not visited in forty years, rented the parsonage to them as the schoolhouse – drawing Hannah's scorn for his mercenary attitude to spreading the gospel in his own parish. The school opened for 140 children in September 1790.

Over ten years, Hannah and Patty established eleven such schools in the region, moving on to Sandford, Banwell, Congresbury, Yatton, Nailsea, Axbridge, Blagdon, and Wedmore. They had up to a thousand pupils at one time. The sisters were constantly shocked by the poverty, squalor, ignorance, and irreligion of the natives – an indication of how ignorant educated people were themselves of the lives of most English people. They considered themselves missionaries bringing Christianity and civilization to one of the dark places of the earth, drawing parallels with the overseas missions of the Clapham sect. Hannah called the Cheddar project "a sort of Botany Bay expedition"; Patty called Nailsea "our little Sierra Leone" and the mothers of Rowberrow "the savages". When Newton visited in 1791, Hannah warned him that he would be shocked by "this dark region where the light of Christianity seems scarcely to have penetrated. We are sending missionaries to our colonies, while our villages are perishing for lack of instruction." In the English working class they were indeed involving themselves in a culture that was utterly alien to them.[6]

Darkest England

The sisters organized annual summer feasts for the combined schools, "as a bribe for good behaviour", as Patty candidly put it. They were hugely popular events, where the sisters came in decorated wagons with beef, plum puddings, cakes, and cider. They also brought along some of their upper-class friends, which added to the appeal of the event. The children marched with flags and horns, ate all they could manage, and were examined by local clergy. Then they sang "God Save the King" and marched to their home villages singing psalms. The promise of such a banquet proved a powerful spur to good behaviour and learning, and the sisters congratulated themselves on treating 517 children for the price of a dinner for eight of their own class. Further "bribery" of fruit, gingerbread, and tarts was needed to keep up attendance throughout the summer when many children would go off looking for birds' nests, nuts, wild strawberries and not so wild apples.

As well as educating children, the Mores wanted to provide more immediate material help, so they decided in 1792 to start a benefit club for women, "the men in this as in most other things, having the advantage of such comforts".[7] According to their plans, each member would pay three halfpennies a week, and in return would receive sick pay when she was off work, and a caudle to drink after childbirth. The one thing the Mores had not thought of was consulting the women themselves, who were keen on a club but wanted the money for their funeral expenses instead of childbirth or sickness. The sisters were appalled at such a waste. Patty reported:

> Those wretches, half-naked, and I believe some of them almost half-starved, had a long contention, with as much fury as they dared exhibit before us, declaring that they would rather relinquish the comforts and blessings of assistance at their lyings-in, to enrich the stock and procure a handsome funeral... This was a pitch of absurdity almost beyond bearing, if one's own lost opportunities did not give a check to impatience, and enable one to endure and submit to their folly and stupidity.[8]

In the end they came to a compromise: members would get 7s. 6d. and caudle on childbirth, 3s. a week sick pay, and 6d. on death. It was more than their weekly subs could cover, and Hannah secretly subsidized the fund constantly.

A much more popular proposal of hers was that the club should give a gift to any bride who had graduated from the school, continued to live by its teachings, and married "with a fair character". She would receive 5s., white stockings made by the women, and a Bible. Another perk of membership was an annual feast, like the schoolchildren's, where members along with the More sisters and their supporters marched in white with blue breast-knots, accompanied by bellringing and music, to take tea and cakes. In return the women had to hear a lecture from one of the sisters. In these, the Mores demanded gratitude and submissiveness toward themselves and God, considering how wonderfully their lives and communities had changed under this new management. They insisted the women's lifestyles be bent to evangelical sensibilities and rebuked them for every way in which village life erred, from gossip to sexual assault. They called on the women to reinforce what their children were being taught, and warned them it was a "very wicked" sin ever to keep them at home without good reason. "They have so little common sense," explained Patty, "and so little sensibility, that we are obliged to beat into their heads continually the good we are doing them."[9]

Such a revealing turn of phrase seems to make it rather unnecessary for anyone else to damn the More sisters' approach to schooling the poor. They clearly provided an invaluable service in their part of the country in aid of literacy and skilled labour, and continued to do so despite increasing criticism throughout the war years. E. P. Thompson's talk of "psychological atrocities" and "religious terrorism" on the basis of the doctrine of heaven and hell is perhaps excessive. Stott points out: "The Mendip schools had to work hard at being popular. If the pupils disliked them, they could simply stay away."[10] But it would be a mistake to imagine that voluntary attendance precludes psychological abuse – indeed, it is a way to keep people one otherwise has no other hold over. The sisters' schemes provided positive incentives and benefits. But their writings, whether about the poor, such as the *Mendip Annals*, or for them, such as the later Cheap Repository tracts, reveal them to be manipulative and arrogantly controlling as well as concerned and generous. Like supporters of the Sunday School Society, their motives were poised between wanting to make life more pleasant for people in hard circumstances and being anxious to keep them in their place. Unlike others such as Wilberforce and Thornton, though, their attitudes were informed by being permanently involved, to some degree, in the lives of the people they wanted to help.

The Slave Trade Continued

After the inconclusive result of the first slave trade abolition debate in 1789, Wilberforce prepared for a second while managing the case for the parliamentary enquiry without Ramsay. He relied on Clarkson, his "abolition walking-stick" as George Stephen called him, and Clarkson's fellow traveller William Dickson, a former secretary to the governor of Barbados. But both were often away on their tours, and they were Wilberforce's co-workers rather than friends and brothers.

The Babingtons and Gisbornes
The breach was filled by a pair of evangelical brothers-in-law from the rural gentry, Thomas Babington and Thomas Gisborne. Gisborne had been Wilberforce's friend at Cambridge, though they hadn't kept in contact since. "There was no one at all like him for powers of entertainment," said Gisborne about their college days.

> *My rooms and his were back to back; and often, when I was raking out my fire at ten o'clock, I heard his melodious voice calling aloud to me to come and sit with him before I went to bed. It was a dangerous thing to do, for his amusing conversation was sure to keep me up so late, that I was behindhand the next morning.*[1]

Despite such distractions, Gisborne graduated as sixth wrangler, and won the chancellor's gold medal for poetry. He inherited family estates in Staffordshire and Derbyshire, but sold the latter, keeping Yoxall Lodge, on the edge of Needwood Forest. He was pressed to stand as MP for Derbyshire, but being a shy country squire who abhorred public and urban life equally, he chose the church instead. Once ordained, he devoted his life to the local parish, his family, art, and writing. He was a prolific and fairly popular writer, publishing books of philosophy, politics, religion, and science, as well as some well received poetry and hymns. He was one of those writers who is a name to their own generation, and completely forgotten by the next.

Thomas Babington was in the same year at St John's, where as a shy and devout evangelical he shunned the unregenerate Wilberforce but became lifelong best friends with Gisborne. The Babingtons could trace their family eminence back to the battles of Agincourt and Bosworth, but the family were best known for the Babington plot, Anthony Babington's Catholic conspiracy in 1586 to assassinate Elizabeth I, for which he and others including Mary Queen of Scots were executed. The family estate, Rothley Temple in Leicestershire, had once belonged to the Templars and later to the Knights Hospitaller, the family buying it during the dissolution of the monasteries, when the head of the Hospitallers was a Babington. Thomas inherited it at the age of seventeen, his father dying just before he went to Cambridge.

Stories of Thomas Babington's youth retold by his granddaughter, Eliza Conybeare, depict a man of exceptional physical and mental strength. Stonebreakers on the road would find granite too hard to smash, and put it aside for the young squire, saying, "He'll be pleased to do it for us; he likes the hard bits." He gashed his leg with an axe and sewed up his own wound with waxed thread, "neat and tight as a seam". At the age of five, unable to get a restive horse across a bridge, he simply kept at it for an hour until he succeeded – the kind of character needed by anyone taking on the British slave trade.[2]

Going up to Cambridge, Babington rode from Rothley Temple on horseback, accompanied by an old steward with a big bag of money for furniture, as he was not using the family's magnificent ancestral rooms at Trinity College. Like Gisborne he gained a first, and then he trained in the law at Lincoln's Inn in London.

Gisborne was always visiting him at Rothley Temple, where the pair of them behaved "like two high-spirited schoolboys", just as Wilberforce, Pitt, and Eliot were at the same time in Wimbledon. Mary Babington, Thomas's only sister, fell desperately in love with Gisborne, who paid her such attention it was generally assumed, not least by her, they would soon be married. The only person who was oblivious to the prospect was Gisborne, and when he failed to pop the question Babington told him he would have to stop coming to the Temple. So he proposed and they married in 1783. Conybeare says, "Uncle Gisborne made a most loverlike husband to the very extremest old age, and it was a thoroughly happy marriage always."[3]

Shortly afterwards, Babington himself fell deeply in love, but the affair ended in tears, and the unnamed young lady married someone else. Conybeare says that even in his seventies her grandfather "never could hear this lady alluded to without emotion". To recover his spirits, Babington went on a solo tour of Scotland and, the inns being few, he stayed at vicarages. At the house of the Revd John Macaulay in Cardross near Inverary, he read Milton to the Misses Macaulay while they span, married the 22-year-old Jean Macaulay, and took her home to Rothley Temple.

Going from daughter of the manse to mistress of the manor was an experience Jean Babington never forgot: the servants lining up to greet her; the mother-in-law stiff, dignified, and bitterly disappointed in her; the husband abandoning her on the first evening to settle business with his steward; the cherry orchards, shrubbery, lawns, orchard, pond, and weir. The couple read together constantly, but his mother hated the habit, considering the reading of either novels or evangelical sermons "a downright sin", so they had to hide their books and read in disused rooms. Thomas set about giving his wife an education fit for her station. "The following words," he said in a reply to a letter from her, "are spelt wrong: bussiness/business, manny/many. Always begin the word God with a great G. Your JJJs and aaa's degenerate rather; be so good as to make a good many of each, which will form your hand." To be fair to him, his letters are also full of unusually uninhibited affection: "Kiss the children for me, my love. I long to be again with you and them."[4] Otherwise, like Thornton, he was famously impassive.

The Babingtons spent half their time at the Gisbornes' house, not least so that Mary Gisborne could teach Jean the arts of housekeeping and pronunciation, and when the Babingtons' first child was born they set a precedent making the history of the Clapham sect even more tangled than it would otherwise be, by naming him in tribute Thomas Gisborne Babington. In 1784 or 1785, Babington paid half the cost of inoculating any in the village who were willing against smallpox.

The Gisbornes and Babingtons actively supported abolition from the start, the two Thomases bringing petitions to Westminster in February 1788, and that is when they met Wilberforce again. He invited them for supper and Babington liked him more than at Cambridge, writing to Jean: "I look up to this little man with a degree of love as well as veneration. What character can be contemplated with more pleasure than a man surrounded by venal politicians but himself pure and disinterested?"[5]

When Gisborne wrote to congratulate Wilberforce on his first abolition speech, Wilberforce's response was to ask for his help in sifting and editing information for the enquiry and the next debate, and Gisborne agreed: "I will employ two or three hours a day in the service of the Africans and yourself."[6] With that, Wilberforce, Gisborne, Babington, and Thornton became close friends.

Gisborne's Moral Philosophy

In 1789, Gisborne made his distinctive contribution to promoting evangelical morality, entering the debate on the philosophical basis for morality, and publishing *The Principles of Moral Philosophy*. Forty years later, writers were still replying to it. Gisborne was answering William Paley's *Principles of Moral and Political Philosophy*, one of the most popular and influential philosophical works of the period, and a set text at Cambridge for almost a century, though it is not considered significant today. Gisborne confronted Paley's utilitarian thesis that, since morality is dictated by God, and God is benevolent, each person is to judge whether an action is right or wrong by "the tendency of that action to promote or diminish general happiness", and that this principle overrides every other moral law. Gisborne agrees that God wills universal happiness, but argues that to prefer one's own assessment of what brings happiness to biblical laws assumes that one has a better view of all the world than God. Paley, he says, is like a workman building St Paul's Cathedral who says: "The architect wanted this church to be excellent, so the best way to fulfil his intentions is to ignore his instructions and do what I consider to be excellent." Paradoxically, Paley's universal happiness principle does not even promote happiness, because it obliges you to commit universally condemned crimes if you believe it is for the best, which is the ethics of despotism.

As an alternative moral principle, Gisborne looks for one that agrees with the explicit commands of the Bible and allows us to apply their basic principles where the Bible is silent. What he finds is the principle of universal human rights. Every person is born with the right fully to enjoy life, freedom, and the produce of the earth. It is wrong to deprive anyone of these things without their consent, except to stop them depriving someone else. Every person's right is an obligation for others. We must use our rights to attain present and eternal happiness for ourselves and others.

Gisborne applies this principle to all kinds of political questions, the most relevant to the story of the Clapham sect being slavery. He denies that all slavery is immoral: it is a just punishment for crime, as long as the slave is treated humanely, for a fair length of time, and without dependants being enslaved as well. Within these limits slaves can be sold, but the buyer must have good reason to believe that the slave is justly held. The British slave trade is flagrantly immoral on every one of these counts and must be stopped.

And yet Gisborne denies that it follows that Caribbean slaves must be freed. While other abolitionists supported emancipation privately but avoided the subject in public, Gisborne is forced by the nature of his book to address the issue, and rules that emancipation is not necessarily morally required: "Slaves, who have been unjustly reduced to their present condition, may yet be detained in it, as long as there is sufficient reason to believe that their liberty, if restored, would be employed in acts of outrage and revenge."[7] It is an extraordinarily shabby-sounding reason. Gisborne is clearly not opposing the release of slaves, but seems prepared to strengthen the case for abolishing the trade by weakening the case for emancipation. Then again, the 1820s anti-slavery campaign was for gradual emancipation, for many reasons, including the safety of the colonists, which largely concedes Gisborne's point.

The French Revolution

The most important event in this period of British history was, paradoxically, the French Revolution. The fear of its spreading to Britain, and the war it brought in its wake, are thoroughly entwined with every part of the story of the Clapham sect. The campaign for moral seriousness and religious renewal could have had no better reinforcements or backdrop than two decades of fear of invasion by French atheists wanting to destroy the British constitution and church.

When in 1789 the National Assembly drafted a constitution dismantling the absolute monarchy, the king's troops joined the rebellion, and Parisians stormed the Bastille prison, the first reaction of the British ruling class was, by and large, delight. They had just celebrated the centenary of their own "Glorious Revolution" of 1688 – where the militant Catholic James II was replaced by William III, by the will of Parliament – seeing this as the foundation of their constitutional monarchy, the envy of all right-thinking people of the world, and hoped the same thing was now happening in France. Thornton welcomed it, and Wilberforce planned to visit Paris in early July, both as a spectator and to try to negotiate a bilateral abolition of the slave trade with the revolutionaries, demolishing the strongest argument against abolition in Britain, that France would take over the commerce which Britain renounced.

As Paris became more chaotic, Wilberforce changed his mind, and instead he paid his momentous visit to Cowslip Green and suggested that "something must be done for Cheddar". In his place, the Abolition Committee sent Clarkson. When the Assembly issued the Declaration of the Rights of Man, recognizing freedom as a universal right, Clarkson believed they were on the verge of "voting away this diabolical traffic in a night", but they never did.

Marianne Sykes's Sketches

The parliamentary committee hearings on the slave trade started in January 1790, with Wilberforce acting as counsel for the abolition, alongside William Smith, a leading Unitarian from Clapham. Wilberforce conferred with Clarkson, Dickson, Pitt, Eliot, and Granville Sharp in his Westminster house and at Clapham. By the autumn, there were thousands of pages of evidence to study in order to pick out its most useful and dangerous points for the coming debate. While the abolitionists were confident that the accumulated evidence was damning to the slave trade, few MPs could be expected to plough through it, so they decided to produce an abridged version. Wilberforce organized a working house party with Thomas Babington at Gisborne's Yoxall Lodge in October. Thornton came with Wilberforce as far as Buxton, where they took the waters, but then had to turn back to Clapham because of his father's failing health. While they were there, however, they met Marianne Sykes, who had made such an impression on Henry eight years before during his abortive visit to Hull: now, aged twenty-five, she was travelling with her brother Daniel.

Sykes had other connections to the Clapham sect too. She had grown up with Wilberforce in Hull, their two families being closely connected. She became a good friend of Jean Babington's, apparently through the Sykeses' connections with the writer Anna Seward, who introduced her to the Gisbornes' circle. The Sykeses were a well-read family, and Marianne grew up discussing politics and metaphysics with Daniel.

She had been reintroduced to Henry through mutual friends the previous year, and became a devout evangelical through his influence. She prayed fervently that Sarah Wilberforce "may be led to decide for her present peace and eternal happiness". In spare moments, she told her mother, "I ramble over these bleak moors in quest of misery. Poverty I always meet but generally so much content as makes me blush – their simplicity pleases me and a few shillings gratifies them, and I leave them I hope not unimproved by the acquaintance."[8] Thornton enjoyed their conversations and reading together, but was convinced God wanted him to remain single, so he was alarmed to find that friends thought they were developing an understanding. He was in a similar spot to Gisborne's with Mary Babington, but was not prepared to marry his way out of a social embarrassment, and so resolved "to use more reserve in enquiring after [her]". Sykes called him "our friend", speaking to her mother, but also assured her that she had only once let him accompany her on her misery rambles. The renewal of their friendship was thus, for now, rather short-lived.

Wilberforce called Smith and Dickson to join him and Babington at Yoxall Lodge. Other guests included Wilberforce's mother and his newly wed sister Sarah with her husband, the Revd Thomas Clarke of Trinity Church in Hull, and Marianne Sykes.

Sykes reported to her mother on the men's slave-trade labours:

> *Mr Wilberforce and Mr Babington have never appeared downstairs since we came except to take a hasty dinner and for half an hour after we have supped. The slave trade now occupies them 9 hours daily. Mr Babington told me last night he had 1400 folio pages to read, to detect the contradictions, and to collect the answers which corroborate Mr W's assertions in his speeches. These with more than 2000 papers to be abridged must be done within a fortnight, they talk of sitting up one night in every week to accomplish it. The two friends begin to look very ill, but they are in excellent spirits, and at this moment I hear them laughing at some absurd question in the examination, proposed by a friend of Wilberforce's.*[9]

Sykes's letters tell us quite a bit about the various members of the group. Wilberforce, whom she remembered from his earlier years, is "now never riotous or noisy, but very cheerful". "Eating beyond what is absolutely necessary for his existence seems quite given up – he has a very slight breakfast – beef or mutton and *nothing else* for dinner, and no more that day except some bread about 10 o'clock." "To me he appears truly *angelic*, and if I had a spark of enthusiasm about me, I should doubt whether he were not a superior being."[10]

His sister Sarah drinks coffee while her new husband, "the happiest being I ever saw", reads to her, keeps forgetting to call her by her married name, and acts "infinitely more loverlike" than when he courted her. Old Mrs Wilberforce, withstanding evangelicalism as ever, a lion in a den of Daniels, grumbles about their early nights and pious days, find her hosts "very good, but very flat", and complains that if she stays "she must give up living in the world". Her hosts look surprised but avoid an argument.

Yoxall Lodge is a delightful place, says Sykes, very large, and every corner is crammed with books. Mr Gisborne is subdued but "seems to be an exemplary father and husband, and rules with the gentlest hand". Mrs Gisborne dresses unfashionably, as that gentle hand requires, in a white gown and pink ribbons. She is "a sweet young woman... and appears to know no more of the English world than of the African".

Mr Babington is very clever and lively, and "in piety he is as exemplary as Mr W". He has "the most affectionate manners and the utmost desire for receiving and doing good to all around him". He loves to debate and promises never to use his strongest argument "if we would but defend our own assertions as long as they were tenable". He exchanges letters daily with Henry Thornton, on subjects that Miss Sykes is not allowed to know about except that John Thornton "is in a very alarming state".[11]

The Last Days of John Thornton

On the morning of Sunday 7 November 1790, in Wilberforce's words, "died what was mortal of John Thornton", aged seventy. In his later years he had given as busily as ever, still trying to buy advowsons and get evangelical ministers into the Church of England, but seeming to meet more resistance than ever. He spent much of this time with his sister Hannah in Blackheath and with William Bull, the Independent minister of Newport Pagnell, or "Bully" as he called him. Thornton gave Bull twenty guineas a year for the poor of the area, and Bull's son, also William, remembered that Thornton "kept a regular account (not for ostentation or the gratification of vanity, but for method) of every pound he gave in a large ledger which he once showed me. I was then a boy, and I remarked on every page was an appropriate text." Thornton's generous friendship was envied by John Wesley, who complained, "I have no access to Mr Thornton: the Calvinists take care to keep him to themselves."[12]

Thornton repeatedly took Bull and other ministers on holidays which were more of a change than a rest, as Thornton was always on the move and expected his companions to preach wherever they came, and even write tracts for the locals. "I shall preach all the skin off my bones," Bull protested to Newton. Ironically, Bull repeatedly wrote to Thornton from home complaining of poor health only to be told it was his own fault for overdoing it: "I can only say", replied Thornton, "if it is too much for you to preach at Surrey Chapel, you ought not to do it; and if you do, you have no right to complain".[13]

They went to the continent to experience the "heathen idolatry" and "farce" of Catholicism, and glory in their two-fold superiority as English evangelicals. Touring Ireland, Thornton came across some ships loaded with tallow, bought the whole cargo and resold it at enough profit to pay for the trip. In his sixty-eighth year, Thornton insisted on taking Bull to Scotland in January, to visit his daughter Jane who had entered the aristocracy, marrying Alexander Leslie-Melville, Lord Balgonie, heir to the earldom of Leven.

One day in September 1790, leading extempore prayers for his servants in Clapham, Thornton got in a muddle and ended by saying the Lord's Prayer twice. When he rapidly worsened, his four children gathered and took him to Bath. He prayed for them and died happily professing his trust in Jesus. "Oh may my last end be like his!" said Wilberforce. Henry was less impressed: his father's mind was worn out, he was talking from mere habit, and, anyway, whose thoughts do not turn to God on their deathbed? "There was nothing very remarkable in the death of my father or mother."[14]

Henry Venn came down to Clapham and preached a funeral sermon – "not", insisted Wilberforce, "to a mourning family; but a family who has abundant cause to rejoice and sing!" "Few of the followers of the Lamb," said Venn, "it may be very truly said, have ever done more to feed the hungry, clothe the naked, and help all that suffer adversity, and to spread the savour of the knowledge of Christ crucified!" Cowper published a poem in his honour: "Heaven gave thee means/To illumine with delight the saddest scenes/...Thou hadst an industry in doing good." Newton told Bull, "I think it probable that no one man in Europe, in private life, will be so much missed at first; but I trust his place will be well supplied, even by those of his own family." Among the many evangelical ministers who preached memorial sermons for him was Scott in the Lock Chapel, who noted

> that his beneficence was not always withheld, even on account of the extreme wickedness of those, that were to receive the advantage of it; but that he was guided in this respect, by the prospect of doing them good... Doing good was the great business of his life, and may more properly be said to have been his occupation, than even his mercantile engagements, which were uniformly considered as subservient to that nobler design.[15]

Hannah Wilberforce had died two years before her brother, and the following year saw the passing of the Countess of Huntingdon and John

Wesley, whose last writing was a letter supporting Wilberforce in the 1791 slave-trade debate.

Bringing Abolition Back to Parliament
When Wilberforce returned to Westminster, in November, plunged back into a world of meetings and dinners and grand careless society, he bitterly missed the merry, holy company of his country friends, "the innocent and edifying hilarity of the Lodge". Wilberforce's second abolition motion was scheduled for December but, to his anger, Pitt put it back to April 1791 to get new taxes through first. Once again the parliamentary enquiry restarted, and Wilberforce had to find witnesses with Clarkson, interview them with Smith, and abridge their evidence with Babington. It was then Eliot's job, along with Lord Montagu, to read the results, amend them, and certify to Parliament that they were a true record. Finally in March, Wilberforce retired to the "rural fastness" of Clapham to master the evidence for the debate in April – work that was hard and important enough that for a second time he worked on a Sunday and missed church.

The evidence he and his co-workers had amassed against the slave trade was so devastating that, in January, according to Middleton, "When these articles are properly authenticated before the Houses, I have little doubt of carrying absolute abolition."[16] But before the debate two events happened that made the issue seem less clear-cut to MPs. First, Tom Paine published *The Rights of Man* in defence of the French Revolution, which appalled the ruling class by arguing against monarchy and for universal male suffrage. Naturally Paine was an abolitionist, and the slavery lobby argued that the two things went together: those who talk of rights and justice and equality for Africans will foment unrest among English workers and are probably closet revolutionaries. Suddenly, said Clarkson, "the very book of the abridgment of the evidence was considered by many members as poisonous as that of the *Rights of Man*".[17]

And then, as if to confirm the point, there was a slave revolt in Dominica. This was not particularly unusual, but managers reported that for the first time the slaves were not demanding better food or clothes but "what they term their 'rights'". British abolitionists did not welcome the slaves' attempts to gain their own freedom, fearing that insurrection would damage the cause in MPs' eyes, as indeed it did.

Making his speech on Monday 18 April 1791, after two years' work, Wilberforce somehow felt himself "most sadly unprepared". He relayed accounts of murder, torture, and rape, and the destruction of Africa, and he argued that abolition would economically leave both Britain and the colonies better off, while making insurrections less likely. But he sensed that the sympathies of MPs were shifting, and vowed that whatever they decided he would continue against the slave trade for as long as it took. After a debate that continued until 3.30 on the Wednesday morning, abolition was rejected by 163 votes to 88.

Sierra Leone: Exodus

As if the moral transformation of Britain and the abolition of slavery throughout its empire were not ambition enough, in 1791 the Clapham sect embarked on the colonization of West Africa. They set up the Sierra Leone Company, with Henry Thornton as chairman and Wilberforce, Sharp, Clarkson, and Babington among the directors, to finance and profit from the settlement of the Sierra Leone estuary with a population of freed slaves. Their purpose was threefold: in Clarkson's words, "the abolition of the slave trade, the civilization of Africa, and the introduction of the gospel there".[1] They would create trading links with Africa to replace the soon to be abolished slave trade, establish British legal, political, and social systems, and infuse Christianity, all financed by investors motivated by the winning combination of philanthropy, proselytism, and profit. It was, though, a long way outside their competence and the most colossal failure of their history.

The Province of Freedom

The colony was not originally their idea. Henry Smeathman, a naturalist who had visited the region, married two local women, and remembered it as a hyper-fertile paradise, had the vision of colonizing it as a settlement for freed slaves. There were thousands of former slaves in British territories: the British had promised freedom for all slaves who came over to their side in the American War of Independence but, on losing the war, had tried to return them to their former owners: 3,000 ended up in Nova Scotia in conditions ever harder to distinguish from slavery, and others came to London where there were already some thousands of former slaves, most in extreme poverty.

John Thornton's friend Jonas Hanway formed the Committee for the Relief of the Black Poor in 1786, and Granville Sharp was also active in providing for them. Smeathman, Hanway, and Sharp promoted the idea of colonizing Sierra Leone, and Sharp created a constitution for the settlement, using, of all things, the Anglo-Saxon system of frankpledge, whereby every hundred households elected a "hundreder" and ten "tithingmen" both to keep the peace and to represent them in a parliament. These would be responsible for "the defence, legislation, public justice, government, and subordination of the settlers, and the union of the whole community, however large and extensive the settlement may hereafter become", giving the settlers self-government and strictly limiting the role of the British colonial company and its agents. He argued that frankpledge "though at present *out of use* is still the *Law of the Land* because it is strictly enjoined in Magna Carta", and published a tract urging its reinstatement in Britain as well as Sierra Leone. It may be a slightly batty-sounding idea but then Sharp had certainly won the right to have his legal lost causes taken seriously, and it was a far more democratic system of government than Britain's. [2]

In 1787 Pitt's government arranged passage for 411 black Londoners to the settlement on the Sierra Leone estuary which they called the Province of Freedom. Olaudah Equiano was appointed storekeeper for the expedition, but was sacked before the ship left Britain in a dispute involving conflicting job descriptions, miscommunication, racial tension, and allegations of theft and insubordination. It was an unhappy but wholly accurate augury for the whole Sierra Leone adventure.

Once in Sierra Leone, the settlers found the land barren, half died in a year, the survivors had to work for slave traders, and in 1789 a local chief burnt the settlement to the ground.

The Sierra Leone Company

The Clapham sect got involved after Thomas Peters, a leader of black Nova Scotians, came to Britain in November 1790 with their petition to be taken to Sierra Leone. Wilberforce, Clarkson, and Thornton decided that reviving the colony with a new settlement called Freetown would be a way of using commerce as a tool for abolition and Christian mission. Failing to persuade the government to establish it as a crown colony, they decided to set up their own joint stock company to manage the scheme. They sent Thomas Clarkson's brother John, a naval officer, to collect the Nova Scotian settlers along with Peters.

Thornton, as chair of the directors, was ultimately responsible for the whole venture, his sole qualification being his successful career as a London banker. He had no experience of the colonies and had not read any of the numerous books about them, much like the other directors. "Our first opinions on this branch of the African subject were, as I now see very crude," he admitted thirteen years later.[3] Thornton brought the Sierra Leone Settlement bill to establish the trading company before Parliament in May 1791. The MP William Devaynes added to mythic hopes for the colony by saying that his own visits to the region showed that "sugar grew almost spontaneously", selling at 2½*d*. for 40lb – a vital point for abolitionists, because if African colonists could produce a good supply of sugar they would undermine the profitability of the Caribbean slave farms. Lord Sheffield complained, "We have enough colonies already," while pro-slavery MPs opposed the bill as giving the company a monopoly on access to Africa via the Sierra Leone estuary, which would have limited the slave trade on that part of the coast.

Thornton dropped the monopolistic clause of the bill, it was passed on 30 May by 87 votes to 9, and the Sierra Leone Company was incorporated. It absorbed Sharp's St George's Bay Company, which had established the original colony, and took Sharp himself onto its board of directors. But he never had a great deal of influence there, because his ideals for the settlement were fundamentally different from theirs. For Sharp, the point of colonizing Sierra Leone was to offer a new start to men and women whose lives had been debased by slavery, and the dignity, freedom, and justice of self-government was essential to that. For Thornton, Wilberforce, and Thomas Clarkson, the colony was a commercial enterprise for the defeat of the slave trade, to be governed by those who knew best (themselves) to that end, and the settlers would work hard for them and submit to their rule out of gratitude, they hoped.

Thomas Clarkson set off on tour once again, this time to drum up investment in the company, while Thornton and Wilberforce retired to Bath to take the waters, from where Thornton lobbied Pitt for a charter to rule the colony as well as trade there. They advertized for a superintendent for the settlement and were disappointed to get only a dozen applications. Accounts of arson, murder, hunger, and disease had evidently not popularized the venture. Despairing of finding anyone better, they appointed Henry Hew Dalrymple, a forty-year-old army officer, to head up a council of officials. He inspired so little confidence on the part of the company that they did not even give him a casting vote in the council.

While they were waiting for news of John Clarkson's success in persuading Nova Scotians to come to Africa, Alexander Falconbridge brought news from Sierra Leone, where they had sent him in 1790 to investigate the state of the existing settlement and surrounding area.

Falconbridge was a former slave-ship's surgeon who had written and testified powerfully against the slave trade. He found sixty-four survivors in Sierra Leone, negotiated a new land agreement with Naimbana (or Nembgana), the king of Koya, a state of the Temne people, and brought Naimbana's son back with him to be educated in England, his wife Anna Maria teaching him to read English *en route*. The prince stayed at Thornton's house in Clapham, was baptized Henry Granville Naimbana with Thornton and Sharp as godfathers, and bought a share in the Sierra Leone Company. The company were delighted with all this and appointed Falconbridge as the commercial agent of the colony with a seat on the council. It seemed a superb indication of their prospects of introducing Christianity, and they hoped Henry Granville would be "as useful to Africa as Alfred and the first Peter were to their respective countries". They told his story in a tract called *The African Prince*, whose cover showed him turning away from an unsuitable book. Their optimism might have been tempered if they had known that the king had sent another son to be educated as a Catholic in France, and a third locally as a Muslim.

Falconbridge started to seem a better choice for superintendent of Freetown than Dalrymple – he certainly thought so himself – but then the longer he was in England the more the directors found him unpunctual, financially irregular, impetuous, provocative, and so bad tempered they were afraid "lest with power in his hands he should be carried to any sudden act of violence". Then again, Dalrymple was looking worse and worse too. "Almost every measure we took was so hastily and wantonly objected to..." reported Thornton, "and in short his extravagance in every sense of the word was thought by all the directors so great that they regretted the hastiness of his appointment." Finally, Dalrymple wanted to rule the colony as a military regime and demanded the company supply 150 soldiers; they refused to send more than fourteen, he took "rather strong offence", and the directors asked for his resignation.[4]

John Clarkson's Triumph

With no one to oversee the settlement and little hope of finding anyone, John Clarkson's report from Nova Scotia arrived like a gift from God. He had gone there with three ships in the hope of taking a hundred people to Freetown. Now, so fervent was the response he inspired, he had 1,196 passengers and had to pull together a fleet of fifteen ships. At first he had found them violently suspicious, so often had they been betrayed and exploited by white people, and afraid the company would sell them back into slavery, or at least bleed them dry with extortionate taxes for settling them in their colony. The black Baptist preacher David George told Clarkson he would not be safe outdoors after dark. At the same time, Clarkson faced obstruction and disinformation from white landowners who saw him trying to make off with their cheap labour. He dealt firmly but diplomatically with the white authorities, and won the black population over with his radical policy of respect and honesty. He dismissed exaggerated accounts of the fertility of the soil in Sierra Leone, promising them hard work and difficult conditions, but assured them that on his ships they would be free passengers with the same rights as any white person, that he would be "happy to redress their grievances and ready to defend them with my life", and on arrival in Freetown he would make sure every family got its agreed share of land – "I would never leave them till each individual assured me he was perfectly satisfied".[5] He meticulously inspected each ship to ensure that passengers would be safe and comfortable, and provided daily meat for all.

What inspired and inspirational leadership, thought the directors of the Sierra Leone Company, and how wonderfully it reflected their own values! The most perfect candidate to oversee their colony was the very man who was about to land there with the Nova Scotian settlers – if only he could be persuaded to stay. Unfortunately Clarkson had a fiancée and comfortable life waiting for him in Suffolk, and had told Thornton that he would stay a month in Freetown and bring news home "but that nothing on earth should induce [him] to remain longer than that time".[6] But at least he might be willing to wait until a half-competent replacement could be sent.

They sent letters to await him in Sierra Leone. Thornton told him that while the directors could hardly hope it would be convenient for him to stay there permanently, "we are extremely anxious that you should be prevailed upon to stay some time at least at Sierra Leone as a point perhaps of the most essential importance to the colony". Wilberforce, who called him "my dear admiral", praised Clarkson's "faithful, spirited and judicious conduct in your late troublesome employment", adding, "I cannot help believing… that when you seriously consider the immense magnitude of the interests which may be involved in your resolving on the measure, you will not long hesitate in your determination at least to hold the situation for a time." He also promised to use his influence to try and gain him a promotion in the navy.[7]

It would take months to get a reply from Clarkson, though, in which time they had to appoint other employees for the colony: clergymen, doctor, surgeon, surveyor, engineer, planter, accountant – all of whom would be on the governing council – and lower officials too. They had to provide supplies, equipment, and transportation, and draw up regulations. They continued to lobby for a charter and grant. And since this was all turning out to be a lot more expensive than they had expected they needed to find much more investment too.

In this, again, John Clarkson was their saviour. His reports from Nova Scotia convinced a lot of people that the colony was both commercially viable and humanitarian. If the abolition campaign had disappointed them, here was a chance to offer a new life of freedom and hope to former slaves, provide Africa with an alternative to the slave trade, export Christianity and European civilization, and make a profit at the same time. Having originally aimed to raise £40,000, the company got £110,000 by the end of the year from more than 500 subscribers, eventually raising almost £240,000. And now instead of desperately trying to find anyone to go out, the directors had the pick of more "safe and respectable" applicants for official posts, and as for general settlers from Britain they were able to select those with useful trades rather than relying on the kind of people who were desperate to leave the country at any price.

Sierra Leone had become a full-time occupation for Thornton, who had to leave the bank to his partners for the foreseeable future, and the directors met in his house in Clapham. He put £2,900 of his own money into the company. He wrote detailed instructions to John Clarkson, hoping that he would stay long enough to put them into practice. He told him that within another year the company would have sunk £30,000, a quarter of their capital, and he doubted whether they could raise any more, so it was vital to get the land cultivated as quickly as possible and keep costs down without compromising their ideals. He proposed a land tax as the quickest way to start recouping "all our huge expenses". Whether farmers should be banned from selling to anyone other than the company he left to Clarkson's discretion. He urged him to suspend any officer who failed to model Christianity to settlers and natives. And he passed on a proposal from Wilberforce for an early experiment in political correctness, that the term "Africans" should be preferred to "Blacks" or "Negroes" "as a more respectable way of speaking of them, and as a means of removing the odium which every other name seems to carry with it".[8]

The Slave Trade

While they waited for news of Clarkson, the Clapham sect pressed on with their more direct efforts to abolish the slave trade, which were now informed by their involvement with Sierra Leone.

Wilberforce felt that, while the defeat of his last bill had exposed the moral decrepitude of the House of Commons, the people as a whole still wanted abolition, so the task now was to mobilize the country to put pressure on Parliament. He published his 1791 speech, while Thomas Clarkson produced a shorter than ever version of the evidence from the enquiry that they had abridged for MPs, this time for the general public. Yet again he took to the road to distribute it and call for petitions, though this time his health failed and he had to hand the reins to Dickson. The Babington and Gisborne families among others secretly organized county petitions – "the interference of the people", as Thomas Babington called it – to try to catch the slavery party off-guard. Babington and Clarkson joined thousands throughout the country in boycotting West Indian sugar, an idea which Wilberforce initially supported but he changed his mind when it proved controversial.

Gisborne and Babington joined Wilberforce in London in March, researching, interviewing, discussing, and writing. Babington wrote home to Jean: "As busy as ever – This morning I have been employed 2 or 3 hours in examining the mate of a vessel which with 5 others fired their cannon for 4 or 5 hours on an African town in last August, because the natives would not sell the slaves so cheap as the captains wished... Sixty or seventy petitions are now by me for presentation." Clarkson tried to persuade Babington to stand in a by-election to get another abolitionist MP into Parliament. "I am not yet quite so mad as he thought I was," he told Jean.[9]

Wilberforce had originally planned to bring his new motion at the start of the session: even assuming it was defeated it would show the country that the campaign was continuing as ever. But Clarkson had convinced him he could win the vote on the back of the coming petitions, so he postponed it until later in the session.

By then though, foreign news had tipped the scales against the abolitionists again. First the French Revolution had turned radical, scaring the British ruling class: the Assembly suspended the king's powers, abolished hereditary nobility, and put bishops and priests up for election. Wilberforce's attempts to dissociate his campaign for the rights of Africans from such revolutionary ideals were not helped when Thomas Clarkson's famous face was seen at a dinner in London celebrating the revolution.

Then came news of a slave revolt in the French colony of St Domingo, modern-day Haiti. They burned sugar fields and wrecked machinery, and several hundred thousand gained their freedom, avenging their years of abuse with execution, mutilation, and rape. The standard of one army was a white child on a spike. The armies of revolutionary France were sent over to return the slaves to the plantations, with British help, and soon a slave war was underway. This, it seemed to many newspaper readers, is what happens if you put notions of liberty, equality, and fraternity in the heads of slaves. And it was spreading: in the British colonies slaves reportedly told their owners: "Slap me again if you please, 'tis your time now, but we shall drink wine before Christmas." The *Gentleman's Magazine* responded: "It is to be hoped, for heaven's sake, we shall hear no more of abolishing the slave trade."[10]

"People here are panic-struck," Wilberforce told Babington, and he was pressed to postpone his motion. When he refused, Pitt threw it out. Wilberforce saw his friendship with the Prime Minister being sacrificed to his mission, but assured Babington that was a price he would pay: "Do not be afraid lest I should give ground... This is a matter wherein all personal, much more all ministerial, attachments must be as dust in the balance. Meanwhile exert yourselves in the country with renewed vigour." He told Gisborne: "Exert yourselves with tenfold earnestness; petition, resolve, etc; if it was before important, it is now indispensable." Newton preached on the subject, as he had before Wilberforce's previous bill, telling William Bull: "I think myself bound in conscience to bear my testimony at least, and to wash my hands from the guilt, which, if persisted in, now things have been so thoroughly investigated and brought to light, will, I think, constitute a national sin of a scarlet and crimson dye... Whatever mischiefs may arise from hurricanes, insurrections, etc. etc., I shall attribute to this cause."[11]

When Wilberforce brought the bill on 2 April 1792, Pitt, despite his initial reluctance, supported it with perhaps the greatest speech of his life, continuing from four in the morning until daybreak. On Wilberforce's suggestion, Pitt drew from the example of Sierra Leone: he talked of how the Roman Empire had enslaved the British saying, "There is a people that will never rise to civilization," and he called on the British senate to stop making the same mistake and to abandon African slavery, letting civilization, commerce, and "the beams of science and philosophy [break] in upon their land". Thornton joined the debate for the first time, reading a letter from Naimbana, and arguing that the slave trade was not just a cause of individual misery but had devastated West Africa. He contrasted the honest commerce of the Sierra Leone Company with the pillage of the slave trade: "It is a *war*, it is not a trade. It is a *crime*, it is not a commerce." He and Wilberforce told stories proving the trade was not the just transportation of African criminals but mere kidnap. Wilberforce also presented Babington's findings, and pointed the House to the 519 petitions abolitionists had sent – more than five times the number of the unprecedented 1788 campaign. The anti-abolitionists were alarmed by these petitions – they managed five themselves – and by their effect on MPs, but the mood of the moment was on their side. "I hope we shall certainly gain ground," reported Thomas to Jean Babington from Westminster, "but by no means expect a victory this year." In fact the Commons voted for a compromise amendment, proposed by the Home Secretary Henry Dundas, phasing out the slave trade over eight years. Dundas was privately opposed to abolition, and while the compromise appealed to less committed MPs, Wilberforce believed it would in effect license the trade to continue indefinitely, and under the cover of abolition make it harder than ever to abolish. He, Pitt, and Fox passionately fought Dundas's amendment, and, failing to stop it, haggled the time-scale for gradual abolition down to four years.[12]

Total abolition of the slave trade by 1 January 1796: it was probably a better result than the abolitionists had any right to expect. "There is a full confession on the part of a very great majority of the House that the S[lave] trade *is a system of enormities...*" Thomas told Jean, "and that it has rec'd its death's wound and cannot long stand". But Wilberforce was less sanguine. Hurt and humiliated by Dundas's intervention, he believed it provided a subtle way to obstruct abolition "so that many who could not avowedly oppose us became our most dangerous enemies". Gisborne wrote a pamphlet denouncing it as "a Bill giving a *licence* for the practice of treachery, and for the commission of murder", and arguing that "no circumstance is so likely to prevent the slave trade from being abolished, as for the country to imagine that it is in fact abolished already".[13] This is how Wilberforce also talked about Dundas's bill in private, but Gisborne made it clear that his book was written without Wilberforce's consent or knowledge, to protect him from the political damage of criticizing the Home Secretary so forcefully.

Prince Henry Granville Naimbana was taken to the Commons to hear the debate and, according to Thornton, was so incensed at the insulting remarks of one MP about Africans that leaving the House he cried: "I will kill that fellow wherever I meet him, for he has told lies of my country." Reminded by his escort of his Christian duty to forgive, he replied that he could forgive an injury against himself and family, but never forgive someone who "takes away the character of black people, [because] that man injures black people all over the world". Told that the instruction "Forgive your enemies" applied even there, "this immediately quieted his rage".[14]

The Clapham sect discussed other bills they could bring to stop the trade in the meantime, but even Grenville, who had helped persuade Wilberforce to start on this road in the first place and was now Pitt's Foreign Secretary, told him he would oppose such irregularity as "an excess of zeal", so there was nothing for it but to wait and watch the bill's fate in the House of Lords. This was not good. The Duke of Clarence, son of George III, led an attempt to throw the bill out, and the result was further compromise: the Lords put the bill to sleep by deciding to hold yet another enquiry into the slave trade before voting on it, hearing seven witnesses before the summer recess, and then holding the business over until the following session.

Sierra Leone:
The Promised Land

Still, in the first half of 1792, the Sierra Leone directors waited with growing anxiety to hear from John Clarkson. There were rumours that the whole group had been murdered. The company negotiated with the owners of Bance Island in the Sierra Leone estuary, with a view to buying it and shutting down its slave station, though this came to nothing. Hearing that Major Houghton of the Africa Association had taken a boat up the Gambia to find Timbuktu, they planned to extend their own trading operations in that direction. Thornton talked with members of Pitt's cabinet and found them keen to back the company's "civilization and cultivation of Africa". In a few years, he was told, once the slave trade was stopped, the government expected to dissolve the Africa Association and transfer its forts and £13,000 annual grant to the Sierra Leone Company. "The colony works me from morning till night," Thornton told Babington; "the importance of the thing strikes me, and fills my mind so much that at present business, politics, friendship seem all suspended for the sake of it."[1]

The directors were relieved to receive a brief report from Freetown in May: John Clarkson had arrived safely and agreed to stay as superintendent but was hampered by illness and inability to act without the consent of the eight-man council. Thornton wrote granting him independent authority if he needed it.

Trouble in Freetown
Finally, in the first week of July 1792, the directors received full dispatches from Clarkson, six months after he had left Nova Scotia. The settlement was a débâcle, and he was furious. The crossing had been extremely rough

and taken seven weeks. Clarkson had been seriously ill – seriously enough in fact to be wrapped in a shroud and taken on deck for burial, but he disturbed his funeral by starting to recover. Eventually all fifteen ships arrived in Sierra Leone intact. Clarkson was dismayed to be greeted, not by Dalrymple the superintendent, but by an ungoverned crowd of British people and a pile of letters imploring him to take on the job himself. Worse still, though the ships bringing supplies and settlers from England had arrived a fortnight before him, the newcomers had done nothing at all but stay in their ships eating and drinking the supplies they had brought. No clearance had been started, no houses or stores built, no shelters set up. Rather than preparing for the arrival of a thousand settlers, they were waiting for them to arrive and make the place comfortable enough for them to disembark. Thus in the moment of his arrival, the fundamental disagreement between Clarkson and the other British employees of the Sierra Leone Company over the meaning of the colony emerged. For Clarkson it was a settlement, existing to offer a new life to the Nova Scotians. For most of the others, it was their own commercial enterprise and the Nova Scotians were their workforce.

The company, via John Clarkson, had promised the Nova Scotians twenty acres of land per man, plus ten per wife and two per child, and they had been persuaded to make the crossing out of personal trust in Clarkson, so he felt unable to leave until he was sure they had got what he had guaranteed them and were in good hands. He was forced, with his fiancée still waiting for him in Suffolk and his fragile health demanding he go home, to take the post of superintendent, and was sworn in on 10 March 1792.

Clarkson quickly found the constitution the company had prepared for Freetown intolerable. Having had sole responsibility for his operations in Nova Scotia and the Atlantic, he now found himself titular superintendent of a council of eight over which his only power was a casting vote (a change the directors had made after sacking Dalrymple). Having previously carried all before him with his energy, charisma, and sense of mission, he could now get nothing done at all. His fellow councillors were worse than useless. He found the doctor Bell an argumentative alcoholic, and it came as something of a relief when he died a week after Clarkson's arrival. The engineer seemed chaotic, the surgeon negligent. Falconbridge was increasingly drunken and difficult and clearly no match for African traders. While every day brought the perilous rainy season nearer, the councillors did nothing but argue; Clarkson could do nothing without them and nothing with them. Their leadership, he complained to Thornton, was "nothing but extravagance, idleness, quarrelling, waste, irregularity in accounts, insubordination" – and they had no respect for the black settlers. For Dr Bell's funeral, the council had insisted on full military honours, which Clarkson vehemently opposed as giving exactly the wrong message to the Nova Scotians, but the council overruled him and demanded his attendance. When the Nova Scotian Thomas Thomas had his arm blown off in the ceremony and later died, Clarkson had a hysterical fit. The directors and investors, he fumed, flattered him with declarations of their total confidence and the importance of the work, so why had they denied him the authority to get on with it? "The present consequences are confusion and disorder, and the future, if not prevented by a speedy alteration will I fear be ruin."[2]

And that was not all. Back in Nova Scotia, white landowners had tried to deter their cheap labour force from leaving by spreading malicious rumours that the Sierra Leone Company would impose such extortionate land taxes ("quitrent") that they would be effectively slaves again. As even the exploitative Canadian landowners had long ago scrapped such hated measures, Clarkson confidently assured his black audiences that there would be no quitrent, but on arriving in Sierra Leone his instructions from Thornton told him that the directors meant "to indemnify ourselves for all our huge expenses at the first by a rent on the lands, which will be more easy to collect than by high profits on trade. I hope the blacks will not consider this as a grievance."[3] It was not exploitation so much as ignorance, but the company was setting the rate higher than it had ever been in North America. The "blacks" would certainly consider it a grievance, and so did Clarkson, and he ignored it. Similarly, Clarkson was unhappy to find that the company had reserved the entire river bank for commercial use, after he had promised the Nova Scotians access to the river and the distribution of all land by lot. He ignored this directive too.

Clarkson was determined to champion the rights of the people he had brought to Sierra Leone against the errors of the directors and the abuse of company officials. And yet his own dealings with the Nova Scotians were not entirely straightforward. One problem about which he said nothing to the company was the conflict between him and Thomas Peters, the black leader. A fortnight after landing, Peters was bringing him complaints about the lack of land and provisions and the imperious white rule of the colony, and did so in such a manner that Clarkson felt Peters was challenging his authority. Two weeks later, Clarkson uncovered what he thought was a conspiracy to replace him with Peters. It turned out to be merely a proposal for a black committee to look after their own affairs under Clarkson's overall government, but Clarkson felt undermined on every side, and generally miserable and unwell, so he refused the request, leaving relations strained all round. Clarkson never entirely recovered from his typhoid fever, and though he was returning to full strength his mood and his memory seemed to be permanently affected.

To cap it all, by the time Clarkson wrote his report, five weeks after landfall, the rains were upon them, the worst, locals told them, in living memory. Tornadoes destroyed what shelters they had got up. Damp destroyed their supplies and ruined their tools and machines. Armies of carnivorous ants attacked at night, followed by packs of rats, and swarms of spiders and cockroaches.

On receiving Clarkson's dispatches, Thornton called an emergency meeting of the directors, Wilberforce dragging himself reluctantly back to London from Bath where he had retired with his sister after a long parliamentary session. Wilberforce sent Clarkson seventy-two bottles of rum to keep his spirits up (he had already sent him a writing-desk), told him he was tempted to see his miraculous recovery as an omen of the success of the colony, and grumbled cheerfully about the cost in "time and labour and confinement" and bad London air he was forced to endure for the sake of the great cause – a somewhat misjudged complaint, perhaps.

The directors extended Clarkson's authority again, making him governor instead of superintendent, giving him open authority to act without the council, and full power to appoint and dismiss councilors. As Thomas put it: "*Everything* is left to your discretion." They recalled Falconbridge themselves "in tolerably civil terms" along with all white soldiers, encouraging Clarkson to do whatever else he thought necessary. "It is to be hoped that you will make a sweep of all the unnecessary whites," Thomas told him.[4] They gave him permission to buy more land as necessary, and sent more supplies. They discussed sending prefabricated buildings so that the colonists could get on with cultivating the land, and fetching more settlers from North America.

The directors also made two important appointments to assist and deputize for Clarkson now that the council was redundant: William Dawes and Zachary Macaulay.

Dawes and Macaulay

Lieutenant Dawes had served with the Royal Navy and been wounded in the American War of Independence, before taking part in the first British settlement of Australia in 1787, going at the age of twenty-five as astronomer for the Board of Longitude and quickly taking on the work of engineer and surveyor too. The astronomy was what interested him – "He is so much engaged with the stars that to mortal eyes he is not always visible,"[5] said his fellow colonist Elizabeth MacArthur – and he built an observatory on what is now Dawes Point, the southern end of Sydney Harbour Bridge. He also produced a dictionary of the Eora people whose land they occupied, with the help of his housekeeper and close friend, the fifteen-year-old girl Patyegarang.

A crisis had come for Dawes in December 1790 when he was ordered to join an expedition to kill two Eora in retaliation for the fatal wounding of a convict who hunted for the governor. Governor Phillips had until then been remarkably understanding of cultural differences and aboriginal taboos, to the point of taking a twelve-foot lance through the shoulder in good part, as ritual recompense for their trespass and depredation, but he now decided that a line had been crossed. Dawes originally refused to go on the expedition, and was prepared to face a court martial for his conscience, but after discussing it with the chaplain Richard Johnson was eventually persuaded – though afterwards he publicly repented. He went in a party of fifty-two men, with two bags for their victims' heads, but no one's heart was in it and they returned, twice, without having managed to catch anyone. Dawes was refused a permanent post because he would not apologize to the governor for his unofficerlike conduct in that affair, and left Australia in December 1791.

Arriving in England in April 1792, Dawes quickly made contact with Wilberforce, with a letter of introduction from Johnson. With his colonial experience, abolitionist conscience, and evangelical spirit, Dawes seemed the ideal person either to take over from Clarkson or to assist him. When they heard that Clarkson meant to stay but without the council, they appointed Dawes as his deputy and sent him out in July, telling Clarkson: "We have also heard of him as a religious man – he seems cool, correct and sensible – he has not yet had much time to be informed of the affairs of the colony, but he is a man of business and I trust he will soon fall into your system, and second your views." Wilberforce recommended him to Clarkson as "a solid man".[6]

Zachary Macaulay, who sailed to Sierra Leone some months after Dawes, was the stiff, puritanical 25-year-old brother of Jean Babington, with a husky voice, faltering speech, and "rather wooden face", and he became a central member of the Clapham sect. Being one of twelve children in the impecunious Macaulay manse in Cardross, he was denied a formal education, but taught himself Latin, Greek, and French – diligence that was encouraged by spending five years without the use of his right arm after an accident at the age of nine. After two years working for a Glasgow merchant, he was dismissed because of an incident that his memoirs decline to go into, except to say that it provoked "a few sober reflections" and led to his leaving the country. A relative, Sir Archibald Campbell, was a former governor of Jamaica and persuaded Zachary's father to send him there, but the connection failed to provide a post for him so he had to take the "laborious, irksome, and degrading" job of bookkeeper on a sugar plantation – a job that, despite its name, was more about managing slaves than paperwork.

The experience shaped him for life. For a start, he found himself in a more brutal world than he ever imagined existed and was sickened by the treatment of the slaves and miserable about his own treatment by his superiors. Worse, he was forced to punish and coerce the slaves himself in ways "the very recollection of which makes my blood run cold". But what appalled him most in retrospect was how quickly he was brutalized himself, losing his squeamishness and conscience, coming to enjoy the work, and gaining promotion. Perhaps there was an element of expiation in the fact that no other person in the Clapham sect devoted more hours or expertise to abolition over the next half century. Whether his dealings with former slaves in Freetown atoned or aggravated is another matter. He gives a striking illustration of how easily a personal commitment to spend one's life in the fight against slavery could sit alongside an utter failure to appreciate their own ideas of freedom and justice.

Macaulay had come back to Britain from Jamaica at the age of twenty-one in 1789, having been offered work by his uncle Angus, but the job fell through. He stayed with his sister and brother-in-law Jean and Thomas Babington, and was shocked at how different he had become from them, and how disagreeable they found him. He was quickly converted to their abolitionism, and took on their evangelical faith as well. Macaulay seized the chance of working for the Clapham sect, and on Thomas Babington's recommendation Thornton sent him on Falconbridge's 1790 reconnaissance trip to Sierra Leone. He returned to England early in 1792, before being sent out to Sierra Leone again in November.

With this new constitution for Freetown settled, Thornton published an optimistic report in the *Gentlemen's Magazine* that the land seemed suitable for coffee and cotton and yielded iron ore, and only two whites and no blacks had died.

Clarkson Versus the Company

In July 1792, the directors started hearing stories from ships' captains returning from Africa about disease engulfing the township and huge numbers dying. So Thornton was somewhat relieved to receive Clarkson's second dispatch on 2 August (written six weeks earlier) and to see no mention of deaths – except a PS to the effect that most deaths were the victims' own fault – and so he started denying the stories. In fact, by 1 July according to Anna Maria Falconbridge, "Five, six, and seven are dying daily, and buried with as little ceremony as so many dogs or cats. It is quite customary of a morning to ask, 'How many died last night?'"[7] Clarkson had not received his full powers from the company by the time he wrote this report (nor Falconbridge his dismissal), and he gave them no information about any progress in cultivation, but only a barrage of complaints. The company was in danger of ruining the colony with this absurd form of government, he said. He swung from declaring that all was already lost to insisting that, if he were given sole power, he could achieve everything he was there for. The company, he said, had sent British settlers out with exaggerated expectations, accompanied by families who added nothing to the labour force, equipped them extravagantly, and seemed to have made appointments as a favour to friends. The supplies they sent were constantly pilfered *en route* and were more geared to commerce than establishing a settlement. The supposedly colonial land was partially occupied by natives who had no idea of having sold it.

Thornton in true evangelical style sincerely thanked Clarkson for his candour – "There are few parts of your character that I more thoroughly approve" – and even told him in a private letter, "You are quite right in most of your observations."[8] Nevertheless Thornton's official reply defended the company at length, pointing out that the "absurd" bureaucracy of the council had not been designed for Clarkson but for the very modestly competent Dalrymple, and until they got Clarkson's first dispatch they had had to assume that Dalrymple would be replaced by someone equally ill-equipped to wield absolute power. Anyway, surely collaborative rule is generally to be preferred to autocracy, in which case the company's only mistake was to appoint poor officials to the council, which they did because they could not find anyone better. Even with such a council, Thornton failed to understand why such a man as Clarkson should not have achieved a great deal already by the famous force of his personality rather than apparently letting the whole project founder. Thornton almost lost his monumental calm over Clarkson's suggestion that he had sacrificed the good of the colony by making appointments to favour friends:

> *I find myself already the poorer for the sums I have expended in order to dispose those among my friends who are servants of the company to go out – I have strained all my interest in a variety of ways, embarked my friends in a world of trouble, sacrificed nearly the whole of my time, and almost entirely neglected a profitable business, in my zeal for the Sierra Leone cause, and chiefly in pursuit of proper persons to go out thither… all my plan of life is made subservient to this primary business.*[9]

Wilberforce applied to the Earl of Chatham, Pitt's brother and First Lord of the Admiralty, for a naval promotion for Clarkson. Chatham could not supply it, and Wilberforce was rebuked by Clarkson's mother for not trying hard enough.

By the time Thornton received Clarkson's complaints, the time lag between London and Freetown was delaying happier news: the rainy season was over, Clarkson was enjoying his full powers, and a proper settlement was underway. By the end of the year the colony seemed settled enough for Clarkson to take leave, sailing from Freetown on 29 December 1792, leaving Dawes as acting governor.

So, on returning to London, Clarkson was finally able to give Thornton some good news. The death rates Thornton had been badgering him for were terrible – two-thirds of the white settlers had died and 14 per cent of the blacks – and Falconbridge had deliberately drunk himself to death after his sacking. But the other survivors of the disastrous rainy season were now all in good health. The survey team had been dividing the land up among the settlers, clearance was properly underway, and the Nova Scotians raised their first fruit and vegetables from Sierra Leone soil. Each family would have received their allotted land within two weeks after he left, he believed. "To make short," he told them, "I believe all the difficulties of forming a new colony were at an end."[10]

He was still furious with derision however at the company's mismanagement. Thornton and Wilberforce found him quite changed from the humble but enthusiastic lieutenant they had sent out – bitter, petulant, unreasonable, an emotional tornado. Illness and experience had transformed him. Judging by his letters, he swung wildly between cheerful optimism and angry despair. He berated the directors for the ludicrous formalities of their meetings. He wanted an immediate dispatch of provisions and pay rises for recommended friends in Freetown, which the company said would not be possible immediately, and he exploded: "They are so ashamed and frightened at their immense and useless expenses… that they have lost all idea of liberality." "I really could not hold my temper," he said, "and very often flew out in abuse of their general plans – this of course did not please them."[11]

The evangelical directorate started to feel that perhaps there was such a thing as too much frankness after all. They granted Clarkson three months' leave and had a house built for him to take back, according to his own design. But while Clarkson waited for a second meeting with them, they received reports from his assistants in Freetown, Dawes and Macaulay, that put what they heard from Clarkson in a new light.

Dawes had served under Clarkson for a few months before he left, and Macaulay arrived ten days after his departure. Both councillors were starchy, strictly pious men compared with Clarkson. Dawes was humane, but his colonial experience was of a penal colony, not of the kind of charismatic leadership the Nova Scotians had enjoyed from Clarkson. As for Macaulay, even Thornton warned Clarkson that he had "no conciliatory manners", might prove inflexible and seemed at first to be utterly without "feeling and tenderness"; also "his appearance is not altogether the most favourable".[12] On the plus side, he was full of zeal for the abolitionist colony, and had an extraordinary capacity for factual research and memorizing the results, so thanks to his year in England he was going to Freetown as something of a theoretical expert on the colony and colonization in general. Taking over from Clarkson, the pair had been befriended by Richard Pepys, the engineer of the original council, who by Clarkson's account was a treacherously oily character, a real-life Uriah Heep. Pepys had assured Clarkson that the ground clearance and allotment could be completed within two weeks after he left, so Clarkson promised the Nova Scotian settlers it would be, then as soon as he left it seems Pepys persuaded Dawes to stop the work altogether in favour of building a fort on Thornton Hill against their neighbours.

Dawes and Macaulay got the impression, not least from Pepys, that Clarkson had been a weak and ineffectual governor, swinging from over-indulgence to rage, constantly consulting instead of acting. A firmer hand was needed, and they set about providing it. And so in their reports to the directors, Dawes and Macaulay each lauded the other, and Pepys, exuberantly; and while Dawes warmly praised the governor for whom he was deputizing, Macaulay made it clear that under Dawes things would be a lot better for everyone than they had been under Clarkson.

This information overturned the directors' whole opinion of events in

Sierra Leone. If Clarkson had been at odds with the whole council, and the directors, and got nothing done in one year because of it, and if his great recommendation – his popularity among the black people – now turned out to be a mixed and exaggerated blessing, then perhaps he was the problem rather than the solution. So, four days after the dispatches arrived, on 23 April, the day Clarkson was due to leave for Suffolk for his wedding, Thornton asked for his resignation.

What Went Wrong?

Clarkson, and indeed the settlers, the investors, and the directors, were victims of the fundamental problem of the Sierra Leone venture: its twin goals of providing a new home for freed slaves, and of starting a commercial enterprise in Africa. Modern accounts of the colony tend to portray the company directors as interested only in profit and not in the black settlers, and, while there is some truth in the accusation, it overlooks the fact that the directors were by no means profiteering – they were fighting the slave trade, and opening a new front in that war by establishing a rival African trade. It was an excellent idea in an excellent cause – if it could be done properly. It required a healthy stream of merchandise to be imported from Freetown, whether produced there or traded, and they needed to start seeing it reasonably soon. If the scheme was to work, land and water supplies needed to be devoted to company agriculture, and supply ships had to carry farming and processing equipment and items for trade. And the work force had to be productive.

The Nova Scotian settlers however had not come to fight the slave trade. They came because they had been promised land, freedom, and equality in recompense for their unjust treatment and their service to the crown; and for Freetown to work as a settlement for former slaves it had to provide those things. But the greater the share of land they received and the higher the quality, and the more freedom they had to farm for their own subsistence and to sell any surplus to whom they chose, and the more money the company spent on houses, food, and domestic equipment for them, the more the company's capital dwindled without seeing any return.

The two aims were not inconsistent: in many ways they complemented each other, British investors providing the necessary capital for the settlement, and the philanthropy of the scheme offering a major incentive to invest. But they ended up pulling in fatally different directions. Clarkson was naturally concerned above all to ensure the welfare of the thousand settlers he had brought from Nova Scotia and to keep his promise of equally divided, self-sufficient, untaxed farming land for all of them. They would never have come if he had offered any less or failed to convince them to put their trust personally in his offer, and it was only what he considered fair and right anyway. Add to this his personal involvement with the exodus, his attachment to the people, and his presence on the ground in Freetown, and it is clear why he would postpone questions of trade and production until the settlement was fully established, and would ignore instructions to raise quitrent and reserve land for the company.

From the point of view of Thornton, Wilberforce, and Thomas Clarkson, giving a new home to a thousand former slaves was a happy side effect of a scheme with the larger goal of preventing 40,000 new victims a year being taken as slaves in British ships. Without commerce, it would never work. The company had taken £240,000 from benevolent subscribers, not as donations toward resettling Nova Scotians but as an investment in abolitionist commerce. While John Clarkson saw the needs of the settlers in close-up and the priorities of the directors in the hazy distance, for Thornton it was the other way around, with the pressures of accounts and accountability in sharp focus. He had sunk one-eighth of their capital, and eighteen months down the line desperately needed to know that there was going to be some return at some point.

Incidental elements conspired to exacerbate the problem: landfall in Freetown too soon before the rainy season, the unprecedented extremity of that season, Clarkson's problems with his original council, and the illness that put him out of action on his arrival and affected him long after. The company seems to have underestimated the work and resources necessary to settle a thousand people before they could be expected to start commercial farming.

Perhaps also Clarkson was a Moses rather than a Joshua, a charismatic figure able to persuade former slaves to leave their home for the promised land, but not so able to govern the land when they got there. Or perhaps if he had stayed long enough to get the settlement established, he would then have got the commercial business up and running too. As it was he left both undone, and through some combination of his own attitude to the directors and their misinformation about his conduct in Freetown, he never got the chance to try again. His successors reversed his priorities without ever having much success with either.

Coming to Clapham

It was in 1792 that Clapham belatedly started to become the geographical focus of the Clapham sect. The watershed was the death of the rector of the parish, Sir James Stonhouse, on 13 April, on the Berkshire estate where he had spent the four decades of his incumbency, finally allowing John Thornton's trustees to appoint an evangelical successor to live in the parish, Henry Venn's son John.

The Clapham Community

Perhaps, considering the timing, this development may have been what persuaded Henry Thornton finally to buy his own house on Clapham Common and set about creating an evangelical community. Battersea Rise was a three-storey Queen Anne house which had been the home of the great banker John Lubbock, and before him William "Single Speech" Hamilton MP. Thornton immediately had the house extended to three times its original size – hating extravagance, but also hating his father's austerity and seeing this as the happy medium. The grounds were huge enough for him to build two more houses there to rent out to religious friends. The first tenants, in 1794, were Edward Elliot, who took the nearer house, Broomfield, and Charles Grant and his family, whose house was called Glenelg and whom we shall meet later in this chapter. The centrepiece of the house was an oval library, apparently designed for Thornton by William Pitt. "Lofty and symmetrical, it was curiously wainscoted with books on every side," according to Sir James Stephen, "except where it opened on a far-extended lawn reposing beneath the giant arms of aged elms and massive tulip trees." Thornton's daughter Marianne recalled in later life, "to the day of my death I shall think nothing so lovely as the trees and the lawn at Battersea Rise".[1]

It seems that Thornton was deliberately building an evangelical community, and not just for the sake of their own fellowship, but to promote the gospel among their friends and acquaintances. Thornton said to Grant in 1793:

> *On the whole, I am in hopes some good may come out of our Clapham system. Wilberforce is a candle that should not be hid under a bushel. The influence of his conversation is, I think, great and striking. I am surprised to find how much religion everybody seems to have when they get into our house. They all seem to submit, and to acknowledge the advantage of a religious life, and we are not at all queer or guilty of carrying things too far.* [2]

Clapham did not just give the sect a name, but changed it from a network to a community. The fellowship they so loved at Rothley and Yoxall was no longer just for summer retreat but part of their daily lives, seamlessly knitting together political deliberation, worship, friendship and, later, family life, insulating them from the world.

The village had changed a lot since the days John and Lucy Thornton were there with Henry and Eling Venn. The draining of the common and improving of the roads had tripled the population and, while it was still a retreat of godless wealthy merchants, there were now many poor families too, and a strong evangelical presence. But Henry rejoiced that his son was being called back to the parish he himself had been called from thirty-three years earlier.

John Venn

The relationship between Henry and John Venn was one of hearty mutual admiration and devotion, dampened only by John's sometimes painful shyness. The rectories of Huddersfield and Yelling were sheltered homes, where, reckoned Henry, his only son "saw no company but of the ministers or children of God; heard no corrupt communication ever come out of any mouth; no praises, in the warmth of a sensual heart, of beauty, good eating, jollity, or wealth". [3]

John's curate, John Cunningham, said that John grew up between the wildly opposite temperaments of his parents, and seemed more often his mother's son than his father's. "Life and joy and energy...", in Cunningham's words, "surrounded the father as a sort of perpetual atmosphere"; he ardently and buoyantly pursued the great goals of his life and saw good in everything – though perhaps "he was less wise in council, than prompt in action". Eling, in contrast, was "easily depressed

– discerning evils at an incredible distance, and peopling earth, sea, skies, with visionary alarms". John suffered a "hidden disease" of depression, according to Cunningham; Henry said, "He rather too much fixes upon the dark side of things." But at other times, preaching, splendid scenery, and being with those he loved could bring out the spirit of his father in him.[4]

John also inherited something even more important to him from his father, which was love. He called him "that dear and admirable man to whom indeed under God I owe almost every blessing I enjoy in life", and told Hannah More, as he told his congregation, that his idea of God's love was simply a magnification of all that was "consoling, tender, affectionate … kind and excellent" in Henry. According to Cunningham, John judged people on the basis of their love for their parents, reading the story of Joseph being separated from Jacob could make him cry, while Absalom's rebellion against David made him redden with indignation. "Of all the men I ever saw," he said, "he most delighted to represent *God* under the image of a *father*. It was to him the most honourable and interesting of all titles, and he transferred it to the Being whom he best loved."[5] He reckoned that the fundamental point that dictated all John Venn's theology and his practice as a minister was the idea of the fatherhood of God, as modelled to him by Henry.

When John was four years old, he announced that, like his father before him, he would be a preacher, and when words proved inadequate would beat repentance out of people with a wooden trowel. "A very pleasing and entertaining child;" recalled Henry, "but altogether earthly, and sensual, and self-willed."[6] He went to Hipperholme Grammar School near Halifax until the headmaster fell ill, and then to Hull Grammar to be taught for a year by Joseph Milner, like Wilberforce who was the same age as John but had left at ten. Milner was best known to posterity for his five-volume *History of the Church of Christ*, which he was so busy writing while John was there, John's son Henry tells us, that the boy's education went backwards for a year, after which Henry sent him to study privately with the headmaster of Hipperholme.

After a couple of years being taught by his father, John started at Cambridge in October 1777. He joined Sidney Sussex College, having been turned down for Trinity because of his father's reputation as a Methodist. He was to be, like Henry before him, a sizar, the lowest of the four ranks of students, who had to perform service in return for a reduction in their fees, which provoked a very unevangelical outburst from Henry to his sister-in-law: "But oh, what a wound to my pride …

Why should not we be a little higher in the world and make some figure? Who can be comfortable or even contented to remain towards the fag end of the gentry, if we are allowed even to rank amongst them?" The lament soon enough lapses into more typical evangelical moralism, and in fact John won a scholarship allowing him to rise a rank in the benighted eyes of the world before the start of term. [7]

Henry was delighted to be asked for advice about university life from his son and replied with a cartload: rise early; shun idleness; read the Bible with prayer; "take care that your bed be thoroughly dry, and lay for the first night in your waistcoat, breeches and stockings"; he advised John not to let religious enthusiasm lead him into arrogance or excess; to be chaste, sober, and humble; to give a stern look to those who scoff at orthodoxy or indulge in *double entendres*; to keep a diary; to study standing up; and "every other morning attend your mouth and clean it well with snuff, which I find of great service to my teeth". [8]

When Henry heard that John was meeting regularly for spiritual talk with two friends at college and wanted spiritual guidance from his father, he replied in ecstasies: "My very dear son, figure to yourself a miser, glorying in his riches; or the child of ambition, exalted to the pinnacle of worldly honour: – their pleasure cannot exceed what your letter, received this day, gives to me." [9]

Henry had always thought that John was brighter than him, and he shone at university. But he was not a hard worker, and like his contemporary Wilberforce he found himself coasting on his natural intelligence rather than studying. When he agreed to stay at the end of term and help a tutor with his new library, Henry told him he was not allowed home until his tutor was satisfied: "In this matter you must do violence to your natural indolence and persevere." [10] Over the course of three years, however, the old Adam prevailed, and John ended up with a thoroughly disappointing third-class degree. A tutor persuaded him to stay another year in the hope of a fellowship, but at the end of it, on the very day of his viva, he offended the tutor by telling a friend what the tutor said about him, and, alone among his friends, failed. Henry, who could see the good hand of God in every evil, said that these troubles taught John a sympathy with his flock that it had taken him years to learn himself.

Days before leaving Cambridge, John finally made friends with his contemporary Charles Simeon. The two remained close friends for life, but Simeon was even closer to Henry. The first time he visited John at Yelling he stayed with Henry in his study until dinner, adopting him as a spiritual father. Simeon was the rector of Holy Trinity, Cambridge, from

1782 until 1836, supported by John Thornton and facing huge hostility for his evangelicalism. For ten years his congregation had to stand because seatholders left, locking their pews, and the churchwardens threw out the benches he put in the aisles, but he became the leader of generations of evangelical ordinands.

When it came to the ordination John Venn had been so long destined for, he was overwhelmed by fear. As he told John Thornton, "Extremely timid by constitution... I confess I startle at my own weakness",[11] and he tried to back out, but Thornton and his father assured him that such fears were good qualifications for the holy calling. His academic qualifications were meagre enough that the only post he could get was as his father's curate – assistance which Henry had never needed before, paid for out of Henry's own pocket. He was ordained on 22 September 1782.

Venn in Little Dunham

After a serious illness, John went to convalesce at John Thornton's, whose care involved having John preach at his church in Camberwell. The congregation included Edward Parry, a director of the East India Company and squire of Little Dunham in Norfolk, who was impressed with his preaching and his references, and invited him to his parish, which had not had a resident minister for seventy-five years, "to introduce the gospel of our Lord Jesus Christ into this dark corner of the kingdom".[12] He became rector in March 1783.

It was not a situation to draw John out of his sluggishness. Little Dunham had a population of precisely 100 adults, and the six-acre rectory with its brewery, "a maid, a boy; a horse, a cow, and two kittens" was, along with the church, some way out of the village. John immediately extended the house with a new parlour, study, two bedrooms, and a cellar. John Thornton said that "Jack had built him a house fit for a squire".[13] John paid for this by enclosing land and raising the tithe in one half of the parish to the same level as the other half, getting himself an income almost twice the size of his father's in Huddersfield.

Despite their difference in approach, John preached the evangelical gospel of his father, and like Henry in Clapham he found his parishioners largely unresponsive. He stirred himself to introduce a second Sunday service and monthly Eucharist, but his timetable allowed him plenty of time to indulge in literature and science, and after a year there Henry told him he should find himself a more demanding parish. Instead, John started holding extra prayer meetings in his own kitchen for his keener parishioners, as Henry did in Yelling, and preached in other nearby churches too. John also emulated his father by visiting alehouses every Sunday to stop sports and "indecent jollity", though unlike Henry he did it in person rather than sending out "Venn men". But in later life he felt – and his successor agreed – that he had never achieved much in his decade in Little Dunham, thanks to his lack of exertion and "unimpressable" parishioners.

In 1789, John decided it was time to marry and, hearing of several suitable young ladies in Hull, he headed north to check them out in May. Top of the list was Kitty King, whose family was another clan of Russia merchants, and whose brother he knew from Hull Grammar School and Cambridge. John and Kitty were introduced by Henry's friend James Stillingfleet. John told her ghost stories and religious anecdotes, and they made good impressions on each other with their agreeableness and piety – something of an achievement for a man as timid as John. He proposed to Kitty by letter in June, and she said that she would like to meet him again before she decided. He visited in August and, after John Thornton supplied glowing references for both of them to their prospective parents-in-law, they married on 22 October in Hull.

Henry Venn, in his *The Complete Duty of Man*, addressed marriage at length, and while his main emphasis, to an unusual degree, was on the mutual duties of love and loyalty, he also emphatically supported the conventional and supposedly biblical values of male rule, so widely unquestioned in eighteenth-century society. The Clapham sect thoroughly subscribed to such principles in theory. But, under his own roof, Henry had let Eling wear the breeches. "She led him entirely.... He was the most uxorious man I ever knew," said Stillingfleet. And when it came to his son's marriage he very much hoped Kitty would take John in hand likewise. "I hope she will stir up her husband", he told Stillingfleet, "and urge him to spend himself in labours."[14]

As indeed she did. She told him: "You may find sufficient work even in this retired place, if you will only put yourself forward." And after two years of marriage Henry said, "I never saw my son so entirely what I would wish as at present." He wrote to Kitty "to congratulate you on the good progress we all perceive in your husband". He was more active, more cheerful, more outgoing, his theology was more positive, and his two pupils (Charles Grant's sons) had made remarkable progress. "Now he is all alive and intent upon laying out his talents for good to the uttermost," Henry told his daughter Eling. "Either in the pulpit or in prayer, I cannot by many degrees reach his attainments."[15]

When the couple visited Henry in November 1789, he was delighted to have all his children under his roof for one last time, "all smiling and affectionate" and united in faith. "It so pleaseth our Heavenly Father to appoint, that after our children, the children of many prayers, are grown up, they are removed to a distance; lest we should settle upon our lees, and give too much of our affection to the children – defrauding him who claims the whole heart for himself."[16]

When John Thornton died in 1790, he left his eleven parishes to a trust comprising three people: Roger Bentley, whom he had appointed to St Giles's, Camberwell; Henry Foster, who had been Romaine's curate at St Andrew's-by-the-Wardrobe in London, but ended up with so many weekly preaching posts that he became a full-time freelance; and John Venn – it would have been Henry but he was now too old. When any of the livings became vacant, one of the three could choose to take it, or find an evangelical rector. As for Clapham itself, Foster was to have first refusal, followed by Venn.

When the rector of Clapham died in April 1792, it was universally assumed that Foster would succeed him, not least because he had no parish and his preaching brought him just £200 a year compared with the £650 on offer at Clapham. So little did John Venn imagine the baton would pass to him that eleven days after Stonhouse's death he formed the Little Dunham Clerical Society, a group like his father's in Huddersfield. But Charles Simeon persuaded Foster not to take it. Simeon told Foster that it would do more for the cause if Venn moved from his obscurity to the prominence of Clapham and he offered to give Foster his whole private fortune if he agreed. Foster agreed, declining compensation.[17]

Venn himself was very reluctant to go to Clapham. "I am almost overwhelmed with the sense of the many and great difficulties I can foresee," he told Kitty. The prominence of the place and the power and prestige of the men he would be preaching to terrified him. "I clearly see myself to be totally unfit for such a sphere."[18] With Kitty's encouragement, he accepted the post in May 1793, but between then and moving down in March 1794 he got cold feet again. Henry wrote him a long letter beseeching him not to fight the Lord as he himself had done on leaving Clapham, assuring him that a sense of his own inadequacy was a good thing, and that the Lord would equip him when the time came.

Banking Crisis

For the rest of the Clapham sect, 1793 was a rather low year. While the Sierra Leone colony struggled and the Proclamation Society plodded, the slave-trade abolition bill foundered in the Lords pending an almost nonexistent enquiry and popular support flagged. The French Revolution, so widely associated with abolition, reached new heights of horror and danger for the British ruling classes. The French invaded the Austrian Netherlands, offering military help to anyone wanting to overthrow their monarchy, and on 21 January executed Louis XVI. Wilberforce was less than thrilled to be declared an honorary French citizen for his services to liberty, equality, and fraternity. The Earl of Abingdon denounced the abolitionists in Parliament as "our Robespierres". Tom Paine's *The Rights of Man* sold 200,000 copies in a few weeks, a failed harvest in 1792 spread misery and unrest throughout Britain, and republican graffiti appeared on monuments. Pitt planned a war to curb French expansion, but the French declared war on 1 February.

When Wilberforce proposed discussions about how to implement the gradual abolition they had agreed in principle, MPs threw out the motion. The Duke of Clarence told the Lords that all abolitionists were "either fanatics or hypocrites". And that month, the British economy crashed, throwing Thornton's bank into crisis.

It was "a season of great commercial distress", Thornton recalled, with runs on banks across the country. The role of bankers' banker on which he had built his wealth suddenly became a liability. "We experienced greater difficulties than most other bankers in consequence of the sudden reductions of very large sums which we had held at interest for some very considerable banks." Like other banks since, they struggled to find the capital to meet the withdrawals, which in retrospect made Thornton question their practice. "There is something, as I now think, like want of honesty in claiming an almost unbounded credit without laying a proportional foundation for it."[19]

The bank weathered the crisis, however, and in fact Thornton's reputation thrived on it. Pitt depended on him for a detailed estimate of the extent of bankruptcies, and later he gave invaluable evidence to the parliamentary enquiry, establishing him as an expert on credit. Baron Auckland, the founder of the National Bank of Ireland, said he was one "of whom and of whose evidence it was difficult to speak in terms of adequate respect".[20]

Thornton's other contribution to the crisis was to give money to people who were struggling. Having been set an extraordinary example in this by his father, Henry surpassed him. His accounts for 1790 show him giving away £2,260, 60 per cent of his total expenditure. As his income increased he kept his personal expenses much the same and simply gave more. In 1792, with its failed harvest, he gave £7,508, which was 82 per cent. In 1793, amid all his own crises, with his other expenses steeper, he still managed to give £6,680. In another year of distress, he gave away £9,000. As he told his children, "I now and then perhaps approached to profusion."[21]

Wilberforce followed the same example, regularly giving away a quarter of his smaller income. The great and revealing difference between them was that Thornton gave with his banker's head, and Wilberforce gave with his heart. Before Thornton would donate to anyone who approached him, he investigated the case to assess how productive his charity was likely to be, while Wilberforce gave to anyone who could convince him that he or she was not a complete crook. Method, love of study, and emotional detachment were at the heart of who Thornton was. Macaulay said that Wilberforce's benevolence was "the more ardent", and that his "active love flies immediately to the object in distress, and gives almost instinctively. Thornton's consideration leads him to weigh the best mode of imparting relief, so as to raise no false hopes, and to produce no future unhappiness." Thornton's approach may be less appealing than Wilberforce's – though not to Macaulay – but it was also more costly to him as well. Time being money, it was "a sacrifice which Mr Macaulay said he did not think overstated at £5,000 per annum more".[22]

Mission to India

In 1793 the Clapham sect also added another front to their campaign to Christianize British imperialism, with an abortive attempt to launch a mission to India. One of the prime movers was Charles Grant, the "long-faced, blue-eyed", 47-year-old member of the East India Board of Trade. Grant was born in Aldourie on Loch Ness in 1746 on the day of the battle of Culloden in which his father was killed fighting to restore the Stuart monarchy in Britain, though Charles himself was of a generation of Scots who increasingly found it in their interests to co-operate with the Hanoverian regime. Charles had a religious upbringing and then grew out of it. Educated at Elgin, he went to Bengal at the age of twenty-one as a military officer in the service of the East India Company, later became a company merchant, and married the beautiful Jane Fraser. He lived a fairly wild life and ran up £20,000 worth of gambling debts. His life was turned around by a devastating series of bereavements: a favourite uncle died in 1774; in 1775 he lost his brother and a close friend; 1776 both of his children died from smallpox within nine days. He was thrown into a spiritual crisis and turned to Kiernander, the Danish minister of the British church in Calcutta, only to find that "my anxious inquiries as to what

I should do to be saved embarrassed and confused him exceedingly".[23] Nevertheless, Grant managed to have an evangelical conversion, and began to thrive materially. He was appointed to the lucrative post of commercial resident at Malda in 1780 and made a fortune from silk-making there. He was appointed to the Board of Trade to reform its commercial system in 1787.

Grant disagreed profoundly with the company's policy of expansionist rule of Bengal for the sake of profit. To his mind, Indians were lost souls and their society horrifically immoral and corrupt, both in desperate need of Christian mission. The company opposed any religious mission as liable to upset Indians and disrupt the colony; as the ambassador Lord Macartney assured the Chinese in 1793: "The English never attempt to disturb or dispute the worship or tenets of others."[24] In 1784, Grant discussed with Wesley and his lieutenant Thomas Coke the possibility of sending missionaries from Britain, but the evangelical disagreed with the Methodists as to whether the mission should be sanctioned by the authorities, and Wesley and Coke were absorbed by other missions. In 1786, Grant and friends, including the clergyman David Brown who came to Bengal to run an orphanage, launched a plan for a mission to India to be sponsored by the crown. They sent proposals to the Archbishop of Canterbury and leading MPs, and asked Wilberforce and Charles Simeon to lead the campaign in Britain. "It is to his influence alone," Brown said of Wilberforce, "that we hope the minister will regard such a project."[25] Wilberforce presented the plans to Pitt, but failed to win his support. But Grant had planted a seed with Wilberforce, and the pair of them remained in contact.

In 1787, Kiernander's Calcutta church was seized by the East India Company because of his debts, and so Grant bought it along with two friends, and when the SPCK failed to provide a permanent minister, David Brown took the post, continuing for twenty-three years without pay, as well as being chaplain to the company. Grant also employed a former ship's surgeon to go to Gumalti as a missionary, though nothing came of this, and gave money for building St John's Church in Calcutta.

Grant decided that paradoxically he would have a better chance of influencing events in India from Britain, and so with his large family he returned in the summer of 1790. He visited John Thornton in the last months of his life, having heard of his religious greatness, and so became friends with Henry – a fact which elicited from Henry a rare tribute to "the worth of my parent". Grant was instantly embraced by Wilberforce's circle as one of their own. He joined the Sierra Leone Company and the slave-trade abolition campaign. He also happened to meet John Venn in August, who was passing through London to visit an advowson bequeathed to him by Lady Smyth, the patron of Yelling. Venn made such a good impression that Grant asked him to take his two sons to Little Dunham as pupils. These were the two boys whose remarkable progress convinced Henry Venn that his son had changed his ways, and Grant was equally impressed. John in turn extolled the "excellent and sensible" Grant to his father.

Grant's sights were set on Parliament's twenty-year renewal of the charter of the East India Company in 1793, in which they might be persuaded to include new regulations requiring a Christian mission to Indians. Colonies were the responsibility of the Home Secretary, Henry Dundas, so in 1792 Grant wrote a detailed essay to present to him, after circulating it around the Clapham sect, outlining the state of Indian society in British Bengal and setting out proposals to civilize and Christianize it.

It was, incidentally, while this was happening that Wilberforce crossed swords with Dundas over his gradual abolition proposals in April 1792. The fact that Wilberforce had to hold in balance these two dealings with Dundas throws some light on his conduct of that debate. On the one hand it explains what might otherwise seem his remarkably positive tone toward Dundas in the debate – praising "his fairness in the manner of bringing forward his propositions" and his "ability and industry" concerning a bill that Wilberforce privately denounced as "a parliamentary licence to rob and murder". But then on the other hand, how easy it would have been for Wilberforce to decide to sell his Indian scheme to Dundas by supporting gradual abolition, telling himself and supporters that compromise over the slave trade was more useful than another defeat – if, that is, evangelism was really more important to him than humanitarianism, and if abolition was a tactic serving his overriding spiritual goal. But instead, politely and amiably, he fought Dundas's gradual abolition with everything he had and without an inch of compromise.

Dundas told Wilberforce that the proposed amendments to the East India Company charter had his support, and so Wilberforce brought them before Parliament in May. His motion obliged the company to appoint chaplains, teachers, and missionaries for the "religious and moral improvement of the Indians" as well as for the colonists. It passed through the early stages smoothly and convincingly – despite, Wilberforce said, "Lord Carhampton abusing me as a mad-man" – and Wilberforce and Grant began to celebrate the victory of the Lord.

In fact the Lord's side was going to have to concede defeat in this battle. Two days before the third reading of the bill, the directors of the East

India Company had an emergency meeting and vehemently denounced it. The wheels of godlessness turned rapidly, and Wilberforce came to the Commons on 24 May to find himself suddenly outnumbered. He tried to assure MPs that his proposals were "not meant to break up by violence existing institutions, and force our faith upon the natives of India; but gravely, silently, and systematically to prepare the way for the gradual diffusion of religious truth." "To reject this measure," he protested, "would be to declare to the world that we are friends to Christianity, not because it is a revelation from heaven, nor even because it is conducive to the happiness of man, but only because it is the established religion of this country". Even Dundas backed the company's objections – "most false and double," cried Wilberforce afterwards, before adding typically, "but, poor fellow! much to be pitied". And in case Clapham hoped to get missionaries into British India unofficially anyway, the new charter made it a high misdemeanour to enter without a licence. Wilberforce told Gisborne of the vote in tones of outrage: "our territories in Hindostan, twenty millions of people included, are left in the undisturbed and peaceable possession, and committed to the providential protection of – Brama". [26]

Wilberforce was devastated by the defeat. Viewing the state of India as he did, thanks to Grant's information, this mission was as important to him as abolition, and he had been thoroughly confident that God was with them, saying three days before the fatal meeting of the company directors: "The hand of Providence was never more visible than in this East Indian Affair." Success would have been a valuable consolation for their other foundering ventures. Moreover, while Wilberforce could keep bringing new slave-trade motions as soon as the Lords' enquiry was finished, nothing could be done about the East India Company charter for ten more years. He suffered agonies of self-doubt, asking whether the failure was "because one so unworthy as I undertook this hallowed cause… Yet where can I go but to the blessed Jesus?"[27] Their one other consolation was that when Cornwallis, the governor-general of the colony, retired in August, Pitt and Dundas – pressed by Grant – made the surprising appointment of an evangelical with no family connections or influence: John Shore. Shore planned to turn down the post, considering himself unworthy and enjoying a comfortable retirement after twenty years in India, until Grant persuaded him, although many historians have considered his first instinct correct. Grant became a director of the company in 1794.

What was at stake in the Clapham sect's proposals for India was a vision for a new kind of empire. The British Empire in Africa was a matter of mere pillage; in the Caribbean, slave-driving; British North America had generally carried on, as far as possible, as if the native people didn't exist; and British India was a secular trading concern. Clapham believed that British presence should improve the world, spiritually, materially, socially, and politically; that Britain had the truest religion, the most benign constitution, and the most advanced society, and was duty-bound to share it. "Wherever the sun shines, let us go round the world with him," Wilberforce told Parliament, "diffusing our beneficence."[28] They attempted this from scratch in Sierra Leone, but if British rule of Bengal accepted the same values it would give them a population of 20 million people to shine upon.

Eliot brought a more modest bill in March on a different subject – corruption in Stockbridge – which failed. Wilberforce brought two little bills in an attempt to keep the abolition cause alive while the Lords sat on the gradual abolition bill. He proposed to stop British ships supplying slaves to the colonies of foreign empires. Before the war, such sales had accounted for two-thirds of the British slave trade, but now they had largely dried up. In other words, all Wilberforce was asking MPs to do was to forbid the future revival of the most unpatriotic branch of a trade they had already committed themselves to abolishing within a few years. As Gisborne pointed out, even those who had previously opposed abolition had at the same time "almost universally reprobated" the foreign slave trade. And yet the bill was defeated by 31 votes to 29 at the third reading. Wilberforce's second motion was to limit the number of slaves that British ships could carry to British colonies, and this was defeated at the first vote.

Sierra Leone: New Management

Long before they heard in May 1793 that John Clarkson had been sacked by the Sierra Leone Company, in fact from the moment Clarkson left the settlement on leave on 29 December 1792, his deputy William Dawes and his assistant Zachary Macaulay discarded Clarkson's principles and priorities. They saw him as an over-indulgent governor, a ruler who had let his people rule him, and therefore achieved nothing. They were determined that the settlement would now be orderly, strict, hardworking, pious, and profitable, however the black settlers protested. Paradoxically, they also turned it into an unprecedented foray into democracy.

Dawes in Freetown
Clarkson had been slightly anxious to hear that his deputy was from a penal colony: "He will find things very different here… he must bear with their ignorance, make any allowances for their change of situation, and must not be hasty with them." But on working with him, he found Dawes wise, tolerant, and firm.[1] Dawes' first innovation in Sierra Leone was extraordinarily progressive. In December 1792, before Clarkson left and with his blessing, Dawes proposed a parliament for the people of Freetown as set out by Granville Sharp, to come into effect the day Dawes took over as acting governor. This was frankpledge with its tithingmen and hundreders elected by all households, which the Province of Freedom had used, and Sharp had pressed Clarkson to do so, without success.

Dawes seems to have expected this parliament to sort out disagreements among the settlers, keep the peace, and provide easier communication between the governor and the people, but it quickly became a more serious political force, which he did not resist. The tithingmen and hundreders presented popular grievances and demands to him, passed rules such as maximum prices, which he ratified, and served as judges in the Petty

Debts Court established in 1795. Dawes was extending Clarkson's policy of giving significant public appointments, such as town clerk, marshal, jurors, and gaoler, to black settlers.

Not only did the Freetown franchise have no property qualification, making it more democratic than in Britain or the United States but, since a third of households were headed by women – "the first women to cast their votes for any kind of public office anywhere in the world", in the words of Simon Schama[2] – it even surpassed that of revolutionary France, though the respective assemblies did not have comparable powers.

Once back in England, sacked and embittered, Clarkson said of Dawes: "He may be well calculated for an arbitrary government, and indeed I know no man more capable of making such a government *tolerable* than himself – but I do not think him a fit or proper person to be at the head of a colony founded on the constitution of Freetown – he would make a much better second."[3] It is clear whom Clarkson thought Dawes ought to be second in command to – and clear that many black Freetowners would have agreed. But the irony is that Clarkson's criticism is a more accurate description of himself than of Dawes. Dawes' government was constrained by the company and by the Freetown representatives, while Clarkson rejected the settlers' requests to take a modest share in it, got his council dismissed, and largely ignored the London directorate. It was Clarkson who made arbitrary government tolerable, while Dawes made a more circumscribed government intolerable.

Macaulay arrived to support Dawes on 8 January 1793, and they decided to add an hour-long morning service to the daily evening service, to which settlers were summoned by the Great Bell. This annoyed less evangelical British settlers such as Anna Maria Falconbridge and Isaac Dubois, two friends of Clarkson's who married on 7 January. They felt that Freetown was being turned into a fanatical religious regime, and calculated that the extra services cost the company £1,500 in lost work time. It was no grievance to the black Freetowners, who had seven churches of their own, Baptist and Methodist ("whose preachers", said Macaulay, "sometimes seem to contend who shall bawl the loudest"), including what remain today the only churches in Lady Huntingdon's Connexion outside England. Their religious affiliations reflected different political attitudes, the Methodist settlers tending to be more rebellious and the Baptists more loyal to the Sierra Leone Company. The black churches worshipped late into the night and treated the official morning prayers as a chance to lie in.

Discontent

More troubling was Dawes' decision in January 1793 to allow Pepys to halt both the land survey which was supposed to deliver the long awaited lots to all settlers and the building of a stone storehouse to protect their supplies. Instead work was diverted to clearing ground for the company's cotton plantation, and constructing company buildings on the waterfront and a fort against possible attack – from foreign powers, slave traders, or their neighbours.

It was not a malicious decision but it could hardly have been more brutal. Dawes wanted to divert resources to commerce, as he had been instructed by Thornton, and to security. He was also unhappy with the way land was being allotted – the company got too little, and the valuable waterfront was divided among the settlers despite Thornton's instruction to reserve it for company use. Dawes had been told to press forward with the all-important trade and production, and had no understanding of the promises of land which had brought the Nova Scotians to Freetown, so he betrayed their trust in Clarkson and in the Sierra Leone Company and denied them their land. Unable to produce enough food for themselves, they would be forced to buy from the company at prices which Dawes raised in some cases to almost twice those under Clarkson, already higher than in Nova Scotia, and Freetowners would be forced to work for the company, at rates and on terms that Dawes dictated.

The settlers were devastated and outraged, but Dawes was determined to rule them. On 24 January, he asked a settler to vacate his hut because the land was needed for part of their fortifications, but a crowd surrounded him and threatened to pull down anything built in their living space until all had their land. As Clarkson had done when facing similar antagonism, Dawes threatened to leave the colony, only to be told, according to Anna Maria Dubois: "Go! go! go! We do not want you here, we cannot get a worse after you."[4]

Dawes retreated for the moment, but on 6 February declared that all allotment of settlers' land was postponed for a year, and that all land within 500 feet of the river belonged to the company, meaning that hundreds of settlers who had houses there would be moved. The furious Freetowners protested that Clarkson had promised them access to the river, and (reported Anna Maria Dubois) that "no distinction should be made here between us and white men; we now claim this promise, we are free British subjects, and expect to be treated as such; we will not tamely submit to be trampled on any longer".[5]

Pepys told them, according to Isaac Dubois, "whatever promises Mr

Clarkson had made them in Nova Scotia were all from himself... he had no authority whatever for what he said and that he believed Mr Clarkson was drunk when he made them... That Mr Clarkson seldom knew or thought of what he said." Pepys, Dubois wrote to Clarkson, "is as black a [*sic*] hearted insinuating a *villain* as this day exists".[6]

The parliament of black settlers drew up an alternative town plan for themselves, and chose two members, Isaac Anderson and the Huntingdonian minister Cato Perkins, to take a petition to the directors in London over the heads of Dawes and Macaulay, clubbing together toward their expenses. Advised by Dubois, the petitioners listed the broken promises and inequalities they had suffered, asking the company to clarify whether they planned to honour Clarkson's assurances, and requesting that Dawes be recalled. "Mr Clarkson behaved as kind and tender to us as if he was our father," they said, adding, in words that ought to have chilled the blood of the fathers of an abolitionist colony, "Mr Dawes seems to wish to rule us just as bad as if we were all slaves." They assured the directors of their humble peaceful obedience – so long as they got what they were owed. "We are sorry to tell your honours that we feel ourselves so distressed because we are not treated as free men that we do not know what to do and nothing but fear of God makes us support it until we know from your honours what footing we are upon."[7]

Meanwhile, Dawes and the Freetowners were not each other's only problems. Naimbana, whose land they were on, died early in 1793, and his son Henry Granville Naimbana, who had been baptized and educated in Clapham, came home, only to die of a fever ten hours from shore. This was a multiple blow to the colonists. It set back their hopes of bringing Christianity to the Africans, it undermined their claim to their land, as in Temne thinking the colonists had bought Naimbana's conditional permission to occupy it rather than an inalienable right, and it wrecked their relations with their neighbours – the prince's brothers accused the British of poisoning him. Dawes appointed armed guards to defend Freetown from them, and several settlers were killed. He also heard that another Temne kingdom nearby had approached European slave traders to negotiate a joint attack on Freetown.

In May a ship from England arrived with an outdated letter from Clarkson telling the settlers he was returning immediately, and a more recent one announcing his dismissal. As Perkins and Anderson were still waiting for a ship for England, the settlers added to their petition a request for his reinstatement. It was now that Freetown heard of the execution of Louis XVI and the French war; in the next dispute over prices, Dawes received a note telling him he was heading the same way as Louis, and that time he bowed to their demands.

While the ship was moored and the captain was away, three sailors took a walk through Freetown and killed a duck belonging to one of the settlers. They were arrested, imprisoned by Dawes, and the next day tried by the Freetown court, as Anna Maria Dubois reported in horror: "not by their peers, but by *Judge* McAuley, and a *jury of twelve blacks*". Being found guilty, one received thirty-nine lashes "by the common whipper", and the others were fined, and kept in irons pending payment. "Poor Jack was dreadfully mortified at being whipped by a black man," she wrote. The captain, when he returned, was outraged, denied the authority of the court to try "white men, the subjects of Great Britain, by a *jury of blacks*" and demanded his men's release. Macaulay protested, but was forced to submit.[8]

Perkins and Anderson finally left for England with their petition in June, on the ship carrying the first cargo of Freetown produce, worth a modest £1,500. Isaac and Anna Maria Dubois left the colony at the same time, returning home on a slave ship via Jamaica, an experience which so "agreeably disappointed" Anna Maria after the horrors she had expected to see that it converted her from abolition.

Slaves in Freetown

Relations with British slave traders caused Freetown serious problems. It was surrounded by slaving stations. The whole point of the colony was to fight the slave trade, and on Wilberforce's request for "damning evidence" of the effects of the trade in Africa for the House of Lords enquiry, Macaulay and Dawes provided him with intelligence. But Clarkson, Dawes, and Macaulay were all forced to trade with them and use their ships for sending letters, etc., and so had to cultivate their friendship. From time to time Freetowners were kidnapped as slaves, and conversely slaves sometimes escaped from prisons and ships and took refuge in Freetown. In July 1793, while Dawes was travelling, five slaves escaped from a nearby ship and were sheltered by Freetowners, and Captain Horrocks complained to Macaulay. Macaulay took a different attitude to this matter from both the directors and Clarkson. Thornton in his instructions to Clarkson said that an escaped slave had "such a clear natural right to protection and freedom that I own I wish much we may find ourselves able to give him full protection if he comes to us", but recognized the dangers of provoking the traders, so he left it up to Clarkson's discretion "whether you will have the strength to maintain the principle of universal freedom or whether you must a while connive and temporize".[9] Clarkson issued a proclamation that a slave was free the moment he or she set foot in Freetown – which had been Sharp's rule for the Province of Freedom too, though he said owners should be recompensed.

But to Macaulay's legalistic mind this made no sense: one wanted the slave trade to be abolished, but as long as it was permitted one had to see the slaves in "the sacred light of property". He did not return the slaves to the captain – the Freetowners had armed them against recapture – but he demanded to know what the Freetowners thought they were doing, and when told what Clarkson had declared would not believe his predecessor had made "so rash and unnecessary a proclamation" until it was confirmed by British colonists. "We had no more power to detain a slave than we had a bale of goods," he told the Freetowners, according to the journal he kept for Thornton. The governors would fight to protect their own people from being taken, but did not have "an emancipating power", so to follow Clarkson's policy would mean that the Sierra Leone Company sanctioned robbery; it would put Freetown in a state of war with neighbouring slave traders, including the African kings; the British government would not help them, as the act incorporating the company explicitly forbade them to injure the rights of traders; and "the company would of course abandon them, for a state of warfare would not suit with their principles".[10]

In the margin of Macaulay's report at this point, the directors have written an emphatic "No". They found themselves in an unhappy position, however. On the one hand, the idea of Freetown returning people to slavery was abhorrent and shameful, and yet they found Macaulay's analysis of the legal and practical position hard to argue with. They seem to have left it to his discretion.

Perkins and Anderson in England

Perkins and Anderson arrived in Portsmouth on 16 August, made their way to London, and presented their petition to Henry Thornton. According to Anna Maria Dubois, he read it sympathetically and took it away to show the other directors, but in the next day or two he received letters from Dawes and Macaulay, rebutting the petitioners' complaints and denying that they spoke on behalf of most of the settlers. Coming to London in the wake of the French regicide and the start of the Revolutionary War, amid fears of republicanism and financial distress, Perkins and Anderson were taking ill-timed industrial action, and Dawes' pre-emptive strike was all the persuasion the directors needed to disregard it. Perkins and Anderson asked for Clarkson's address, which the directors refused to give them.

While they waited for a proper meeting and an official response to their petition, their money ran out and they applied to the directors for more. One, the Clapham merchant Samuel Parker, offered money in return for mortgaging their land in Freetown. When they declined, Thornton arranged for them to earn a living as servants, while the Huntingdon family got Perkins the chance to attend college.

Wilberforce again requested a naval promotion for John Clarkson and again failed, and this time Thomas Clarkson complained that Wilberforce lobbied Chatham repeatedly "with singular zeal and warmth", but had not absolutely insisted on it face to face. He also included side-swipes at Pitt and Thornton. Wilberforce wrote a bristly letter, pointing out that what Clarkson was demanding from him he would condemn, rightly, as political corruption if he exercised it on behalf of any other friend. He wanted to see John promoted, but would not be cajoled into pulling more strings (or offended into pulling fewer) than was right.

Eventually in October Perkins and Anderson were given John Clarkson's address in the Fens, by Isaac and Anna Maria Dubois who were now in London, and they sent him a copy of their petition. Clarkson wrote to Thornton suggesting a joint meeting "to explain the promises you authorized me to make them", which Thornton ignored, so Clarkson sent a second letter, unsealed, via Perkins and Anderson, which they delivered to the next meeting of directors in November.

Instead of agreeing to a meeting, Thornton told the delegates to present any questions they wanted answered in writing, which they did with rapidly evaporating deference: "We did not think, gentlemen, anything more was necessary than the petition we brought, and delivered to you from the people we represent; but as you do not seem to treat that petition with the attention we expected, you oblige us to say something more on the subject." Clarkson, they said, had convinced them that his promises had the company's authority.

We certainly hope your Honours intend making good those promises, and we beg to know whether you do or not? – We beg to have grants for the land we at present occupy, and a promise in writing for the remainder…

We will not be governed by your present agents in Africa, nor can we think of submitting our grievances to them, which we understand is the intention of your Honours, for it is inconsistent to suppose justice will be shewn us, by the men who have injured us, and we cannot help expressing our surprise that you would even hint such a thing.

Their petition had said Christian duty would stop the settlers taking things into their own hands until the directors had had a chance to act;

> *but we are sorry to say, we do not think you seem disposed to listen to our complaints, and if we are obliged to return to Sierra Leone, impressed with those sentiments… it is impossible for us to say what the consequences may be, but we will make bold and tell your Honours, on the [an]swer we get, depends the success of your colony….*
>
> *The manner you have treated us, has been just the same as if we were slaves, come to tell our masters of the cruelties and severe behaviour of an overseer.*[11]

The directors were outraged. Both the tone and content of the letter assured them they were facing their own revolution. They dismissed the two men from the room, then Thornton sent them a note asking them to put all Clarkson's promises in writing. When they did so, the directors' only response was to interrogate them about who was helping them write. Isaac Dubois was sacked soon afterwards, and Perkins and Anderson left for Sierra Leone in February 1794 with nothing.

Anna Maria Dubois (under her former name of Falconbridge) published an account of her stay in Sierra Leone, exposing the disarray and death rate, and the mistreatment of Perkins and Anderson. She made no secret of the fact that she did so in anger having failed to get money she reckoned due to her from Thornton, but it was a great embarrassment and they responded immediately with a public report on the colony.

Giving full weight to the fact that we have only one side of the story, the treatment of Perkins and Anderson still seems inescapably shabby. Race, class, politics, and self-satisfaction appear to have combined to ensure that two of the very few "clients" that Thornton and Wilberforce ever met were received with fear and contempt. Though not full members of the Clapham sect yet, Dawes and Macaulay had gained a share of the love and trust that bound them together, and one of Clapham's weaknesses was that – much as they welcomed each other's censure – criticism from the outside made them close ranks. Above all, it is the perfect example of their paternalism and perhaps sentimentality that, in the abstract, injustices done to African people inspired agonies and rage (or calmer equivalents in Thornton's case) and unwearying struggle to deliver justice, whereas two African people arriving in their office to claim justice for themselves was more than they could cope with.

The Pen

In the summer of 1793, the French Revolution became more unhelpful still for the abolition movement in Britain. The Convention declared that Christianity was superseded by the cult of reason. Facing famine, civil war, and invasion, they decreed "the Terror", and up to 40,000 suspected traitors went to the guillotine, including further members of the royal family. The slave revolt in St Domingo became a war, with Britain and Spain supporting the slaves, and so the French commander Sonthonax decided the only way to keep the island for France was to declare the slaves free, which he did on 29 August 1793. The Convention then abolished slavery throughout the empire on 4 February 1794.

The crushing irony was that French abolition removed the most powerful argument against British abolition – that if British ships gave up the slave trade they would merely be handing it over to the French – and yet the British moneyed classes were so horrified by the revolution that the effect of French abolition was to damn the British campaign by association. Wilberforce's brother-in-law Thomas Clarke told him: "I do not imagine that we could meet with twenty persons in Hull at present who would sign a petition, that are not republicans. People connect democratical principles with the abolition of the slave trade and will not hear it mentioned."[1] The British invaded St Domingo in September 1793, supported by French plantation owners, and resisted by Toussaint L'Ouverture's army of freed slaves. It took five years and 40,000 deaths before the British admitted defeat.

Pitt and Grenville assured Wilberforce that in the 1794 session the Lords would finally complete the enquiry that was grounding his abolition bill, and the Clapham sect spent the winter preparing evidence for it, including their new supply from Dawes and Macaulay. Thomas Clarkson embarked once again on five months of travel to find witnesses.

In February 1794, Wilberforce renewed his motion against the slave trade to foreign empires which had been narrowly defeated the previous May. This time, despite tirades against the Frenchness of abolition and the "wild and visionary opinions" of abolitionists, it passed through the Commons, but the Lords, resenting the interruption of their own purported enquiry, shelved it. And yet when the Bishop of Rochester proposed restarting that enquiry in March, they refused. When they eventually got around to it, they interviewed a total of two witnesses, and then having, as Gisborne put it, over two or three years spent "parts of some few days" on it, "the hearing of evidence was entirely discontinued".[2]

It was finally too much for Thomas Clarkson, who had a nervous breakdown. He left the Abolition Committee, moved to the Lake District and invested the pension Wilberforce raised for him into farming. The committee had long suffered from falling donations, and now gave up its rooms and reduced its meetings to two a year.

The idea of Wilberforce as the holy pragmatist who would do anything within reason to sell evangelicalism to the ruling classes, and for whom abolition was a way of recruiting the nation to that cause, is very severely dented by his conduct of the abolition campaign through these lean years. The people in general had lost interest in it, while to many in the upper classes it was an abomination. As a means to an end, a far more sensible alternative would have been to give up. And yet he kept at it relentlessly, because in truth the only ends to which it was a means were human happiness and acquitting himself before God.

Campaigning for Peace

Less pragmatic still was the Clapham sect's opposition to the war with France. Wilberforce had spoken against it from the start, being generally opposed to war for humanitarian reasons. He fruitlessly entreated Pitt to be more conciliatory to the French, and told Parliament: "War I consider at all times the greatest of human evils, and never more pregnant with injury than at the present moment." Thornton took the revolutionary threat more seriously, saying, "The war, being a war in defence of our constitution, appeared to me to be more just than almost any other in the British history," but French victories soon persuaded him as "a general lover of peace" that Wilberforce was right, and that coming to terms would be more sensible than waging a long war whose hardships only encouraged republicanism at home. Pitt was absolutely committed, though, and used the King's Speech that opened the 1795 parliamentary session to insist there could be no peace without counter-revolution in

France. This was the matter over which the Clapham sect chose to fight the Prime Minister. It was a momentous decision, and Wilberforce lost sleep over it. As independent as they were as MPs, they had supported Pitt, personally and politically, in everything of significance, and they knew he would take it hard. They also knew the war was very popular in Parliament and in the country, so they had no chance of winning the vote, only of losing support for their other causes, and forfeiting their invaluable influence with Pitt. There was in other words nothing very much to be said for their defection, other than that it was the right thing to do – and that, as Wilberforce wrote in his journal, becoming more unpopular "may not be bad for me in spiritual things".[3]

Sure enough, his peace amendment was easily defeated, by 246 votes to 73. William Windham, the Secretary for War, publicly condemned it as a motion for "submission, humiliation, degradation before an inveterate and insolent enemy", privately condemned Wilberforce as a "wicked little fanatical imp", and told Lady Spencer: "Your friend Mr Wilberforce will be very happy any morning to hand your ladyship to the guillotine."[4] The King publicly snubbed him, and he was estranged from Pitt for months. Even friends such as Isaac Milner and William Hey disapproved.

And sure enough when Wilberforce brought his next abolition bill to the Commons, in February 1795, it was trounced. The House had voted to abolish the slave trade by the end of that year, and so, as it was still possible for the Lords to pass Dundas's bill, Wilberforce proposed new legislation merely to confirm and detail their decision, but it was rejected at the first reading. Sharp's Abolition Committee issued a report which concluded that in the light of Parliament's decision "we are reduced to the sad necessity of informing our friends, that all hopes from *that quarter* are nearly vanished". The plantation owner Stephen Fuller wrote home from London that abolition was defeated and they should hear no more of it. And yet, despite all this, Thornton said, looking back at the peace motion nine years later: "There is hardly any vote of which I am less disposed to repent than that for which our party were so much displeased with us."[5]

More's Books

Throughout the 1790s, the Clapham sect applied themselves to the moral and spiritual regeneration of Britain through the printed word. More and Gisborne kept up their steady flow of books. ("Gisborne another book!" wrote Wilberforce to a friend in 1798. "He deserves to live in a forest.") In February 1791, More followed her *Thoughts on the Importance of the Manners of the Great*, again anonymously, with *An Estimate of the Religion of the Fashionable World*. This was a far more warlike book. Spurred on by the danger of the times, she was no longer satisfied urging the godly to be better, and now confronted the mass of people who believed and worshipped as Christians, but failed to live up to evangelical standards in their daily lives. She insisted they were guilty of greater sin than outright infidels: "Christianity, like its divine Author... is *betrayed* by the... treacherous disciple, even while he cries, 'Hail, Master!'" She bemoaned the "moral revolution in the national manners and principles" and "the almost total extermination of religion in fashionable families". Children were no longer trained in godliness, and the dissolute no longer bothered to repent on their deathbeds. The laws of the sabbath were heard in church and ignored for the rest of the day. Gamblers offered up the happiness of wives and children "to the demon of play". They needed to realize that true Christianity is not simply accepting dogma or performing rites, "it is not a name, but a nature: it is a turning the whole mind to God: it is a concentration of all the powers and affections of the soul into one steady point, an uniform desire to please *Him*". Instead of seeing themselves as reasonably good people, they needed to recognize the profound corruption of their souls and commit themselves to daily wrestling them into submission.[6]

Much of this reads like the apologetics of Doddridge and Venn, but More's concerns were more political. She warns readers that their own dissoluteness will make the working classes dangerously profligate. "It is no less absurd than cruel, in such of the great as lead disorderly lives, to expect to prevent vice by the laws they make to restrain or punish it, while their own example is a perpetual source of temptation to commit it." She imagined a boy, taught in a charity school such as hers to give devout thanks for his meal of barley bread, being taken on as servant to a noble family where he sees his master sit down daily "to a repast for which every element is plundered, and every climate impoverished; for which nature is ransacked, and art is exhausted, without even the formal ceremony of a slight acknowledgment". How can such people be expected to stick to their training in virtue?[7]

More imagines readers protesting that their private lives may be permissive, but they are moral people because they give generously to good causes. She concedes that they are living in "the age of benevolence", but it will not save their souls or their society. They relieve poverty with their giving, but create far more poverty by setting the poor an example of drunkenness, gambling, sexual licence, luxury, and waste. True charity is a matter of directing one's whole life to helping others for God's sake;

it is evidence of Christianity, whereas fashionable charity is a substitute for it. "The most valuable species of charity is that which prevents distress by preventing or lessening vice, the greatest and most inevitable cause of want", so attempts such as hers and Patty's to control the habits of working people were, she maintained, more genuinely generous than mere giving. Her readers had similar opportunities to impress Christianity on their servants, by instruction and example, remembering that "to keep an immortal being in a state of spiritual darkness, is a positive disobedience to [God's] law". [8]

The book went through five editions in two years. Its greatest importance, reckoned Newton, was that More's style and name put evangelical apologetics into the hands of fashionable people who would never otherwise read them. In 1793, Wilberforce decided to write a similar book showing how average Christians failed biblical standards. He had considered writing such a book in 1789, but decided that any good it did would be outweighed by his being seen as a fanatic, diminishing his influence on the government and political allies. Now four years later his religion was well known, he was more confident and better supported in it – and with his plans for the slave trade, Sierra Leone, and India running aground, he had less to lose. He began writing at Bath in August, and expected to finish the book by the autumn. But Wilberforce did not have the concentration of More and Gisborne, and the book took him four years.

More turned to a new audience in 1793, with *Village Politics: Addressed to All the Mechanics, Journeymen, and Day-Labourers of Great Britain*, an antidote to radical politics that she wrote under the pseudonym of "Will Chip, country carpenter", being so determined to keep her identity secret she used a different publisher. She succeeded for slightly over a month. It was a new direction in the Clapham sect's tactics of social influence. Their policy of trying to directly control the lower classes while winning around the higher with reasoned arguments had started to look inadequate, thanks to the popularity of Tom Paine and the republican movement: the lower classes turned out to be people who could be swayed by arguments and books, and needed to be swayed back.

Village Politics is a dialogue in which Jack Anvil the blacksmith, who has just been convinced by *The Rights of Man*, is won back by the conservative common sense of Tom Hod the mason. Jack has discovered how unhappy his life is – "which I would never have known if I had not had the good luck to meet with this book" – and wants the equality and freedom the French have seized for themselves. Tom explains that theirs is the freedom to hang from the next lamppost anyone they do not like the look of, circumstances under which no kind of equality could last long. Why follow the French? "They only began all this mischief at first, in order to be just what we are already." They have gone from tyrannical monarchy to tyrannical anarchy, while Britain has enjoyed a free and just society all along. The radicals are like the local squire's new wife who wanted "to pull down yonder fine old castle, and build it up in her frippery way" just because "there may be a trifling fault or two and… a few decays may want stopping". Society needs both rulers and workers, and without aristocracy we would starve for want of government and philanthropy; "the poor have as much share in the government as they well know how to manage".[9]

The book contains an interesting exchange which, without a good dose of double standards, sounds like a striking self-condemnation of the moral reform programme of the Clapham sect:

Tom. *I'm a friend to the people. I want a reform.*

Jack. *Then the shortest way is to mend thyself.*

Tom. *But I want a general reform.*

Jack. *Then let every one mend one.*[10]

Equally ironic is the fact that, just as More used the unladylike profession of essayist to urge women to keep to their traditional spheres, so she was urging the lower classes to leave politics to their betters, in a way that addressed them directly as political creatures and engaged them in political debate.

More returned to her traditional readership with another bestseller, *Remarks on the Speech of M. Dupont*, addressing the horrors and threats of the French Revolution. Arguing that it was fundamentally a rebellion against God, she said the way to guard against it spreading to Britain was moral regeneration. "If we would fly from the deadly contagion of atheism, let us fly from those seemingly remote, but not very indirect paths which lead to it."[11]

Gisborne's Books
In 1794 Gisborne published a successful book of poems called *Walks in a Forest*. He was also a flautist and painter, touring the Lake District with William Gilpin, the pioneer of the "picturesque", and Joseph Wright,

who painted an affectionate portrait of Thomas and Mary. All this sets
him apart from the rest of the Clapham sect, whose attitude to the arts
was grim. They had no interest in music or art, disapproved of opera,
theatre, and novels, and judged poetry more by theological than aesthetic
standards. Gisborne passed that test, finding an abundance of spiritual
lessons in the forest. His second volume of verse was called *Poems Sacred
and Moral.*

He continued his philosophical approach to moral reform with *An
Enquiry into the Duties of Men in the Higher and Middle Classes*, which
practically applied *The Principles of Moral Philosophy* to the lives of British
men from king down to tradesman – going no further on the ground
that working men were unlikely to read a 900-page moral treatise. It was
widely acclaimed, and Gisborne produced a sequel in October 1796, the
much shorter *An Enquiry into the Duties of the Female Sex.* Contemporary
readers, male and female, found both books strict and in many cases
puritanical or idealistic, "receipt-books… to make human angels".[12] To
a modern reader, though, what Gisborne says about women's roles in
relation to men is appallingly repressive and breathtakingly patronizing.
As most of his original readers would see it, he was defending a moderate,
common-sense position that welcomed the liberation of women from their
closeted and uneducated lives of years gone by, while maintaining their
subordinate role. Gisborne very briefly addresses Mary Wollstonecraft's
groundbreaking *A Vindication of the Rights of Woman*, describing it as
"upholding the perfect equality of injured woman and usurping man in
language so little guarded, as scarcely to permit the latter to consider the
labours of the camp and of the senate as exclusively pertaining to himself",
an absurdity which apparently leaves no further criticism necessary. He
argues that God has given men and women different kinds of body,
mind, and work. God made men physically stronger, to labour and fight,
while compensating women "by symmetry and expression, by elegance
and grace", and the power to enchant.[13] He gave man powers of reason
and concentration for the purposes of government, war, commerce, and
philosophy. Women, being incapable of these things, have other powers,
also very important in their own way:

> *in sprightliness and vivacity, in quickness of perception, in fertility of
> invention, in powers adapted to unbend the brow of the learned, to
> refresh the over-laboured faculties of the wise, and to diffuse throughout
> the family circle the enlivening and endearing smile of cheerfulness, the
> superiority of the female mind is unrivalled.*[14]

God has commanded wives to obey their husbands – in everything moral and reasonable – and designed them to do so, planting in them "a remarkable tendency to conform to the wishes and example of those for whom they feel a warmth of regard".[15] Probably the most shocking gulf between Gisborne and modern readers is in the fact that he spends two chapters instructing parents and educators on girls' duties, before starting to include the women themselves among his readers, as if men are moral agents while women are primarily objects of morality.

In 1797, Gisborne published a school-book, *A Familiar Survey of the Christian Religion*, encouraging schools to teach "Christian fear and love of God" as the basis for morality.

The Cheap Repository Tracts

From 1795 to 1798, More extended *Village Politics* into a monthly series of tracts, the Cheap Repository. This is often said to be in response to Tom Paine's *The Age of Reason*, which argued for Deism, against British Christianity and French Atheism, for a dangerously democratic 3*d*. a copy. Dozens of writers did respond to it, including Thomas Scott. Bishop Porteus, by this time president of the Proclamation Society and a great fan of *Village Politics* (he wrote to More as "Mrs Chip", telling her that her husband was "one of the finest writers of the age"), told More "the eyes of many are fixed on *you* at this important crisis"; their expectation was "a kind of call upon you from heaven" to publish a very plain defence of Christianity, "brought down to the level of Will Chip and Jack Anvil".[16] But More declined, saying she did not have the ability.

The Cheap Repository did not provide apologetics for Christianity it was more concerned with improving the politics, morality, and religion of working people. They bought a great deal of literature, but not in the form or through the channels that More was used to, rather through broadsides and chap-books – cheap sheets and booklets containing stories and songs of a kind that often grossly offended evangelical sensibilities, "poor, licentious, and injurious trash", as the Revd William Jay, a Dissenter friend of the Clapham sect put it, or in Thornton's words, "corrupt and vicious little books and ballads which have been hung out at windows in the most alluring forms, or hawked through town and country".[17] They could be sexually explicit, blasphemous, or peppered with four-letter words; even, as in the song of the exhausting wife who damns her husband by demanding satisfaction during church time, all three at once. If More and her collaborators could produce a steady stream of stories and songs in a popular style but with a Christian content, through the same channels and for the same price, they might colonize the literature of the British heathen.

Chap-books were crudely produced, illustrated paperback books usually from four to twenty-four pages long, often telling stories – traditional romances, British victories, the crimes and executions of outlaws – but also offering information and advice on anything from sex to witchcraft. Others contained songs, jokes, prophecies, and sermons. Broadsides were single sheets, often containing ballads and generally illustrated, and were used to decorate people's walls as much as for their contents.

More described her project as "a plan for abolishing ballad singing, and trying to substitute religious papers". She told Sir Charles Middleton in November 1794: "I am getting acquaintance with all the hawkers, pedlars and matchwomen in town and country, and to secure a stall at country fairs I propose to make a friendship in Bath and Bristol, with all such gentry as stick out penny literature in little shops in lanes and alleys."[18]

The first tract she wrote was *The Shepherd of Salisbury Plain: Part One*, a story in which a gentleman discovers a shepherd living in overwhelming poverty with his wife and eight children in a leaky hovel. They make the most of their lives through economy and superhuman cheerfulness, remaining clean and tidy because "poor people who have but little regard to appearances will seldom be found to have any great regard for honesty and goodness".[19] They treasure everything in their lives gratefully as blessings from God, however unlikely, knowing that all things are ultimately for the best, that they could have had it so much worse, and that a heavenly mansion awaits their patient faith. The shepherd reads the Bible daily and even the smallest children work every moment they can. The gentleman ends up envying the shepherd's contentment, and gives him five shillings, whose value we are assured is hugely magnified by the family's frugality and pious appreciation.

The lessons that the poor were supposed to take from the story hardly need spelling out – it would seem a remarkably manipulative piece of work if it had some subtlety, but it's like being force-fed syrup while being repeatedly poked in the ribs. However, the tract also has its eye on middle-class readers, showing them how beneficial for everyone working-class piety is, reminding them to set a good example and to support efforts to evangelize them, and demonstrating the right level of charity – enough to put a smile on their faces without materially changing their lot in life.

More launched the *Cheap Repository* at a breakfast at William Jay's house. Jay was a Dissenting preacher whose sermons More often attended outside the hours of Church of England services. John Thornton had helped pay for his education, but did not want him to go to university, saying, "God has opened the young man's mouth, and for many years to come we dare not shut it." More asked Jay to read the tract to their guests: "This I did," he says, "not without difficulty, being affected to tears with some of its exquisite touches."[20]

With the approval and donations of those guests and other useful friends, More set about producing and marketing the tracts, which included edifying ballads, hymns, and sermons as well as stories, at a rate of three a month. Virtue was rewarded, trials endured, blasphemers struck down; slippery slopes took promising youngsters to the gallows, clergy and gentry shone like stars, and the pious poor enjoyed their poverty more than might have been expected. Some titles left little room for curiosity, such as the ballad *The Story of Sinful Sally, Told by Herself, shewing how from being Sally of the Green she was first led to become Sinful Sally, and afterwards Drunken Sal, and how at last she came to a most melancholy and almost hopeless end; being therein a warning to all young women both in town and country*. Other titles were calculated to appeal to the buyers of wicked tracts, and then wean them off them, such as *Tawney Rachel; or, The Fortune Teller: With some account of dreams, omens and conjurers*. In *The History of Mr Fantom, the new-fashioned philosopher and his man William*, Fantom denies the afterlife, which persuades William to run off with his port and silver spoons and get himself hanged. All the tracts were anonymous and, while More wrote the majority herself, her sisters Patty and Sally wrote a good number and she also drew on a circle of contributors, the most prolific of whom was, surprisingly, Henry Thornton, though he had some qualms about the morality of writing fiction. His tracts included *Religious Advantages of the Present Inhabitants of Great Britain*, and the parable *The Beggarly Boy* where a miserable urchin refuses to exchange his awful lot for the well-dressed, well-fed life of servant to a gracious gentleman, mirroring the folly of those who refuse God's grace. Other contributors included John Newton, John Venn, and Zachary Macaulay. The acclaimed poet William Mason submitted six ballads, four of which More rejected as containing too much politics or love.

The first set was published in March 1795, and the series continued monthly until 1798. Some 300,000 were sold in the first fortnight and 2 million by the end of the year, not counting the Irish edition. The printer struggled to keep up with the demand. Selling them at a price determined to undercut the existing supply, and with promotional discounts, More talked of losing £500 or a thousand pounds by the end of the year.

Thornton became treasurer of the venture and published a prospectus soliciting donations. The Clapham sect touted the cause around their friends, bringing in gifts from as far afield as Pitt and William Gilpin, as well as from the usual pockets. The Proclamation Society gave More a vote of hearty thanks and a small subscription. A number of local societies were set up by middle-class supporters to distribute the tracts, promoting them to shops and giving them away in hospitals, workhouses, schools, and prisons. They were also circulated in the armed forces.

The *Cheap Repository* had support from the bishops, especially Porteus whom More found with a thousand copies of the "sublime and immortal publication" on his desk to promote among his associates and give to passing hawkers. The Bishop of Worcester on the other hand warned that the scheme was encouraging the poor to read, and then "who shall hinder them from reading *bad* books as well as good?". The Duchess of Gloucester and Edinburgh, sister-in-law to the King, on meeting More for the first time quoted *The Shepherd of Salisbury Plain* to her two or three times: "I took the opportunity of saying stronger things of a religious kind than perhaps she had ever heard," reported More. Wilberforce, commenting toward the end of his life on the genius but lack of religion in Walter Scott, said: "I would rather go to render up my account at the last day, carrying up with me *The Shepherd of Salisbury Plain*."[21]

And yet how popular the *Cheap Repository* was among the people it was supposed to be aimed at is very hard to estimate. Certainly some tracts were sold by the hawkers of chap-books and broadsides, but how that number compares with those that were bought by middle-class people to give away (or keep) is impossible to say. Even so they must have had a certain level of popularity to find so many givers and takers. The duality of the repository is illustrated by the fact that More and Thornton soon decided to print two versions, one on cheap paper for the poor and a higher-quality edition that could be handsomely bound for the gentry, at a profit, and which sold very well. They became popular as middle-class children's stories, thanks to their simple style and morality – though presumably in collections without the likes of Sinful Sally. A writer for *Notes and Queries* in 1863 remembered them as second only to *Pilgrim's Progress*. This means that even if they missed their intended audience they found a large one, susceptible to their moral teachings, over a long period. The repository certainly failed in More's ambition to abolish chap-books and broadsides, which sold well throughout the nineteenth century. Instead she provided a pious alternative that competed alongside the more earthy fare. Still, the number of tracts printed was something like one for every two people in Britain, so, even if we assume a large majority were never read, the audience that More found for the values of the Clapham sect must have been phenomenal.

Sons and Lovers:
Macaulay and Stephen

Cato Perkins and Isaac Anderson arrived back in Freetown in June 1794 with the news that the directors had rejected their petition, like firebrands in a powder keg. Dawes had returned to England to recover his health and marry, leaving Macaulay as governor, and the settlers were more dissatisfied with colonial rule than ever.

On 30 November 1793, the company's ship had caught fire in the harbour with £15,000 worth of cargo on board, and settlers not only refused to raise a fire brigade but, says Macaulay, openly "rejoic[ed] in the calamity as a just judgment of God on their oppressors".[1]

On 16 June 1794, Macaulay enraged the Freetowners by sacking two of them, Robert Keeling and Scipio Channel, for "disrespectful conduct" after they rounded up a crowd to harass the slave captain Alexander Grierson, who had got into an argument with them and told them "in what manner he would use them if he had them in the West Indies". As the Sierra Leone Company had made itself their only way of getting a living, the parliament of tithingmen and hundreders demanded their reinstatement on pain of mass resignation, and proposed that no one should be dismissed without the consent of their peers. Macaulay refused, telling them: "No one within the colony has a right to censure the governor." Freetowners insulted and threatened him. On 20 June the loyal black town marshal Richard Corakapone was threatened with hanging when he tried to break up a mob, and when he tried to arrest the leaders the tithingmen and hundreders refused to back him. Settlers were on the point of revolution, and prepared to attack Macaulay that night.

Macaulay announced that from the first act of violence all salaries would be stopped, and he armed white employees and black loyalists under David George against the insurgents. There was rioting through the night and Pepys made three arrests. When a crowd gathered outside Macaulay's house demanding their release, he set a cannon at the gate. Rioting continued through the next day, but there was no attack on Macaulay or his officials, and by Sunday 22nd it had blown over. He issued a proclamation to be read in all churches warning them that if they threw off the yolk of the company they would lose the employment, education, and civilization it provided and be "reduced to the situation of the natives", in all probability ending up as slaves again; and that they would also wreck their mission to civilize and Christianize Africa. He offered free transportation back to Nova Scotia for any who wanted it and went as far as to fit up a ship, but no one sailed. Those who stayed, he said, had to accept his government, including the right to dismiss employees, "which he will always exercise".[2] He dismissed all known rioters and sent eight rebels to England to be tried, along with seven witnesses. Granville Sharp pleaded for leniency and they were banished from Freetown for life.

Invasion

On 28 September 1794, Freetown was attacked by the French. A flotilla of warships appeared in the estuary and bombarded the town for an hour and a half. One seven-year-old child was cut in half in his mother's arms, while many lost limbs. Macaulay noted that the flotilla was piloted by a local slave trader, Mr Newell, who had lost two slaves to Freetown. Macaulay surrendered the colony immediately and it was plundered by the sailors for two weeks. They stole or burned stores and crops, killed livestock, burned buildings, wrecked machinery, ruined medical supplies, and desecrated churches. Macaulay said they came in rags and left dressed in seven plundered suits at once, or depending on luck and taste in "women's shifts, gowns and petticoats". "We... passed the time in moralizing," Macaulay wrote.[3]

The French had planned to burn the whole town, but the black settlers persuaded the commander that, being at war with the British, he might leave the property of African Americans out of it. They were largely left alone, and managed to rescue food and materials from company buildings. They fed white colonists and sheltered them from heavy rain. They saved their lives: "I am afraid we should actually have starved," said the company botanist. Macaulay was aware how easy it would have been for settlers to have taken their revenge and how graciously they behaved. He was "gratified by the warm congratulations of the settlers on our health and safety", and noted that there was "no instance of any of them, even of those who were most disaffected, showing a disposition to insult any of us". Pepys could not believe in their forgiveness and ran with his family into the forest crying "like a child", Macaulay said, refusing accommodation as he was convinced there was a price on his head, and dying there a week later.[4]

"On Saturday I received the full account of the calamities at Sierra Leone…" noted Thornton in his diary. "I trust in some measure I resorted to the reflection that all these things come not without the appointment of the Providence of God."[5]

The settlers' treatment of company officials was more generous than Macaulay's response. The settlers considered what they had saved from destruction to be theirs by right of salvage, Macaulay having unconditionally surrendered Freetown to the French. As soon as the ships left, Macaulay told the parliament that he was prepared to let the settlers keep rice, molasses, and rum, but everything else (£1,000 worth of goods by the company's estimate) had to be returned, on pain not only of dismissal but of losing the vote and rights to schooling and medical care for one's whole family. When the parliament protested he simply told them he had already made his decision. He commandeered the best houses for dispossessed officials and a hundred prisoners dumped by the French. Settlers accused him of having betrayed Freetown to the French, and having urged the invaders to carry them off as slaves.

Macaulay drew up a pledge of allegiance and acquiescence that Freetowners had to sign to retain their rights, but could only get 120 signatures. If only he had had the courtesy "to come and ask us in a fair manner if we would bestow these things to the company", some settlers wrote to Clarkson in November, "God only knows we would give it up with all respect."[6] Since he left, they said, Freetown had become "a town of slavery". The majority who refused to sign the pledge armed themselves once again against a raid by Macaulay's forces, and set up their own school.

Incredibly, Macaulay decided this was the moment to start levying the quitrent that Thornton had proposed and Clarkson ignored. Their land grant certificates had been burned by the French, so Macaulay issued new ones, inserting new conditions including an annual quitrent of a shilling per acre. The parliament told settlers not to accept grants and three-quarters did not, so once again Macaulay imposed sanctions on them, painting black arrows on houses to mark them out. He drafted all remaining men into a militia against further attack, where black soldiers who had experience from the American War of Independence were put in command of white men. In 1795, Dawes returned to Freetown from his furlough, and Macaulay, being ill himself, came back to England.

James Stephen

As he did so, another addition to the Clapham sect was settling down on return from the colonies. James Stephen, who had been secretly supplying intelligence to Wilberforce from St Kitts since they met in 1789, was too rough-edged and religiously moderate for the inner circle of Clapham as yet, but he was already an important ally and over the next six years made his way to the heart of it.

Stephen was the perfect antidote to Zachary Macaulay, as fiery and furious as Macaulay was placid and cerebral. Macaulay said his greatest temptation was arrogance; Stephen, duelling. Like Thornton, he wrote a memoir for his children, but while Thornton's was surprisingly frank in his opinions of his father, Stephen's candour about his own personal life is astonishing. His conscious aim was "to illustrate the ways of providence", cataloguing the disasters and moral failings which turned out to be part of God's plans to prosper and use him. In the process though, he produced an entertaining drama, which, for all his latter-day contempt for the "trash" produced by novelists, is thoroughly Dickensian, if somewhat steamier. The only fault in the story is that he never finished it. His son James set about writing his biography but decided it was unpublishable, and the memoir was not printed until 1954, by Stephen's great-granddaughter.

James Stephen's father, also James, was a Scottish trader in French wine who met his wife in 1752, when he was nineteen, as a result of a shipwreck. He was taking a cargo to Scotland to settle there as a merchant, but was wrecked on the Dorset coast. Guarding the surviving wine from smugglers with the help of the Collector of Customs, Milner, he and Milner's fifteen-year-old daughter Sibella fell in love. The Act of Parliament invalidating clandestine marriage was pending, so thinking "now or never" James and Sibella secretly married. When all was revealed the family were furious about her disobedience, but they forgave her, and James went into business with them.

"But heaven had not yet ratified her forgiveness," said Stephen. She blamed her life of misfortunes on the sin of dishonouring her parents, and he agreed: "There is no species of sin against which I have so strikingly and uniformly seen the displeasure of God manifested in his temporal retributions."[7]

The business failed, and in the fall-out the hotheaded James quarrelled with Sibella's family and his own brother, whom he had involved. James went to London to raise money for a wharf, while Sibella took baby James ("Jem") and his brother William to stay with his grandfather, yet another James Stephen, a contraband trader in Aberdeenshire. The boys came down to London when Jem was five, and Sibella, who had come two years earlier, could not understand them without her husband's interpretation. They went to school in Vauxhall, where their teacher, Peter Arnett, had recently done hard labour for attacking the credibility of the Old Testament, and he quickly cured the Scottish with which they had been "infected". Outside school hours the brothers played cricket and cards, made boats out of yellow cucumbers they found floating in the Thames, indulged a sensitive love of flowers and insects, and blew up live frogs with a straw.

When Jem was nine, the family moved back to Dorset, where the boys were teased for speaking without "provincial corruptions". Jem got into a fight which ended with him hiding naked in a sandpit until his friends found him and brought him clothes. Aged ten, Jem fell desperately in love with the master's fifteen-year-old daughter, obsessing over her at the expense of his lessons, and longing, when she was visited by boys of her own age, to be old enough for duelling.

His father was appointed by Sir John Webb to manage the development of his Dorset estate into an industrial town. Stephen had got as far as building a lot of houses, constructing a ship in their own yard, selling clay from their pits to London and sinking a coal mine (though not finding usable coal), when Webb got cold feet and tried to cancel their contracts. They fell out, but Webb could not get rid of Stephen – except that Sir Robert Herries had lent Stephen £1,500 as security for his brother to sail with the East India Company, so Webb bought the debt from Herries and sued him for it.

Meanwhile, Stephen was also in the throes of a violent quarrel with another brother, Thomas, over their partnership in a brewery. Thomas took the opportunity of Webb's attack to sue James too. Young Jem walked thirty miles with his father for the court case, and while there met his uncle Thomas on the stairs. Thomas stopped to kiss him to show there were no hard feelings; Jem punched him in the gut and walked on.

His father ended up as a debtor in King's Bench Prison in London. He called Sibella to bring the children and live there with him – which shocked her, but she dutifully obeyed. Arriving to find him dishevelled, in a dirty room stinking of meat and liquor with the bed up against the wall, she screamed and burst into tears. A friend got William a job in a

London counting-house, and eventually Sibella got lodging for herself and the children with William's employer, spending her days in the prison and her evenings in tears.

Whatever his faults, James Stephen senior never lacked energy or ambition, and his answer to his present predicament was to try to get imprisonment for debt ruled illegal. He argued the case before Lord Mansfield, the Lord Chief Justice whom a few years later Granville Sharp would force to concede that slavery was illegal in Britain. Stephen did not manage the same miracle, but he continued to publish on the subject and, failing to persuade the radical politician John Wilkes to take up the cause, was drawn into a war of words with him in the opposition press. Stephen organized a break-out of prisoners, planning to march on Westminster and demand their freedom, but found when it came to it that many had backed out, so they went back inside.

It was a change of heart from Sir John Webb that finally secured James Stephen's release. Webb cancelled the debt, paid him £500, and gave Sibella an annual pension of £40. Warming to his experience of the law, Stephen tried to become a barrister but made it impossible by continuing his outspoken public disputes. He operated as a kind of underground lawyer, meeting clients in taverns to discuss business that other lawyers turned down.

They lived in Lambeth, and Jem was taught Latin at Kennington Green by a failed cheesemonger. His best schoolfriend was his neighbour Thomas Stent, whose family originally forbade him to play with the prison boy, but eventually embraced him as an honorary member of the family. Thomas had a sister Jem's age; though fourteen, she was "quite the woman in appearance, in understanding and manners", redheaded with lovely eyes, lively, and affectionate. The pair were soon madly in love, and with Tom's help they kept their romance secret, thinking little – Stephen sadly reflected later – of "the sin of filial undutifulness" they were committing. They were found out by Nancy's parents, who forbade her and Tom to see James ever again.

He went to Winchester College for six months in 1773, thanks to a cousin dying and vacating his place, and had a miserable time, having the Latin of boys half his age and no Greek. He left school because of financial and family difficulties, and his mother's consumption forced the family to move to Stoke Newington, three miles north of London, for country air. For fifteen months, he watched his mother die. She struggled heroically with the demands of three daughters and a toddler, and with the "painful mortifications" of her reduced circumstances, and she talked to them of the goodness of God and the world to come. On 21 March 1775, James went to the lending library on the Strand, called for his father on the way back, and heard she was dead. He ran all the way home, and jumped over the gate. For a week, he says, he verged on madness and suicide. The burial "was like my own living heart's inhumation". She was dearer to him than anything in the world. When he was about ten she had had pleurisy, was told she would die, and sent for him. Not realizing the seriousness of her illness, he talked for a bit then started looking at pictures, and she burst into tears at his indifference. "Dear woman!" he wrote, "she did me an injustice… No – my beloved Mother, want of affection for you was not among the number of my faults. My filial love and reverence for you were great indeed, and are still deeply engraved upon my heart, though 45 years have now elapsed since I first wept over your grave." [8]

But, looking back, it was all part of God's ineffable plan. If he had stayed at Winchester he would have gone on to Cambridge and become a good scholar and a bad person. Instead his mother's last year taught him lessons in goodness and godliness that were worth more than Latin and Greek. They took rather a while to take root, though.

James considered going to fight under Washington in the War of Independence, but ended up training in the law, with the help of a generous uncle. He entered Lincoln's Inn in October 1775, then spent two years at Aberdeen University, working all hours to catch up and avoid humiliation, constantly terrified that his massive deficiency in languages would be discovered. He returned home to find the family in poverty, living in a labourer's cottage, his sisters riding pigs on Stoke Newington common, and his six-year-old brother drinking in the alehouse. He worked for his father's seedy legal business, learning "a smattering of everything", which was of great use in his later work.

Meeting a mutual acquaintance, James enquired after Nancy's family. The parents were separated following an affair, Mr Stent all but ruined, Tom in the navy and a prisoner of war, Nancy still single and living with a friend of her mother's, Mrs Thomas in Vauxhall. James spied on Mrs Thomas's house from a pub with a pocket telescope, making a cup of tea last two hours, until he contrived to bump into Nancy. Though she resisted, they were soon in love again, and met secretly. It turned out though that Nancy was engaged to Mrs Thomas's son, who was returning from the Caribbean to marry her. After a scene of hysterical melodrama, she broke off the engagement, becoming estranged from her father and expelled from her lodgings in the process.

After his father died, James became a parliamentary reporter for the

Morning Post in the days before note-taking was allowed. He briefly lodged with Nancy's friend Maria, whom her brother Tom planned to marry when he returned to England. James and the girls spent their time together. He took them to hear a debate on slavery at Coachmakers' Hall, and secretly prepared a speech, delivering it to thunderous applause, "the best and by far the best received I have ever made in my life". The girls were thrilled, and James realized that Maria had fallen for him and he for her. "I have been told, that no man can love two women at once; but I am confident that this is an error… Beyond doubt, I loved them both, fondly loved them." James and Maria tried to stop seeing each other, but failed, even when her guardians matched her with an army officer. The officer told Maria he would duel with James, then when James came up to him in the street with pistols he backed down.[9]

James's choice between them seemed to have become easier when in 1780 he got Maria pregnant – until Nancy, still devoted to him, told him to marry Maria with such nobility that he realized he could never give her up for Maria. Then Tom returned to marry Maria, James told him everything, there were tears all round, and Tom left the country forever.

Nothing but the hand of God could redeem the situation, and so, Stephen believed, it did. His brother William had been in St Kitts since 1775 working for their uncle, who now died leaving William his fortune, which he shared with James. In the nick of time, he could afford to take Maria somewhere discreet to have the baby and then leave him with a nurse, and to pay for a doctor. Baby William was born in 1781. After a last brief fling with a mistress of the Duke of Gordon, Stephen secretly married Nancy, Maria married another man, and Stephen sailed to St Kitts to restart his legal career, Nancy and baby William following later.

Colonial maritime legal practice offered good money, especially after the outbreak of war in 1793. It also gave Stephen an insight into the workings of the slave trade and slavery which no one in Britain could match. Unwell but well off, he came home with Nancy and their three children at the end of 1794, and transferred his trade to the Prize Appeal Court of the Privy Council, unaffectionately known as the Cockpit.

Zachary Macaulay

Zachary Macaulay slotted right into the Clapham sect on his return to England in the summer of 1795, thanks to his abolitionist intelligence, evangelical strictness, and family connections. He stayed in London and Clapham with Thornton and Wilberforce, as well as with the Babingtons who were spending a year in Sidmouth in Devon for the sake of Jean's health. He visited Rothley Temple alone to pay homage to the scene of his conversion, saying, "To this place I owe myself," and developed a profound admiration for Thornton and his cold, methodical intellect.

Thornton brought Macaulay to visit Hannah and Patty More at Cowslip Green, who took to him and put him to work writing tracts for the Cheap Repository. While he was there, Macaulay rather uncharacteristically fell deeply in love with Selina Mills. Five years his senior at twenty-nine, Mills was the evangelical daughter of a Quaker Bristol bookseller, mild-mannered, and a close friend of the More sisters, especially Patty. She had been a favourite pupil and took over their school for young ladies near Bristol when the sisters retired in 1789. She unwittingly involved the school in a national scandal in 1791 when a fourteen-year-old pupil, Clementina Clerke, who had just been left £6,000 a year by her uncle, gave her a note from a sick aunt, asking if Clementina could visit for a few hours. Mills let her go, but the sick aunt turned out to be Richard Vining Perry, a Bristol surgeon, who took Clementina to Gretna Green to marry her. Friends and family chased the couple there and then to Flanders. Hannah offered £1,000 reward for her return and eventually sued Perry, but the law was on his side and all she achieved was to publicize their humiliation.

Macaulay's visit to Cowslip Green was brief. He was due to sail for Freetown to relieve Dawes (who apparently meant to go to the South Seas again, this time as a missionary, though nothing ever came of the scheme), and the Sierra Leone Company planned to keep him busy in London until then. Anyway, he saw little in himself to appeal to a pretty young woman. So he left without saying anything to Mills, and "resolved to suppress [these feelings] as unfavourable to my repose".[10]

Generally, feelings Zachary Macaulay resolved to suppress stayed suppressed, but Hannah More's eagle eye had spotted something, and thanks to a few sly questions he told her everything, without realizing he had said anything. She was aghast, knowing Patty would be devastated to lose Mills, and was determined to stop them getting married. She talked to Thornton, who questioned Macaulay, who in turn realized he had betrayed himself.

Sleeping dogs would have had a good long rest if Hannah and Patty had not kept writing to Macaulay insisting that he visit them again for a few days before sailing. He visited them in Bath at new year 1796 with Jean and Thomas Babington, who encouraged him to court Mills. Hannah tried to avoid talking about any possible romance and, when Macaulay insisted, told him that there was absolutely no chance of Mills being interested in him, making him promise not to pursue the matter. He resolved once again to give Mills no idea how he felt, to the extent of spending dinner without looking at her – and therefore having no idea how upset she was herself. When he and the Babingtons took leave of the sisters, Mills was nowhere around, and good as his word Macaulay did not ask after her.

But between the parlour and the carriage he caught a chance glimpse of her, crying bitterly, and realized all was not as it seemed. They exchanged letters, and turned out to be in love. "I love to dwell on this unexpected occurrence," he said later, "because… it confirms me in an opinion, founded indeed mainly on other and better grounds, that our first meeting… was under supreme direction."[11]

And yet on 25 January 1796 Hannah wrote to Thomas Babington to say Mills had "resolved not to entangle herself". She was a woman "of a very calm composed mind", More explained, unintentionally underlining how perfect the match was, "has no violent passions, but is of an orderly regular spirit and though not *deficient* in sensibility has not those acute sort of feelings that torment the possessor". She hoped this information would give Macaulay "that sort of reasonable consolation which is all that, sorry as I am to say it, the state of the case admits".[12]

As this did not ring true, Macaulay and the Babingtons paid a third visit to have it out. On arriving Macaulay tested the water by asking Patty how Mills was, and she replied "with such a repulsive coldness as quite surprised me". He and Mills forced the issue, the Mores could no longer deny her feelings, and they reluctantly agreed to their engagement. The sisters persuaded Mills that she should not go to Sierra Leone though, so the marriage was postponed until Macaulay retired from the colony, and the sisters insisted that the engagement should be kept secret in the meantime, something to which Macaulay unhappily agreed. With that he left for London "with an impression", he told Jean, "which I strive to combat, that our friends have not dealt kindly and candidly with me". Jean told him his impression was absolutely right, and that even Thomas had lost his self-possession over the business. Macaulay left Clapham for Sierra Leone on 10 February, "composed on the eve of such a destination", reported Marianne Sykes to Jean Babington, "cheerful though separated from those he most loved".[13]

Husbands and Wives

In stark contrast to Wilberforce's humane idealism over the war and the slave trade, there was a far more reactionary and ruthless seam running through his politics when it came to civil liberties. In 1794, Pitt suspended habeas corpus, allowing the state to imprison suspected revolutionaries without trial for the sake of wartime security. When the opposition brought the first of many motions to lift the suspension in January 1795, Wilberforce stridently supported Pitt's authoritarianism, arguing that it was vital to "strengthen the hands of government for the repression of and punishment of the factions". This might have looked like a pragmatic move to atone for his recent defection from Pitt's camp over the war, but in fact he was as ideologically committed to such repression as he was to abolition and peace, and supported such policies throughout his career. He considered radical politics a threat to the freedoms of the British constitution, and believed this "seasonable sacrifice" would preserve them in the long run. It is possible, though, that his discomfort over having hurt Pitt made him more vocal than he would have been otherwise.

Thornton had had a more liberal political upbringing than Wilberforce, absorbing his mother's attitude as a religious Dissenter – "she had taught me… to suspect no danger of carrying liberty to an extreme and to consider the constitution as intended rather to guard the rights than to restrain the vices of the people"[1] – but he found himself coming around to Wilberforce's conservatism.

Wilberforce and Pitt were gradually reconciled, and summer found them at Eliot's house in Clapham, just as in the old days. This did not stop Wilberforce bringing a new motion to stop the war on 27 May 1795, but he did it with Pitt's permission. He told the House that the alliance against France was collapsing, that the end of civil war in France put the enemy in a stronger position than ever, and that the hardships of antirevolutionary war were only feeding revolutionary movements in Britain. He was defeated by 201 votes to 86.

His arguments were justified in the autumn of 1795, however. Austria was Britain's only remaining ally. The St Domingo war dragged on disastrously, and the free black Maroons in Jamaica were now at war with the British too. A failed harvest at home doubled bread prices, and revolutionary tracts and posters appeared throughout the country. Rioters broke the windows of 10 Downing Street, and allegedly shot at the King's coach. Pitt responded with the Seditious Meetings Act and the Treasonable and Seditious Practices Act, giving magistrates power to disperse meetings of more than fifty people, break up small political clubs, and arrest those involved in either. They also imposed severe penalties for attacking the British constitution.

Again Wilberforce adamantly supported Pitt's repressive bills, telling Parliament they defended legitimate debate, and thus "raise new bastions to defend the bulwarks of British liberty". Hearing that a meeting of Yorkshire voters was called to protest against the bills in two days, Wilberforce dropped everything, borrowed Pitt's coach and four, and raced up – on a Sunday. Appearing from nowhere, he gave a thundering defence of Pitt's gagging measures, reciting shocking passages from radical tracts, to cheers and the air full of hats. He won the vote, returned with petitions, and Pitt's bills were passed.

Wilberforce in this performance was clearly acting on genuine personal principle rather than as any kind of political machination – he had gone up thinking it would probably cost him his seat in the 1796 election. And yet he suddenly found himself fêted as a hero of the establishment, an effect that was amplified a week later when the government announced it was seeking peace with France – his own pressing for peace now seemed far-sighted rather than premature. Thornton believed that Wilberforce's peace motion had "had some influence in producing a disposition to negotiate in the ministry".[2]

Wilberforce's feat also made it less easy to conflate abolition with revolution. As Gisborne said: "Even they who... stigmatized all the friends of the abolition as patrons of anarchy, and proselytes of Jacobinism, may perhaps be ashamed of their outcry; when they still see, what they have often seen already, those men who have done themselves most honour by zealous opposition to anarchy and Jacobinism, distinguishing themselves no less honourably by unremitting hostility to the slave trade."[3]

The pay-off came on 18 February 1796: Wilberforce brought a new abolition motion and to his amazement it passed the first stage by 93 votes to 67. For the first time in almost four years he was allowed to draft the terms of a new bill. At the second reading, leading anti-abolitionists made a sly attempt to get it thrown out before most MPs had come from dinner. Alerted, Wilberforce rushed in and kept talking until the House had filled enough to carry the vote. The final debate was a close contest in which Dundas argued that abolition would endanger Britain's £20 million investment in its Caribbean colonies. The bill was defeated by four votes – and, reckoning that more than four abolitionists had missed the debate in favour of the new comic opera *The Two Hunchbacks*, Wilberforce was sick with disappointment.

Henry Thornton and Marianne Sykes

It seems that love was in the air for the Clapham sect. Henry Thornton decided to ask Marianne Sykes for her hand in marriage, fifteen years after their first meeting and six after their slight entanglement. Babington and Wilberforce recommended her to Thornton, apparently after he confided his struggles in combining holiness with the single life. After their earlier embarrassment, Thornton felt the situation was too delicate for him to visit Sykes himself – going to Hull on any pretext would set tongues wagging, he feared. So he sent John Venn on an undercover mission there, to test the water. Unfortunately his cover was a bit too good. He went to Hull with Edward Parry, the squire of Little Dunham, philanthropist, and director of the East India Company, who enjoyed the visit enough to ask Sykes to marry him.

Mrs Sykes pressed her daughter to accept, but Marianne gave Parry what Thornton considered to be a definite no and Parry understood rather more subtly. Then she came down to London herself, and Thornton overcame his anxieties and met her in person. Before Parry could make his next move, on the evening of Saturday 1 February, the day after Macaulay's engagement, Thornton sent her his proposal. He acknowledged Parry's prior claim and his excellent character, but said that as he understood it she had turned him down permanently. He explained his change of heart about marriage, sounding very like Benedick in *Much Ado About Nothing*: "When I said I would die a bachelor, I did not think I should live till I were married." He assured her he was in complete control of his heart and had chosen her rationally, but if she did not forbid it she would have his heart too. As for what he hoped would be their future together, he said he did not believe there was any such thing as a lot of happiness in this life. He asked her not to reply without granting him a personal interview.[4]

Receiving his letter the following morning, Sykes replied with the perfect answer to the statesman of evangelicalism – she told him off for expecting her to deal with such matters on a Sunday. She turned him down emphatically, saying she considered herself bound by any promises that Parry believed her to have made until she talked to him again, adding: "I sometimes think I should be more useful as his wife than as yours, though I think if I follow my own inclinations it will be to remain unmarried for the present." She hoped they would stay friends and said she was doing him a favour by refusing him, "for indeed I should not at all increase your present stock of happiness".[5]

Thornton let the matter rest for the remainder of the sabbath, but visited her the next day and managed with the benefit of face-to-face conversation to get an ardent yes. Good businessman that he was, he wrote the following morning asking if he could have it in writing, "while you are not under so immediate an influence". Equally practically, "Can you find out what your fortune is to be – it runs in my head that I once heard it was to be large." And, by comparison, almost gushing: "I assure you that though I shall bear your faults, and persist in telling you of them as in old times, I perceive in you what is far more prominent in my eyes, a most delightful humility and sincerity, which promise me more happiness than I ever expected to enjoy in this world."[6]

They wrote to Parry and her parents to announce the engagement. She apologized to her father "for the only *apparent* want of duty and respect I have ever been guilty of, in promising to give away my hand without consulting you". She told her mother that she would not be coming back to West Ella for the wedding because "the council at Battersea Rise have decreed that it will be much more eligible to be married in town", which Marianne reconciled herself to by imagining how distraught she would have been to leave West Ella for the last time. Mrs Sykes mourned the loss of "my sensible companion, my confidential friend, my dutiful affectionate child, the sweet soother of every care", but consoled herself that being a friend of Wilberforce and Babington made Thornton "one of the excellent of the earth".[7]

Marianne and Henry argued about the decoration of their town house and carriage. She was shocked by the extravagance, but eventually accepted his explanation that it was their Christian mission "to gain an influence over the minds of our equals... which cannot be done if we are not equally free from austerity and ostentation".[8]

Henry was busy with Sierra Leone business and that month's slave trade debate, and while Wilberforce teased Sykes that "all business has been at a stand since [she] came to town", Thornton had to get up at five to spend a few hours with her before the business of the day. At work, Macaulay was disconcerted to see the tumultuous state of mind of his hero of cool methodical application: "Even when talking to him on serious business he would all at once interrupt the conversation by proposing some question, or entering into some details respecting Miss Sykes."[9]

In the fourth week of their engagement, Henry told her that "owing to parliamentary business etc." the wedding would have to be within the next few days, and so they were married on 1 March 1796. Henry asked her parents, who were not present, to think of Battersea Rise as their new home, but Mrs Sykes insisted she was not so much gaining a home as losing a daughter. She spent the day of the wedding "weeping, praying and watching the weather", she told Marianne. "Mr Thornton talks of bringing you the latter end of the summer, but who knows what a day may bring forth?" She died ten days after the wedding.[10]

The Bettering Society

In March 1796 Napoleon took control of the Italian campaign against the Austrians, Britain's last remaining ally, with devastating effect. While the Royal Navy made its colonies and trade routes pretty secure, French domination of western Europe was equally invulnerable. Radical politicians in Ireland waited for French forces to come and help them cast off the English yoke. The outlook was bad enough for Pitt's administration to try to come to terms with the French, and for the French not to try very hard to come to terms with the British. There was great satisfaction in Clapham at the prospect of peace, and Wilberforce used his influence to persuade Pitt and Dundas to include proposals for a convention against the slave trade.

They were also concerned with the economic troubles of wartime. The bad harvest of 1795 had sent prices soaring and, though Pitt's repressive legislation was containing unrest, both the social conscience and the self-preservation instinct of the wealthier classes said that something needed to be done to ease the troubles of the rest of the country. A group of magistrates in Berkshire introduced the Speenhamland system of topping up wages from parish funds in line with inflated bread prices, and Pitt tried to nationalize it, telling MPs it would "disarm the Jacobins of their most potent weapon", but they rejected it as too expensive.

Against this background, in December 1796, Wilberforce and Eliot joined Thomas Bernard and Shute Barrington to found the Society for Bettering the Condition and Increasing the Comforts of the Poor.

Bernard was the treasurer of the Foundling Hospital, a JP, and a member of the Proclamation Society. Barrington was his cousin and the Bishop of Durham.

The idea of the Bettering Society was to publish reports on the activities of innovative philanthropists across the country, to encourage others to try similar schemes and establish best practice. Its first volume was published in May 1797, and it included accounts of a free spinning school, a parish windmill, and a friendly society providing medical insurance to members, as well as a recipe for ox-head soup at 2½d. per gallon to feed poor neighbours and teach them better eating habits. Thomas Gisborne wrote about setting up a dairy farm to provide cheaper milk, and about credit shops for miners with repayments taken out of monthly earnings to discourage them from splurging. W. M. Pitt, the Prime Minister's cousin, reported on a scheme letting inmates in Dorchester prison work for money. Edward Parry told readers about enclosing land in Little Dunham to provide fuel for the poor. Bernard's many contributions included an account of how as a magistrate he kept a book on how industrious the various poor people of Stoke were, so that charity could be adjusted to desert.

One scheme that brought together most of the various concerns of the society was the village shop set up by the parish of Mongewell in Oxfordshire, which Bishop Barrington described. It sold good quality bacon, cheese, candles, and soap at an average rate of 21 per cent less than villagers would pay at market. They were materially better off, he said, not just because of the lower prices but because they could work instead of travelling to market. The farmer who employed them benefited from not losing labourers on market day, while ratepayers – a constant theme in the reports – profited from not having to finance so much charity. Morals improved because a trip to the market generally involved the alehouse too. And the villagers' incentive to work was not being undermined by charity but bolstered by making their money go further.

The society wanted not only to improve the circumstances of the poor, but to improve charity. Traditional parish charity relieved people's immediate needs, but the Bettering Society believed the money should be channelled into permanently improving their lives. They aimed to make recipients both less and more independent: on the one hand, they avoided hand-outs, preferring schemes to help people help themselves; on the other, they also preferred schemes that induced people to change their behaviour, using charity to "improve" the poor. We shall return to this theme with the Clapham Bettering Society.

On 12 December 1796, James Stephen's beloved wife Nancy died in childbirth. She left seven children, including her adopted son William, who was now fifteen. James broke with Protestant orthodoxy to pray every day of his life for her forgiveness and the happiness of her departed spirit. He was broken with grief, but Wilberforce, who had started spiritual conversations with him before, forced himself into his misery with the consolations of friendship and religion. Stephen gradually embraced his friend's faith and came to be accepted into his clique.

Stephen brought to the Clapham sect a far more critical attitude to the Prime Minister – and indeed to Wilberforce. Pitt had helped to set Wilberforce on the road to abolition and consistently supported the cause in Parliament, but it was a personal commitment rather than a political priority, and he could never throw his government's weight behind it. "Mr. Pitt," complained Stephen, "unhappily for himself, his country and mankind, is not zealous enough in the cause of the negroes, to contend for them as decisively as he ought, in the Cabinet any more than in Parliament."[11] Stephen did not trust him, and he distrusted the effects of Wilberforce's trusting friendship with him.

Stephen's fears were fed by the events surrounding a motion by the plantation-owning MP Charles Rose Ellis on 6 April 1797. Claiming to be an abolitionist at heart, Ellis argued that immediate abolition would drive the slave trade underground, so the best thing that could be done for slaves was to improve their lives through moral instruction and better living conditions; but it was the colonial governments' job, not Parliament's, to make laws for the colonies, and they were making excellent progress, so the one practical proposal of the bill was to send a message to the planters telling them to keep up the good work. Under a pretence of abolition, it did nothing but undermine Parliament's claim to the right to legislate about the slave trade. And yet Pitt suggested to Wilberforce that they try to improve the bill by amendment rather than to vote it out. Wilberforce opposed it head-on, and lost. Pitt supported him in the Commons, but he seemed to be tiring of the abolition campaign, which had achieved nothing in ten years and divided Parliament during a gruelling war. The popular movement had evaporated, Clarkson was writing a three-volume history of Quakerism, and Sharp's Abolition Committee met for the last time and conceded failure. Stephen's unquenchable fury against the trade could not have been more desperately needed.

William Wilberforce and Barbara Spooner

In 1797, Wilberforce finally completed the book he had been writing since 1793, and it came out in April, after last-minute editing by

Babington, under the title *A Practical View of the Religious System of Professed Christians in the Higher and Middle Classes Contrasted with Real Christianity*. Its detailed critique argued that "nominal Christians" grossly underestimate the corruption of human nature, the standard necessary to satisfy God, the cost to Christ of our salvation, and the response required. To nominal Christians, God's mercy to believers means that he lowers his standards to indulge those who assent to the creed, perform some basic, undemanding religious rites, and are not especially bad compared with some others they could mention. In truth, says Wilberforce, God's standards cannot be lowered and we are all damnable sinners in his eyes. His mercy is the ultimate sacrifice of his own son to atone for our sin, and the only way to avail ourselves of it is to see the worthlessness of our own supposed goodness, repent of our sin, and be forgiven. Then we will receive the Holy Spirit to enable us to live radically holy lives, which is not just a matter of doing good and avoiding sin, but living every moment of our lives to the glory of God. It involves strict morality; it is incompatible with idleness and ambition, and the love of pleasure or wealth; and it is a matter of passion, however unfashionable. And as with More's writings, there is the lesson of France: deserting religion destroys civilization; renewing religion saves it.

The publisher had no confidence in the demand for such a book, printing 500 copies purely because it had Wilberforce's name on it. It was out of print in five days, and within six months he had sold 7,500 copies. Newton told him: "I have *devoured* it... I deem it the most valuable and important publication of the present age, that I have seen: especially because it is *yours*."[12] On the one hand it caused a stir because it was an utter condemnation of the religion of the British establishment by a man who was at the heart of it; on the other hand, as Newton said, it was read by people who would never lower themselves to hear an evangelical preacher. It was praised and despised, inspiring attacks and defences, but not ignored. "Eloquent, animated, and frequently sublime, how can it be read without a glow of piety and of delight, by any thinking Christian?" asked one reviewer. Another, complaining he was forced to cover it because everyone was talking about it, said: "His notions of *the nature of religion* have made him a censorious bigot... he has written... an apology for fanaticism."[13] The Clapham sect were making evangelical faith and morals a perennial subject for magazines. Edmund Burke spent the last two days of his life reading the book.

It was now Wilberforce's turn to find love, again through the help of Thomas Babington. The day after *A Practical View* was published,

28 April, Maundy Thursday, Babington recommended to him Barbara Spooner, the pious daughter of a worldly family of Birmingham merchants and a niece of Lord Calthorpe. They met in Bath on the Saturday and Wilberforce was utterly smitten. He found his mind wandering in the Easter service and told his journal: "My heart has been tender; but I fear it has been too much animal *heat* and emotion." He saw her every day and lost sleep every night. "My heart gone." Thornton, More and Babington all urged him to take his time – "though they imperfect judges", noted Wilberforce. A week after first meeting, he proposed and was accepted. They spent hours in conversation over the next few days, "one of Barbara's hands in mine; the other in her mother's".[14]

To Wilberforce's dismay and the relief of his friends, he had to go to Westminster for a month when Pitt called him to vote for a subsidy in an unsuccessful attempt to stop Austria conceding to France. While in town Wilberforce took the opportunity to make his seventh full abolition motion, which he lost on 15 May 1797, saying: "I have been too long used to it to feel much disappointment." Without repenting his engagement, he regretted that he had been whipped along by "the forces of affection or impulse of appetite". After attending a Proclamation Society meeting, and getting Pitt's assurance that he would try to end the war, he returned to Bath on 29 May and married Barbara the following morning. "In evening to Beacon Hill. My dearest – desired me to join in prayers with her. Retired to bed early." Their honeymoon was a tour of the Mendip schools. They lived in Wilberforce's town house and Eliot's house in Clapham.[15]

The War Years
The collapse of Austria came after a winter in which French attempts to land in Ireland were defeated merely by the weather, a run on the Bank of England nearly emptied its gold reserves, and sailors mutinied at Spithead and the Nore from April to June 1797 over low pay. Britain was terribly vulnerable, and so in the summer Pitt's government once again negotiated with the French. Stephen pointed out to Wilberforce that the proposed treaty included an agreement to return to slavery those who had gained their freedom in the conflict, and urged him not to let friendship with the Prime Minister deter him from fighting "this wicked and invidious proposition". "You..." Stephen said, "are the Moses of these Israelites, though at the same time a courtier of Pharaoh."[16] Stephen also wrote about it in the *Morning Chronicle*, though Wilberforce warned him that attacking the proposal in the opposition press would only endear

it to the government, and if he really wanted them to listen he should publish pamphlets. As it was, the peace talks collapsed after the French government was overthrown in a pro-war coup.

Like other evangelical commentators, Stephen saw Britain's troubles as divine retribution for the slave trade, but he went beyond them in prophesying total destruction. At God's decree, he told Wilberforce, Pitt would continue to pour the last remaining British forces into the St Domingo war, "and you and your friends will support Pitt", and so with poetic justice Britain, the "most implacable enemy" of African people, would be consumed by Caribbean war. Stephen was unhappy being an undercover abolitionist – it smacked of holding something back from the cause, which he could not stand. His legal practice had demanded secrecy for eight years, but his career was now secure enough for him to tell Wilberforce to lift the veil: "I no longer wish for any reserve as to anything I have done, or may do, in relation to that subject." As if to emphasize his allegiance, he moved with his children to Clapham.[17]

John Shore was stepping down as governor-general of British India in 1797, where, avoiding intervention or expansion, he had reformed the judiciary and revenue from the organization of a trading colony into the bureaucracy of a state. He intended to come and join the evangelical community in Clapham, though that took another five years. The Clapham sect pressed Edward Eliot to take the India post to maintain the evangelical presence there, and he had the support of Dundas and Cornwallis, but he declined because of ill health. He died on 20 September. The effect on Pitt of his brother-in-law's death was beyond conception, reported Wilberforce; and as for himself, he told Hannah More, "except Henry Thornton, there is no one living with whom I was so much in the habit of consulting, and whose death so breaks in on all my plans in all directions. We were engaged in a multitude of pursuits together, and he was a bond of connexion, which was sure never to fail, between me and Pitt." Wilberforce's brother-in-law Thomas Clarke died that summer too, leaving Sarah "pretty well, and more composed than I could have expected", he told More.[18]

For Thornton, 1797 was another year of national financial crisis out of which he emerged rather well. Down, Thornton, Free, and Cornwall, as it now was, had enough subscribed capital to ride out the invasion panic quite comfortably, and with his insight into monetary theory he was called upon to give evidence to the parliamentary enquiry into the suspension of the gold standard. He supported it with such authority that he made a name for himself as an economic expert, which did his banking career no harm at all. He testified to finance committees in both houses and the following year was invited to join the Commons committee.

In February 1798, Stephen reprimanded Wilberforce about two pro-slavery measures that Pitt had let slip past. The first was an Order in Council arranging for a permanent supply of slaves to Spain's colonies, disregarding the bill against the foreign slave trade passed by the Commons. Wilberforce persuaded Pitt to get the order revoked.

The second was less straightforward. In 1797, Britain had taken Trinidad from the Spanish and Demerara from the Dutch, and Pitt supported a scheme which prohibited the import of new slaves to cultivate them, but allowed their transfer from existing British plantations. Stephen spotted that while this sounded like abolitionist principle in action, it would be the opposite in practice. The cultivation would require vast numbers of slaves; it was considerably more dangerous than ordinary sugar-farming, so numbers would fall sharply; this would allow the owners to tout it as a failure of abolitionist principles; meanwhile it would cause misery to slaves; and managers would simply replace the slaves they had transferred with fresh imports to the old colonies anyway, so the prohibition was meaningless. "Lloyd's Coffee House is a roar of merriment, at the dextrous compromise," he told Wilberforce. Wilberforce privately appealed to Pitt to stop the proposals, which he eventually did, but Stephen was appalled that it had taken his own intervention to stop such a transparent ploy and wanted Wilberforce to attack Pitt publicly. "I still clearly think, that you have been improperly silent," he told Wilberforce, "and that when you see the government loading the bloody altars of commerce... you are bound by the situation wherein you have placed yourself to cry aloud against it." He accused him of putting friendship with Pitt and his cabinet – "those high priests of Moloch" – before duty, and told him that without that friendship the slave trade would already have been abolished.[19]

Nobody talked to Wilberforce like this. Stephen would have had good reason to think he was sacrificing his burgeoning friendship with Wilberforce to his duty of speaking the truth to power, but in fact it only deepened their friendship, being exactly the fearless candour that Wilberforce felt he needed.

Go on, my dear sir, and welcome. Believe me, I wish you not to abate anything of the force or frankness of your animadversions.... Openness is the only foundation and preservative of friendship, and though by it I have lost some friends, or I should rather say have discovered that I never possessed them, yet it has cemented and attached me still more closely to the two best I have in the world.

He told his diary, on the other hand: "I trust that I have preserved the due medium: all think me wrong."[20]

The 1798 parliamentary session brought an eighth abolition motion from Wilberforce, and now he was supported by George Canning, the rising star of Pitt's party. Thornton contributed a report from Sierra Leone: pro-slavery MPs argued that the trade rescued African captives from execution; Thornton demonstrated that captives were taken purely to supply the trade and were killed if unsold. It caused such depopulation, he said, that towns on the Sierra Leone coast were one-tenth the size of those of the Foulah area inland. It was a close defeat this year, 87 votes to 83, and the abolitionists told themselves they were steadily gaining ground: their opponents now completely conceded the evils of the slave trade and were left arguing that abolition was not the most effective way to stop it.

Thornton brought his own bill on 4 May, drawn up with the help of Stephen and Wilberforce, to close parts of the African coast to slave traders, and the abolitionists brought another bill to limit slave numbers on ships, but Pitt put them both off to the next session.

Sierra Leone and Ireland

Macaulay was pleasantly surprised to arrive back in Freetown on 18 March 1796 to a warm welcome from the settlers, so it is unfortunate that he came with instructions to clear them off the waterfront and collect the long overdue quitrent.

Macaulay's Rule

The confrontation over the first issue never amounted to much. Nathaniel Snowball, Luke Jordan, and others who still lived on what they called Brothers Street and the British called Discontented Row were brought to court with Macaulay presiding, and the jury acquitted them – the only "unjust decision I have ever known a Sierra Leone jury to come to", said Macaulay. The quitrent he announced would come into force, at a shilling per acre, from 1 January 1797. This was going to be more of a problem.

In the meantime, Freetown was on constant alert for attack from French ships or neighbouring kings or slave traders or an alliance. After their ordeal in 1794, it was a terrifying prospect, and the town was evacuated more than once on false alarms. "I have thanked God a thousand times", Macaulay told Babington, "for having crossed my wishes so far that [Miss Mills] should not be here."[1]

As a lesser irritation, Macaulay had brought with him from England a consignment of Wesleyan Methodist missionaries appointed by Thomas Coke, who had given them a letter of introduction to the king of the Foulah people, signed "Thomas Coke, Minister of the Most High God and Teacher of the Law of Nations". Macaulay was disgusted by their pretensions, especially since they expected to be maintained by the Foulah without working, in gratitude for their holy presence. "To their astonishment Freetown resembled neither London nor Portsmouth," said Macaulay; "they could find no pastrycooks' shops nor any gingerbread to buy for their children." They complained about the scarcity of bread in Freetown, and he told them they were coming to "a country where neither wheat nor wheaten bread was ever seen". He had tried to discourage their illusions *en route*, only to find that Coke had warned them not to listen to his gloomy talk. Now he told them what he thought the Foulah would make of their plan to be paid in land and food for their preaching and, when the day came for him to take them there, they announced they wanted to go home instead, and he agreed wholeheartedly. "One who cannot live on rice," he said, "ought not to turn missionary."[2]

Macaulay started a school in his house for twenty or so African children from the surrounding region. He also ran Sunday schools, modelled on the More sisters', for them and 200 Freetown children, with prizes such as hats and handkerchiefs, and annual feasts.

In May Macaulay took the liberty of rescuing four local people from a British slave trader, Captain Peters. They were a man and three girls who had fallen out of favour with King Jammy and been sold by him. To Macaulay this was a clear-cut case of the slave trade at its most obviously inexcusable – "No crime alleged, no plea of being born in slavery, no debt exists in any of the cases" – but fortunately he was not forced to violate Peters's property rights. He simply sent a message politely requesting their return, and Peters was frightened enough to send them. The girls stayed in Freetown and joined Macaulay's school, while the man returned home, stealing Macaulay's forks and spoons. "He could not be convinced that he had committed a crime," recorded Macaulay when he was caught: "he had only taken what he wanted, and what I could spare. I was quite amused with finding in a savage African the grand principle of the modern refined system of politics."[3]

Macaulay exchanged letters with Mills, assuring her he would give up anything in the world for her sake, and her for God's sake. He heard from Dawes and the Freetown doctor Winterbottom, who had arrived at Clapham and been sent by Thornton on the standard pilgrimage to Cowslip Green and the More schools. Winterbottom, clearly in on their secret, reported that Mills interrogated him about Macaulay's work. "When engaged in business," said Winterbottom, "[Macaulay's] look was so grave as to almost frighten me." She sighed: "How happy should I be in some of his anxious moments to sooth his cares!" Mills then went to stay at Babington's, who reported to Macaulay, "I have been trying to point out particular faults… yet I can fix on nothing prominent."[4]

The institution of quitrent was all the more disruptive coming on 1 January 1797, straight after the Freetown elections in December.

Macaulay tried to soften their result by selling land to the British colonists for the first time, entitling them to vote and stand. This provoked outrage from his stauncher opponents, such as Ishmael York and Stephen Peters, who protested against the white encroachment into their political rights. Ill-equipped to grasp the issue, Macaulay told the directors: "There was something so unique in making a white face a civil disqualification that really provoked me to laughter." He explained to them the advantages of "the election of some of the whites, of whose superior information it would be well if they availed themselves", with predictable results. The election was a landslide for "the most ignorant and perverse of our colonists".[5]

When the time came to collect the first half-year's quitrent on 1 July 1797, Freetown was split as usual along church lines, David George telling the Baptists to pay, Huntingdonian ministers saying their members could make their own minds up but they themselves would pay nothing, and other Methodist churches declaring they would expel anyone who paid. Macaulay summoned the whole settlement to hear his thoughts on the matter, but the parliament told them to boycott the speech, which half of them did. He spoke for an hour and forty minutes and took no questions, claiming – in ignorance rather than dishonesty – that they had received no land grant before sailing from Nova Scotia and had been told of the quitrent before they left. He did not stay for the ensuing debate, in which Anderson read passages from Dubois's book which contradicted him. Methodist leaders, according to Macaulay, told settlers to return any land grants that mentioned quitrent, and threatened to burn the houses of those who paid. Macaulay said he would hang anyone who burned a house, and stationed soldiers on Thornton Hill. The conflict again reached stalemate.

In September 1797, Macaulay heard from several sources that some settlers were negotiating with their neighbour King Tirama to overthrow Macaulay and liberate Freetown from the Sierra Leone Company. Again he mobilized soldiers and announced that he knew about the conspiracy, and again it fizzled out. Increasingly, disenchanted settlers moved out of the town to country farms, or to a breakaway settlement in Pirate's Bay led by Snowball.

Macaulay decreed that from the election of December 1797 women would no longer have the right to vote, which as well as the obvious disenfranchisement reduced the number of black households who could vote, and for the first time two out of twenty-four tithingmen were white.

Macaulay received an eight-line note from Thornton in reply to his latest report on the situation there, which "was long enough to give me the satisfaction of knowing that he had nothing particularly to blame: a negative, but from Henry Thornton no mean praise". Macaulay thoroughly approved of Thornton's emotional economy. When Mills wrote to him repeating some warm expression of Thornton's regard for Macaulay, he seemed almost disappointed, explaining that he had been betrayed into relaxing his habitual restraint. "He wishes at no time to give praise unnecessarily... knowing that in the main it is hurtful. He wishes at no time to utter a needless expression of regard..."[6]

By 1798, Macaulay was ready to return to England and his fiancée, and in April Thomas Ludlam arrived to take over. Macaulay's one reservation about leaving concerned the African children he taught in his house. He loved them and was thrilled by their progress in Christianity and British manners, and could not trust anyone else to take on the class. But that summer he received a letter from the Scottish minister Robert Haldane, asking him to find thirty to forty children who could be sent to Scotland, taught there, and then sent back to Africa as missionaries. Macaulay agreed to bring his children, as long as he could help supervise the scheme.

Macaulay's last six months in Sierra Leone were dominated by the threat of attack from neighbouring kingdoms. Freetown had given asylum to slaves that King Tirama planned to sell, and Macaulay refused in a different tone from the one he felt necessary in dealing with British traders. Tirama plotted a coup, the town was on alert for some months, and Macaulay slept with loaded guns by his bed. Yet more instructions came from the directors to collect quitrent, but Macaulay sailed for England in April without having received any at all, and passed the problem on to Ludlam.

He sailed with the twenty-five African children bound for Scotland. They met a pirate ship and were chased for thirty-five hours. It looked likely that they would be caught, in which case Macaulay expected the children to be taken as slaves to South America. "I had resolved on accompanying them," he told Mills afterwards, but luckily for the children, and for the patient couple, the ship reached Plymouth safely in May.

The Frustrated Wedding

Macaulay left the children to sail around the coast to London while he went ahead to prepare for their arrival. He planned to settle them in Clapham temporarily while he went to Bath to marry, at last, after three years' delay. So he was stunned to arrive at Clapham and find that as far as Thornton and Wilberforce were concerned there was no question of his going to Bath, because they had put his name down as a key witness in a

House of Lords enquiry for Thornton's slave trade limitation bill. The bill absolutely depended on his evidence, they insisted. As his granddaughter and biographer puts it: "Macaulay's habitual patience appears to have failed him." He went to bed pleading a fever, wrote anxiously to Mills to explain his delay – "I have acted as I believe you would have advised me to act" – received a reply assuring him he was right, and got on with it.[7]

It was a renewal of the bill that Pitt had postponed the previous year. First, Wilberforce had gone through the motions of a tenth abolition bill on 25 February 1799, and despite a brilliant performance from Canning was defeated by 84 votes to 54. Thornton brought his bill on 5 March, and after Pitt held it up again for the sake of other business – causing a minor falling out between Thornton and Wilberforce – it was passed by the House of Commons on 12 April. Grenville led the support for the bill in the Lords, but opponents demanded a new enquiry before voting, and so the Clapham sect moved in, with Stephen as counsel, Macaulay and Dawes as witnesses, and Wilberforce and Babington coaching them through their evidence.

Unfortunately for Macaulay, their opponents' main purpose and tactic in the enquiry was procrastination, and it dragged on through June before he got a chance to speak. In the meantime he attended to his African children, who entertained his friends at Clapham and impressed Hannah More with their Christian knowledge. John Campbell, a missionary come from Scotland to inspect them, reported that he initially found some of them missing, which turned out to be because "the neighbouring mansions, astonished to see a cloud of young Africans, [sent] out their manservants to try and catch some of them and bring them before them. They fancied all were their friends, and most willingly went with any who asked them."[8]

Campbell could not take them to Scotland straight away because Macaulay had booked them into hospital for inoculation against smallpox. He felt increasingly reluctant to hand them over, and when someone warned him that Haldane was a Calvinistic Baptist democrat, Macaulay told him that he had decided it was better for him to oversee the children's training himself – and that, since Haldane had originated the scheme, he might remain involved by footing the bill. Haldane rejected the compromise, and so Macaulay kept them in Clapham.

In the Lords' enquiry Dawes was interrogated and bullied for three days by the Duke of Clarence, and impressed his hearers more with his honesty than his memory. Macaulay finally took the stand on 24 June, suffering from malaria. He ended up feeling frustrated that, rather than having the chance to carry all before him with his total recall and his understanding of how the slave trade hampered the colonizing of Africa, Clarence kept him regurgitating information they had already heard. Stephen summed up, according to Macaulay, with a compelling speech that "was not sufficiently condensed for their lordship's patience" and failed to grasp Macaulay's point about colonization.

"We have at length the strongest probability of carrying the Slave Limitation Bill," said Wilberforce shortly before the debate on 5 July; and shortly afterwards: "Never so disappointed and grieved by any defeat." He was all the more grieved to hear from Grenville that they had only lost, by seven votes, because fourteen proxies had been mislaid, all on their side.

At least for Macaulay it was all over, and he told Mills he would be with her very soon. So one cannot judge him too harshly for being annoyed when Wilberforce and Thornton announced they had another time-consuming job lined up for him, helping them draft applications for a royal charter for Sierra Leone and arrangements for the Jamaican Maroons in Nova Scotia to be resettled there. "I am ashamed to tell you," he wrote to Mills, "that I have felt an unjustifiable degree of mortification on this occasion, and have been venting my feelings a little too strongly to both of them. They laugh at me and blame my own rashness in making promises. Is it not quite provoking? I had been valuing myself on my patience."[9] They married finally on 26 August 1799, and lived in Lambeth. He discovered a shocking and saddening fact about his wife in the early years of their marriage: she did not like the Clapham sect. The Mores, of course, and the Babingtons she loved, but the Thorntons, Wilberforces, Venns, and Stephens she could do without. During Zachary's perpetual visits she claimed illness and stayed at home reading. It was a happy marriage – all Clapham's were, without exception – but dreams of introducing her to the happy holy band had sustained him through tough times in Freetown, and he was deeply disappointed. Zachary became secretary to the Sierra Leone Company, and established a school in Clapham for the African children with William Greaves as the teacher. Among their many visitors was John Newton, who was able to talk with two or three in the language he learned as a prisoner on Plantain Island.

Ireland

The influence that events in Ireland had in finally bringing the abolition of the slave trade to completion has rarely been given its due. It was totally unforeseen at the time, and forgotten soon after. Ireland was in the unhappy position of being a separate kingdom, ruled by the King of

Great Britain; with its own Parliament, whose Acts had to be approved in England; and with a 90-per-cent Roman Catholic majority who were forbidden to own land or hold public office, and only gained the vote in 1793. From the English point of view, since the start of the Revolutionary War Irish nationalism offered a back door into Britain for the French, and in 1798 Irish rebels rose against British rule, though only a small French force got through the British naval blockade to support them. Up to 30,000 people were killed in the aftermath. Pitt recognized that the spirit of the French Revolution had reached Ireland, and that, war or no war, 4 million Irish Catholics could not be kept disenfranchised forever. Once they dominated the Dublin Parliament it would be much harder for the British government to control it and Protestant landlords would be at their mercy. So in November 1798, Pitt proposed to incorporate Britain and Ireland into the United Kingdom, abolishing the Dublin Parliament and adding 100 Irish MPs to the 558 in Westminster, and 32 members to the House of Lords. If Irish Catholics were subsequently allowed to stand, they would form a powerful bloc in Westminster, rather than controlling their own Parliament. This would prevent Irish independence and bolster British security.

For Wilberforce and Thornton, the issue was primarily about Irish Catholics having their political disabilities removed. Both, like other evangelicals, had very low opinions of Catholicism and Catholics, though Thornton supported their political rights. Wilberforce originally opposed the union as giving too much power to the Roman Catholic Church. Gisborne felt it would lower the tone of Parliament. But on the other hand it should help to alleviate the extreme inequality of Irish society, and for that reason Wilberforce and Thornton voted for it. Pitt spent £1.5 million buying the acquiescence of MPs in Dublin. The Act of Union was passed in Westminster in the summer of 1799, and the following year in Dublin, and the union took place on 1 January 1801.

What does not seem to have occurred to anyone, understandably, is that, Ireland having no slave trade, the Act brought into the British Parliament 100 new MPs who had no reason to oppose its abolition. The conditions of the campaign that the abolitionists had been waging in Parliament for more than ten years, to all appearances pointlessly, had now suddenly and totally changed. The extent to which they failed to realize this, and the cost of that oversight, are illustrated by the fact that for one reason or another Wilberforce let four years go by without bringing an abolition bill.

Church Missionary Society

Henry Venn was seventy in 1795, and for over a year had been too frail to go beyond the fields around Yelling rectory. "Yet I enjoy liberty," he said. "I soar to heaven; and mix in the society of cherubim and seraphim." He enjoyed Milner's church history, a present from John, and was sustained through sleepless nights by visions of his happy, holy family. Since his second wife died in 1793, his daughter Jane had kept his house, and in 1796 the pair of them moved to Clapham to live next door to John and Kitty and their family. His other daughter Eling Elliott was already living in Clapham with her husband Charles. In June 1797 the doctor told Henry he was about to die, but believed the news so cheered him up it kept him alive another fortnight.[1]

John Venn at Clapham
John had thrived at Clapham. "Don't tell JV unless you feel it right," Henry wrote to Kitty shortly after he started, "that his preaching is very acceptable. His brother, [Charles] Elliott, thinks that he is among the best preachers." His congregations numbered up to a thousand, but he was distressed by how hard it was to get the poor to church. So he started a Sunday evening meeting in the old church (in addition to the morning and afternoon services at Holy Trinity) to teach children the catechism "in the plainest manner", and then persuaded their parents to come as well. He also started an evening service in Holy Trinity, in the face of protests from the parish, who were alarmed at the extremism of a three-sermon Sunday and "shocked to think that a matter so pernicious to the morals of the place... was being proposed".[2]

In 1796 Venn oversaw the extension and improvement of Clapham workhouse, and finding the parish rates insufficient to provide for all in need, he started the Clapham Poor Society, which sold bread, coal, and potatoes to them at reduced rates. Following the lead of the Bettering Society, in February 1799 he founded the Society for Bettering the Condition of the Poor at Clapham. The thirty members divided the poor families of the village among them and kept a close eye on their needs – using charity to improve the bond between rich and poor being one of the ideals of the national Bettering Society. They collected a large fund, set up two schools for knitting, spinning, and reading, regularly visited their clients, and gave them help ranging from grants to fumigation. Venn kept up to date with the latest medical ideas, and used the society to promote a progressive regime of hygiene, quarantine, and inoculation. In 1800, four years after Jenner's first vaccination, Venn saved Clapham from a smallpox epidemic through vaccination.

Venn's society demonstrated both the strengths and weaknesses of the Bettering Society's tactic of permanent improvement instead of indiscriminate payments. It certainly avoided what today's aid agencies would call "fostering a culture of dependency". "There is a spring and energy in an independent spirit which is capable of great exertions," said Venn. "Nothing damps, nothing extinguishes that independence of mind so much as the habitual reception of alms." Thus they aimed to keep down food prices for everyone rather than simply giving out food, and instead of simply making payments to expectant mothers they asked them to save five shillings and then doubled it. While the gospel told Christians to feed the poor and clothe the naked, Venn believed he could do better: "Let the aim of the society be to say, not merely that this man was hungry and we fed him, but this man was naked and behold he is clothed by his own industry." On the other hand, the society was a means of stringent social control. "Before any relief is granted," instructed Venn, "information should be particularly sought concerning the moral character of the applicant, particularly if he is accustomed to attend public worship." The system was explicitly intended not just to encourage the poor to work and provide for themselves, but to reform them, weeding out debauchery, idleness, and gaming, and teaching them religion. The Cheap Repository shows that the Clapham sect was converted to the use of reason and rhyme to win the lower classes for the Lord that still did not preclude more coercive methods.[3]

In April 1798, as Napoleon apparently prepared to invade England, Venn founded – and acted as chair, treasurer, and chaplain for – the Clapham Armed Association, a militia of 270 volunteers who paraded on the cricket pitch and kept their guns and pikes in the vestry. He maintained it long after the invasion scare passed, intending it as much for English revolutionaries as French, "to defend our liberty and property against foreign invasion or internal commotion".[4]

Church Missionary Society

In 1799, Venn became a founder member of the Church Missionary Society. It grew out of the Eclectic Society, a discussion group for ministers formed by John Newton in 1783 in a pub in Aldersgate Street, the Castle and Falcon. The Eclectic Society included Henry Foster and Thomas Scott, and later on John Venn and Charles Simeon. At each meeting a member tabled a question, and they talked about subjects from family prayers to how to combat smuggling. Foreign mission was a perennial topic. In February 1796 Simeon raised the question of a new Anglican missionary society, but the majority rejected the idea as stepping on the toes of the Society for the Propagation of the Gospel (SPG) and Society for Promoting Christian Knowledge (SPCK). Simeon took the idea to Clapham, though, and had a number of meetings with Wilberforce, Thornton, Grant, and Venn. He impressed them with his ardour, but nothing concrete came from their talks.

On 18 March 1799, Venn revived the issue with a discussion of general principles for foreign mission. He argued that the Church of England's existing societies were hampered by having to send out clergy, but the need was too urgent for that. For evangelicals, however special the role of minister was, it was the duty of all Christians to spread the gospel, so Venn wanted to send lay preachers. The London Missionary Society did this and so had sent thirty missionaries at once, but the LMS was non-denominational and, much as Venn approved of their work, any churches he helped plant overseas would have to be Anglican. They should start small, he argued, not with bishops and patrons and fundraising, but with prayer and study and promoting the idea. Simeon enthusiastically agreed: "Not a moment to be lost. We have been dreaming these four years, while all Europe is awake."[5]

They agreed to form a society on those principles, and did so at the Castle and Falcon on 12 April. They declared that it was the duty of all Christians to spread the faith among the heathen, and that since the efforts of the SPCK and SPG were confined to the West Indies and North America they would take on the task of mission to "Africa, or the other parts of the heathen world". The committee of twenty-four was a rather less dazzling array than most of Clapham's, including thirteen clergy (among them Newton, and with Scott as secretary), only four of whom had parishes. As well as Venn's brother-in-law Charles Elliott, it included a sculptor, a tea-broker, and a skinner. Vice-presidents included Wilberforce, Grant, Samuel Thornton, and Edward Parry, and Henry Thornton was of course treasurer. But no bishop or member of the aristocracy had anything to do with it. The Archbishop of Canterbury refused to receive a delegation from the committee, telling Wilberforce "he could not with propriety at once express his full concurrence or approbation". Even Porteus was cool toward them, while Wilberforce himself refused to be president.

There were several reasons why even those who agreed with the aims of the CMS were cautious in their support. The idea of lay missionaries was extremely controversial – even Newton objected, and so Venn cut all mention of the policy from the society's prospectus. Moreover, the CMS was an unmistakable challenge to the SPG and SPCK – it was Clapham at its most sectarian, forming a society to do something evangelically that was already being done by the church's official missionary organizations. And despite the society's links with Sierra Leone, and vague talk of "other parts of the heathen world", it obviously had India in view, the colony that was becoming the heart of the British economy. The East India Company was resolutely opposed to mission there, believing it would throw the colony into turmoil, and the British establishment bowed to their authority, so to try to circumvent their opposition for the sake of the gospel looked a lot like "methodistical" fanaticism. The committee found it equally difficult to recruit missionaries themselves, and after three years of appeals across the nationwide evangelical network recorded "that they do not have it in their power to report that any missionaries are actually engaged in fulfilling the pious designs of the society".[6]

Civil War in Sierra Leone

Thomas Ludlam, who became governor of Sierra Leone late in 1799, was twenty-four years old, "gentle and unassuming" with "mild conciliatory manners".[7] He immediately restored free education for all, regardless of politics, reopening four schools, and he went on to abolish the job of quitrent collector. But the revolutionary spirit had gone too far in Freetown for such measures to satisfy the parliament, who presented Ludlam with a bill of grievances in March 1800, and independently appointed James Robinson as judge in April. Ludlam repeated Macaulay's arguments against such appointments, adding that under the forthcoming royal charter any challenge to company appointments would be treason.

In other words, if they were going to overthrow the governor they should make it quick. Isaac Anderson was appointed head of a revolutionary council. All the hundreders and half the tithingmen supported an uprising.

On 3 September they met in Cato Perkins's church and drew up "The Law of the Sierra Leone Settler" to take effect on 25 September. The governor would cede all authority to the parliament, except to manage company trade, and supporters of the deposed governor would be fined £20. They set fines and maximum prices. "All that come from Nova Scotia," they declared, "shall be under this law or quit the place." It was signed by three hundreders, Anderson, Robinson, and Anzel Zizer, and by Nathaniel Wansey the head tithingman.[8]

On 25 September, Ludlam called British colonists and loyal Nova Scotians to Thornton Hill fort and armed them. Hearing that Anderson, Robinson, Zizer, and Wansey were meeting he sent Marshal Corakapone to arrest them. According to Ludlam, Robinson hit Corakapone in the face with a rice-threshing stick and Corakapone beat him back until he surrendered, then Wansey knocked down another constable and was stabbed. Others said that the four were unarmed, Corakapone fired on them, and they fought back with fence posts. Either way, Robinson and Zizer were captured and Anderson and Wansey escaped.

On Saturday 27 September, Anderson set up camp with fifty young men at the bridge on the road to Granville Town. Ludlam had a force of eighty-two, thanks to reinforcements from forty African seamen, but feared that King Tom would join the insurgents' side. Anderson demanded the release of Robinson and Zizer, which Ludlam refused. Still Anderson held off, and all hung in the balance until ten on Tuesday morning, when, in Ludlam's words, "Behold! A most unexpected intervention of providence": the ship carrying the 500 Maroons from Nova Scotia and 45 British troops came into view. The Maroon chiefs agreed to Ludlam's terms of settlement, and when he told them the allocation of land was delayed by an insurrection they offered to fight for him. Still refusing to surrender, Anderson's forces were quickly dispersed, and gradually captured.

Fifty-five people were tried after the battle, thirty-two of them, including Robinson, being banished from Freetown on pain of 300 lashes and their property divided among the Maroons. When the royal charter arrived on 12 October it still did not give Ludlam authority to punish treason, so Anderson was executed for sending him a threatening letter, and a second conspirator, Patrick, for stealing a gun.

Ludlam resigned before the trials were over, and Dawes took over for a third time. He abolished the system of hundreders and tithingmen and the colony was governed by company officials. On 18 November 1801, Freetown was attacked by an alliance of King Tom's forces and exiled Freetowners led by Nathaniel Wansey. After a destructive battle in which eighteen Freetowners including Corakapone were killed and Dawes was wounded, the attackers were repelled.

Under Addington

James Stephen cemented his place in the Clapham sect in 1800 by marrying Wilberforce's widowed sister Sarah. William was not sure about the marriage – "It seemed like my sister's beginning life again, and going to sea once more in a crazy vessel"[9] – however: "Stephen is an improved and improving character, one of those whom religion has transformed, and in whom it has triumphed by conquering some strong natural infirmities." Stephen's grandson, Sir Leslie Stephen, remembered Sarah as:

> *a rather eccentric but very vigorous woman. She spent all her income, some £300 or £400 a year, on charity, reserving £10 for her clothes. She was often to be seen parading Clapham in rags and tatters. Thomas Gisborne, a light of the sect, once tore her skirt from top to bottom at his house, Yoxall Lodge, saying "Now, Mrs. Stephen, you must buy a new dress". She calmly stitched it together and appeared in it next day.*[10]

The year 1800 was the first since the enquiry of 1790 that Wilberforce decided not to present an abolition bill. The sugar colonies had achieved what the Sierra Leone Company failed to do and created a slump in prices through over-production, so in February a group of major Caribbean plantation owners proposed to Pitt a five-year suspension in the slave trade to limit production. As negotiations went on the abolitionists held off their motion, but in June the West Indian proprietors overwhelmingly rejected the suspension, by which time it was too late for an abolition motion. That December, Babington decided he was as mad as Clarkson thought after all, and stood as MP for Leicester, a borough notorious for expensive elections, carrying it, Thornton said, "against a treating, bribing, and extravagant sort of antagonist". The Macaulays spent the winter at Rothley Temple, Zachary taking the only recorded holiday of his life on account of having broken both arms.

In the 1801 session, Pitt tried to remove the political disabilities of Irish Catholics, as he had promised before the Act of Union, but George III vehemently opposed him, his cabinet was divided, and Pitt resigned on 5 February 1801. The new Prime Minister was Henry Addington, who was committed to peace with France and opposed abolition. He began negotiations with Napoleon at Amiens immediately. Because all the slave powers were involved, Wilberforce believed he could get multilateral abolition of the slave trade inserted into the treaty, and talked to Stephen of "streaks of light indicating the opening day, and rewarding all our past sufferings". It was for this that he let a second session go past without an abolition motion, the first session of the united Parliament of Britain and Ireland. The preliminary peace agreements were signed in Amiens in October; the Gisbornes celebrated with fireworks at Yoxall Lodge and Wilberforce outlined his international "grand abolition plan" to Addington, arguing that it neutralized the strongest argument against abolition – that other nations would continue it when Britain stopped – and pointing out that, after all Wilberforce's work, the credit for abolition would then go to Addington: "It is not... without emotion that I relinquish the idea of being myself the active and chief agent in terminating the greatest of all human evils." But Addington declined the credit and rejected the proposal. Wilberforce warned Addington that he would console himself by bombarding the Commons with abolitionist bills, but in terms that showed how far he despaired of their achieving anything beyond keeping the debate in the newspapers: "I own to you however that I shall go to the performance of this duty with a heavy heart; for I am not sanguine in my hopes of effecting much through the medium of Parliament... But I must do my duty and acquit my conscience."[11]

Two months after the preliminary peace agreement, a French fleet took 34,000 soldiers to reconquer St Domingo from Toussaint. Napoleon had a lot of sympathy in Britain for this counter-revolutionary campaign, but Stephen published a series of letters to Addington, under the title *The Crisis of the Sugar Colonies*, urging that Britain and its colonies should at least remain neutral. Napoleon would almost certainly fail, he argued, leaving St Domingo an experienced, confident black military republic, with a grudge against its British neighbours if they helped; and even the unlikely event of Britain helping the French to victory would leave St Domingo with 70,000 slave soldiers "at the door of our most valuable settlement, and ready to assist the ambition of the Republic for... conquering the slave peopled islands of Great Britain!" With slave revolution a live cause in the Caribbean, Stephen added, Britain urgently needed to reform its colonies, improving the lives and increasing the freedom of the slaves. He mentioned with telling pessimism how abolishing the slave trade "would have been" the best way to do this, but that there was no prospect of Parliament passing it, and it was now probably too late anyway. All that remained was for Britain "to be taught by experience alone, the inseparable connection between morality and true wisdom". Addington was not persuaded by Stephen's arguments, and gave his full approval to the French reconquest of the slaves. In May Napoleon officially reinstated slavery in St Domingo, as Stephen predicted, and by the time he conceded defeat had lost 50,000 men.[12]

The Blagdon Scandal

Hannah and Patty More had expanded their educational empire throughout the 1790s, opening the ninth and last school in Wedmore in August 1798, despite the misgivings of anti-Methodist clergy and farmers. In 1799, Hannah published *Strictures on the Modern System of Female Education*, a long discourse on how upper-class women should be taught and should behave. She ridiculed the idea of women's rights, arguing that women did not have the same mental abilities as men, but also protested that women were condemned to inferior education that could not do them justice, giving them silly accomplishments such as dancing, drawing, and music rather than moral and rational training. Education should be more serious and better equip women for this life and the next – in aid of which More gave an exposition of evangelical theology and how to inculcate it. The book sold well and provoked the usual diverse reactions. "Society has been essentially benefited," by More's books, and they "ameliorate the state of man. Miss More deserves great praise." Alternatively, she might be seen as viewing the world through the mists of Methodism, whose "absurd strictness will render our sabbaths the most uncomfortable and most unwelcome days of our lives". The following year a large society ball for children featured her in effigy, she told Thornton, "with a large rod in my hand prepared to punish them all for such naughty doings!"[13]

She got into more serious trouble over her school in Blagdon, when she quarrelled with the curate, Thomas Bere, and his wife Sarah. They had complained that her teacher there, Henry Young, led Methodist meetings in the evenings, prayed in his own words, was rude about the curate, and suggested to the curate's wife that she was not a Christian. Unsatisfied by More's response, Bere appealed to the absentee rector; More parried by sending the rector reports that Bere denied the divinity of Christ. So Bere dealt with the matter himself as the local magistrate, taking affidavits from parishioners that Young held secret meetings, praying extempore and for the French. Bere called a meeting of local magistrates in November 1800 who agreed that Young must be dismissed, so More closed the school.

The next month, though, she met the rector in London, and persuaded him that Bere was a heretic. He was dismissed on 23 January 1801 and More reopened the school two days later. Bere refused to go, protesting that he had been punished without even hearing the charges against him. He published a book about the affair, to which More, insisting that she would "not answer the book though it accuses me of all the crimes committed since the murder of Abel", got a friend to reply instead. Bere published a second book; he was reinstated in August, and in September the school closed again. Bere opened his own, to which More sent anonymous donations.

This was the end of the local controversy, but as the books had been assiduously reviewed by the *Anti-Jacobin*, it was now a national controversy. In two years, twenty-three books were published on the subject. The *Gentleman's Magazine* surveyed the literature and concluded that it exposed the "insinuation and artifice" with which Methodists infiltrated the church: under the cover of Sunday schools for children they started midweek meetings for adults that were really conventicles for anti-Anglican teaching and worship. The *Anti-Jacobin* reckoned that evangelicalism was not only religiously but politically subversive: "The Sunday schools which happen to be under *their* superintendence are to be dreaded as the cradles of anarchy and murder." It uncovered "an organized confederation" for sabotaging the Church of England with Methodism, and announced "Clapham Common is the seat of its power", promising a more detailed exposé later. It also complained about their support from bishops: "*Every* parish may be convulsed, and *every* clergyman maybe oppressed, if the *cunning of* Mrs. More can thus … conjure up even good spirits, even the very angels of the church, to do her work of mischief for her." Beyond the *Anti-Jacobin*, even advocates for Sunday schools concluded that church authorities should take control of them before they became "the gates of sectarianism, fanaticism and bigotry".[14]

A panicked Porteus suggested More should close the schools, but Wilberforce insisted she do no such thing: "the Bishop never saw the schools: he never saw the country in its former, and in its present state. He has no adequate notion of the degree in which it has pleased God to bless your and your sister's efforts." In April 1802, lamenting the fact that the controversy was still raging, the *Anti-Jacobin* added thirteen more pages to it, culminating in the revelation "of her having received the SACRAMENT from the hands of a layman!!!". The layman was the Dissenting minister William Jay.[15]

This was the high-water mark of the scandal. Wilberforce, Thornton, Porteus, and More worked their network to get assurances of support for the schools. Her ally John Boak, the curate of Cheddar, published a book compiling testimony from nine local vicars that contradicted Bere's accusations. Another High Church magazine, the *British Critic*, judged that

Bere's campaign against More had failed and had shown an "uncharitable and atrociously revengeful spirit", asking why no evidence for More's supposed Methodist leanings could be found in her eight-volume works, published the previous year. No bishops came out against her, leaving the *Anti-Jacobin* in the embarrassing position of standing alone for the church against the Bishop of London and, though its February 1802 issue promised damaging revelations against him too, they never came. Alarming and upsetting as it was, the Blagdon controversy was in the end valuable to Clapham, demonstrating that the ecclesiastical establishment did not see evangelicalism as a threat to be countered, but had come to accept it as part of the church.

The Christian Observer

In January 1802, the Clapham sect launched its own magazine, the *Christian Observer*. The idea seems to have come first from William Hey, the Leeds surgeon, who got the backing of Wilberforce, Thornton, and Babington in 1798. Josiah Pratt, who was married to Hey's niece, then raised the subject for discussion by the Eclectic Society. Pratt was a London curate who had been converted at the age of seventeen by the words "Let us pray" before a sermon. The point of the magazine was to use news and reviews to promote an evangelical worldview, "to correct the false sentiments of the religious world", as Pratt said, by offering an evangelical analysis of current affairs, literature, and everything else. Hey wanted Thomas Scott, now fifty-five, to be the editor, but Clapham rejected him: "Mr. Scott is a *rough* diamond, and almost incapable of polish from his time of life and natural temper," said Wilberforce.[16] Instead Pratt took the post, but found it fantastically demanding and left after three issues in favour of Macaulay, who combined it with his work for the Sierra Leone Company. (Later that year Pratt took charge of the Church Missionary Society from Scott, who took over from Dawes as its teacher of Arabic and Susu, having to learn both for the purpose.) The magazine's editorial committee included Thornton, Wilberforce, Grant, and Venn, but their only contribution, Macaulay said, was to criticize articles after they were published.

The magazine included essays, the majority on religious subjects, but also covering matters as diverse as geology, travel, the ethics of hunting, the female character, botany, suttee, gypsies, and budgeting for students. It offered extensive news reports from home and abroad, covering religion, politics, slavery, scientific advances, archaeological discoveries, literature, and technology. There were reviews, largely of religious books, with very generous and positive coverage of anything by the Clapham circle – though

Hannah More's habit of anonymity got Macaulay into trouble when he inadvertently published a mixed review of her religious novel *Coelebs in Search of a Wife* in 1809. Her bitter complaint, and the grovelling of the *Christian Observer*'s recantation suggest that Macaulay had found the limits of evangelical frankness. A section of the magazine called "review of reviews", was for thoroughly frank criticism of rival publications, such as the *Edinburgh Review*, also launched in 1802, with its "strange opinions … unfair arguments" and "talent to do mischief". The *Review* in turn condemned the *Christian Observer* as "a publication which appears to have no other method of discussing a question fairly open to discussion, than that of accusing their antagonists of infidelity".[17]

Editing such a magazine, sixty-four pages a month, as a part-time job alongside colonial management would have been quite demanding enough, but Macaulay ended up writing a lot of it too, including essays, sermons, news, and reviews. It was attacked heatedly by both Dissenters and High Church for siding with the other. Even Scott, who contributed to the magazine, said no Calvinist could be happy with its attitude, while Dean Kipling of Peterborough accused the editors of being Calvinist schismatics plotting to kill the King. Another correspondent complained there was too much about Calvinism and Arminianism, and could there not be a bit more for the ladies? In Macaulay's hands the magazine was never going to be full of laughs – More said that it was valuable "but wants a little essential salt" and Wilberforce, "if it be not enlivened it will sink". It did however have the inestimable advantage of costing one shilling, compared with 2s. 6d. for its cheapest rival, and it continued until 1877. There were a huge number of magazines on offer, so it is fair to assume that the *Christian Observer* preached to the converted, but it played a part in the success of the Clapham sect by equipping evangelical readers with information, arguments, and a more comprehensive evangelical outook.

Thornton published *An Enquiry into the Nature and Effects of the Paper Credit of Great Britain* in 1802, expounding the case he had made in Parliament over the last five years: that the amount of paper money in circulation did not have to reflect the amount of gold in the Bank of England. Reducing paper would undermine credit and disrupt commerce, and injure the bank, the government, and the nation. Instead, the amount of paper money should match levels of public confidence. The book became a seminal text in classical economics. F. A. Hayek, rediscovering it in 1939, considered: "It is not too much to say that the appearance of the *Paper Credit* in 1802 marks the beginning of a new epoch in the development of monetary theory."[18]

Vice

In 1801, the Macaulays surrendered to gravity and moved to a relatively modest house in Clapham. They were the least wealthy family of the sect, and Thornton always paid for their doctors and lent them servants and horses. The following year John Shore, now Baron Teignmouth, moved with his family into the village. This was the peak for Clapham as an evangelical community, with the Thorntons, Wilberforces, Stephens, Macaulays, Venns, Elliotts, Grants, and Shores all there.

Family Life

While Battersea Rise had started out as a bachelor castle, it was now a family home, and Henry Thornton himself was changed in the process. His eldest and favourite child, Marianne, was now five. Henry played with his children, painted for them, wrote them poems, read to them, and prayed over them as they slept. "Mr H T really is become a *reformed* character," his wife told Hannah More. That said, he wrote Marianne a warning against the dangers of the world at the age of four and an analysis of her faults at six.

Marianne was a timid girl, terrified of the dark, the sea, horses, and parts of their garden. Henry gently insisted she sit on his horse with him, until at six she rode her own pony, accompanying him daily to London and being escorted home. She had to go in the sea twice a week on their holidays, and the part of the grounds she refused to visit after being scared by a dog they turned into a garden for her.

Just as the Clapham sect abhorred wasting time in leisure or pleasure, Henry believed that children's naughtiness arose from idleness, and set Marianne to work as soon and as often as possible. She happily churned butter daily for breakfast, waited on her parents, took messages to the butler, and read from the *Morning Chronicle*. As soon as she could do sums she was employed on the household accounts, which "amused and interested me extremely and gave me a pleasant idea of the meaning of the word economy". When she could write legibly, she copied documents and wrote letters for Henry "whose friends must have been astonished at receiving notes of invitation written in a child's round text hand". Similarly James Stephen's son George made duplicates of confidential abolition correspondence so that his father did not have to trust a secretary, and eavesdropped on their fascinating discussions. Henry discussed politics with Marianne, and came to her bed to tell her the results of votes in Parliament. This respect for children's minds was shared throughout the Clapham sect. Thomas Babington's granddaughter says that at sixteen they "were allowed to exchange ideas with them absolutely as equals. The word 'encouraging' would not at all describe their relations to us. I really think they were not conscious of any distance between us."[1]

The Thornton family was close to the Grants, though Charles was a distant, majestic figure – his children called him "the Director". Charles Grant became MP for Inverness-shire in 1802 after buying a massive estate on Skye, and was acknowledged as the most influential spokesperson for East India Company interests, a position he used to fiercely defend its trading monopoly. He got a college opened in Haileybury in Hertfordshire to train company officials in an effort to root out corruption. The Grant children were years older than Marianne, but enchanted her with stories, took her on long walks and taught her poems. "Our houses and ground were almost common property," she said, and the same applied to the Venns. Another highlight of her happy childhood memories was the visits of Hannah More:

> *"May is coming and then Hannah will be with us" was one of the earliest hopes of my childhood. And when she did arrive I always felt I had a fresh companion just my own age, ready to sympathize with all my pleasures and troubles… she discoursed with me about Joseph and his brethren and all the wonderful adventures of the children of Israel with such eloquence and force that I fancied she must have lived amongst them herself.*[2]

Another favourite of More's was Thomas Babington Macaulay, born in 1799, and an intellectual prodigy. Tom's earliest memory was in his second year seeing smoke pouring out of a chimney and asking his father if it was hell. From the age of three, he read incessantly and talked in "quite printed words", as their maid put it. When he was four he had hot coffee spilt on his legs, and when his hostess asked if he felt better, replied, "Thank you madam, the agony is abated." At the age of eight, he wrote a history of the world from the creation, an essay to convert Indians, poems after the style of Scott and Virgil, and many hymns, while memorizing long poems on a single reading. His mother rarely praised or indeed spoke of his remarkable abilities to him, his father never at all, but their severity was balanced by the celebration of family and friends. When he was eight the Mores had him standing on a chair and preaching to local labourers.

Family prayers were central to the faith of all the Clapham sect. If church was a religious duty, worship with dearest friends and family was very heaven. "If there be happiness in this world, this is it," said Henry Thornton of the Venn family prayers. For the servants forced to sit through it, it was generally more of a duty, often incomprehensible, though those who did not object to their puritanical standards seemed to find the Clapham sect generous employers. The Thorntons often let them borrow the carriage, while Wilberforce kept his personal secretary long after he lost his sight.

The African children fared as badly in England as the British in Sierra Leone, and died at a distressing rate. In 1805 fourteen were baptized at Holy Trinity, but by the end of the year the majority of the original twenty-five had died. Most of the survivors returned to Freetown to join the school there. Greaves kept the school open for the sons of the Clapham sect. Selina Macaulay sent Tom, telling him he would have to start studying without his habitual supply of bread and butter, and was told, "Yes, Mama, industry shall be my bread and attention my butter."

Trinidad

The issue which kept Wilberforce from bringing an abolition bill in 1802 was Trinidad. With the war over, Addington decided to sell the 1,800 square miles of fertile crown land to investors to cultivate plantations. Stephen had argued in his letters to Addington that this would mean investing £20–30,000 of British capital in land that could be quickly lost to the French, who had tens of thousands of troops in the Caribbean, and the more it was cultivated, the more enticing it would be. "To found a new slave colony in that neighbourhood, seems to me scarcely less irrational, than it would be to build a town near the crater of Vesuvius." At least Addington should wait until the French were gone.[3] Canning planned a bill to prevent the cultivation of Trinidad, and Wilberforce delayed his abolition bill until he brought it, which he finally did on 27 May. Canning repeated Stephen's arguments, but Addington dismissed the motion, saying no legislation was needed until the island had been surveyed, when there would be a parliamentary enquiry. Wilberforce decided even at this butt-end of the session to bring an abolition motion as a matter of principle, but it was evidently not going to get anywhere, and he gave it up before any debate.

In 1797, the Proclamation Society secured the conviction of the London bookseller Thomas Williams for publishing Paine's *The Age of Reason*. Their prosecuting counsel was, bizarrely, Thomas Erskine, the founder of the Society of the Friends of the Liberty of Press who had defended Paine himself over *The Rights of Man*. Apparently Erskine was persuaded that, as a religious rather than political polemic, *The Age of Reason* deserved suppression, but in the interval between verdict and sentence, Erskine repented and asked the society to recommend clemency. He claimed this was on new information: Williams's starving wife had dragged him to see their ten-foot apartment, where she tended three children with smallpox and her husband sewed religious tracts as his main line of work. In disinterested remorse, Williams asked Erskine to burn the books for him, if he could get them back. Here, Erskine told the society, was an "opportunity of manifesting their charity and Christian forbearance" by telling the judge they wanted no further punishment for Williams. The committee unanimously refused, Erskine resigned his brief, and Williams did twelve months' hard labour.

It is not the noblest moment in the history of the Clapham sect, but it is given a new light by the autobiography that Francis Place, a collaborator of Williams, wrote in the 1820s. According to Place, Erskine's story was complete fiction: Williams, a fat jolly man, lived in a three-storey house, which Erskine had visited several times; he made pretty good money from selling books, none of which were religious, and neither was he; and he had sold 7,000 copies of *The Age of Reason*, which made collecting them an unlikely prospect.[4] If the committee knew Erskine's story was merely an attempt to save face after a volte-face, they had better reason to refuse his appeal than would otherwise appear.

The Vice Society

For others, though, the problem with the Proclamation Society was not its goals or methods but its ineffectiveness in pursuing them, and from 1802 it was superseded by the more efficient Society for the Suppression of Vice. Though it did not take them long to throw themselves into it, the Clapham sect were not founders of the Vice Society, and had an ambivalent relationship with it. It was led by the High Church barrister and pamphleteer John Bowles, and unlike the top-heavy Proclamation Society was a thoroughly middle-class initiative, its founding meeting of twenty-nine men containing no nobles, bishops, or MPs. Its subscription rate for members was half that of the Proclamation Society, and within a year it had nearly four times as many members, a third of whom were women. The Vice Society was the more reactionary in one respect: it refused membership to Dissenters, who according to Bowles "with exceptions… encouraged and promoted, to the utmost of their power, the French Revolution, because it was founded upon their own principles".[5] This discrimination provoked a series of pungent satires in the *Christian Observer* on the "society of the Friends of Immorality, Vice, and Irreligion", arguing that the Vice Society promoted bigotry and religious discord. These satires have been attributed to Thornton but were in fact the work of William Jay, the Dissenting minister and friend of Wilberforce and More.[6]

The committee met weekly and there were sub-committees for their three main areas of interest: the sabbath; fraud and obscenity; disreputable houses, and cruelty to animals. In their first year over 200 publicans, grocers and butchers were convicted of Sunday trading, and in the second that figure tripled. Thousands were issued with printed warnings. They may not have had position, but the society had energy and organization. They showed the Proclamation Society how it was done, and its members quickly joined. Only three of the original members had been in both groups; by the second year forty had joined, including most of the Clapham sect.

One new tactic of the society was to discover obsolete laws against behaviour of which they disapproved, and revive them. This had its disadvantages: the law against Sunday trading, for example, set fines of 5s. for a barber and 10s. for a publican, stringent enough 200 years previously, but now an amount traders could take in their stride. It also made the society unpopular with magistrates: "If the same zeal was pursued in prosecuting thieves," complained William Fielding, "more advantage would be derived to society. We have had our office loaded with miserable informations, by a society of miserable sectaries, the penalty being only five shillings; and we could do no otherwise than impose the fines."[7] The society's first annual report listed 487 convictions in London, 440 for profaning the sabbath. Other vices proved more elusive though, and in two years the society only managed seven convictions for obscene publications – three of them involving the same man – despite claiming that between 6,000 and 8,000 people were involved.

More controversial was their policy of using paid investigators. Members acted as self-appointed police themselves and subsidized existing parish officers, but most of their prosecutions came from their task force of spies. Sydney Smith argued that such a hated job as prying and snitching could only attract desperate and unscrupulous people, spreading distrust and subterfuge. Bowles answered: "The rat is only to be hunted to his hole by the ferret."[8]

What alarmed Clapham most were reports that the society allowed its agents to use deceitful methods to ferret out the rats. Macaulay argued that doing evil that good may come was moral and political fanaticism, evidently enjoying the rare chance to turn the F-word on his High Church critics. His stance as editor of the *Christian Observer* was to welcome the "well-intentioned zeal" of the society in a good cause, with several caveats, such as an objection to their picking on the vices of the poor, and even more to their publicly admitting it. His affirming tone was balanced by Jay's ridicule. Bowles's second report in 1805 replied to Macaulay by justifying deception on biblical grounds: Jesus on the road to Emmaus pretended to the disciples that he was going further than he was, and so "preferred crooked means to those which were direct and straightforward, in order, that by the assistance and light of his own example, a rule of human conduct might be deduced". Jay responded by giving the same words to his Society of the Friends of Immorality, adding that, if they had also been inserted into a Vice Society publication, it must have been a fraud "intended to bring that useful and respectable society into disrepute with the public". Wilberforce wrote to Lord Dartmouth (son of Newton's and Venn's supporter), its president, warning that the society would be wrecked by resignations.[9]

The Clapham sect raised the issue at the Vice Society's 1805 annual meeting and Wilberforce was shocked by "the extremes to which the justifiers of artifice hurried". After a short debate they agreed to a private meeting of six people on 28 May, where, presumably by repeating his threat to lead mass resignation, Wilberforce secured from Bowles a promise not to practise falsehood, which was then written into the rules, reconciling the Clapham sect to the society, until its next scandal.

The first thing that stopped Wilberforce bringing an abolition bill in 1803 was flu. Then the King announced that Napoleon was once again preparing an invasion force and the country should get ready to defend itself. Sea forts were built, volunteer regiments organized. "My wife is advised by some of our friends to leave London," said Thornton, "for the sake of avoiding the danger of being surrounded by a French soldiery, and I am hearing day by day new accounts of slaughter and insurrection in Ireland."[10]

"My poor slaves!" cried Wilberforce; it would be "improper to bring forward my intended motion… when the whole attention of government is justly called to the state of the country". The bill would be routed, he reckoned, and would turn the Irish MPs against him permanently.[11] In May, Addington's government declared war on France, opposed by Wilberforce and Thornton before a hostile House. Teignmouth was appointed Lord Lieutenant of Surrey, in charge of a home army of 8,000, and Macaulay marched at the head of the Clapham volunteers. Marianne Thornton believed that Napoleon would cut down their tulip tree, while Tom Macaulay assured her that Napoleon "would merely stab all the little children in their beds". By 1804, Napoleon had 100,000 soldiers ready in the English Channel.

The Bible Society

Not everything had to stop for Napoleon, and in 1804 the Clapham sect became founding members of the Bible Society. It began because of the scarcity of Bibles in Welsh. The last edition had been printed in 1770, and ministers were finding it impossible to get hold of copies. John Thornton's Naval and Military Bible Society provided twenty-five to an applicant in 1787, but had to buy them from the SPCK, whose stocks were limited and prices steep, so in 1791 the same anonymous minister raised money and applied directly to the SPCK for a new edition, but they were doubtful about the demand and costs, and it was eight years before the run of 10,000 was printed. Even then, the organizers had vastly underestimated the demand and were deluged with complaints from ministers who received only half their order or none at all.

The SPCK repeatedly refused to consider any further editions, so in December 1802 Thomas Charles, a minister from Bala, asked for the help of the Religious Tract Society, an interdenominational evangelical organization founded in 1799 to fill the gap left by the Cheap Repository with more specifically religious material. The Tract Society thought the plan should be expanded to provide Bibles to any part of the country, and indeed the world, where they were hard to get hold of. They put the idea to Charles Grant, who introduced them to Wilberforce. Wilberforce told them to conduct a nationwide survey of Bible shortage, and in March 1803 the British and Foreign Bible Society was formed.

It was an interdenominational society, and the tensions between Anglicans and Dissenters had to be carefully managed. Thus the committee officially consisted only of laymen: fifteen Anglicans, fifteen Nonconformists, and six foreigners, but all ministers in the society were to act as unofficial committee members. The first committee was chaired by Sharp, and included Wilberforce, Macaulay, Stephen, Grant, Babington, and Thomas Bernard, with Thornton as treasurer. The president was John Shore, Lord Teignmouth, and vice-presidents included Bishops Porteus and Barrington. Local societies raised money and distributed Bibles.

Thomas Charles prepared an updated and amended edition of the Welsh Bible, but the SPCK disapproved of the very idea, so they and the Bible Society agreed to print 20,000 copies each of the existing version. Similarly they printed 20,000 Gaelic Bibles alongside the Scottish SPCK's print run. They produced French and Spanish Bibles for prisoners of war, and English Bibles for churches, prisons, and hospitals.

The society immediately stirred up a surprising amount of controversy. The Revd Thomas Sikes denounced it for including Dissenters, who, he said, wanted to distribute Bibles to undermine the church: "supply these men with Bibles..." said Sikes, "and you supply them with arms against yourself". Thomas Twining, the tea merchant, heard that the society was planning Indian translations and wrote a tract against the dangers of disturbing the Indians, which created enough of a storm for both Teignmouth and Porteus to write replies. Teignmouth was also drawn into controversy with the chaplain to the Archbishop of Canterbury, who accused the society of diverting funds from the SPCK. A Cambridge divinity professor wrote that encouraging the Bible Society would do nothing to advance the established church "and might contribute even to its dissolution". "It is ever vigilant," warned the *Anti-Jacobin,* "ever active, and ever will continue so, till the church is destroyed." One prominent defender of the society in these debates was William Dealtry, the future rector of Clapham.[12]

It is hard to understand such a panicked reaction, or to credit the fear that the distribution of Bibles by Anglicans and Dissenters was an attack on the Church of England. The great anxiety of the times was the backdrop for it. Dissenters and evangelicals, two great villains in High Church eyes, were both rapidly increasing, and the Bible Society brought them together not only in a central committee but in cells springing up all over the country. This revived the age-old fear of established churches that if ordinary people get hold of the Bible they will find the bits that sound misleadingly like heresy and concoct a new religion. But to calmer observers, this paranoia was absurd, and they were gradually vindicated. It was another conflict out of which the evangelicals emerged looking more reasonable, moderate, and indeed Christian than their accusers.

This was not so true for the Vellore mutiny. Indian troops in Vellore, near Madras, revolted in 1806, ostensibly over a new uniform that violated both Hindu and Muslim rules, perhaps as part of a wider anti-British movement. Some 350 Indians and 114 British were killed. The news caused uproar in Britain, revealing how insecure its rule in India was. Twining argued that the East India Company had always said missionaries would cause a revolt, missionaries were in India, the revolt had happened, therefore missionaries were to blame and should all be expelled. Teignmouth among many others defended the missionaries; Sydney Smith among many others ridiculed and denounced them. Grant stopped the company from expelling the missionaries, but it became much harder for them to enter or travel within British India.

The Resurrection of Abolition

By the time Parliament met in 1804, there was again talk from major plantation owners about suspending the slave trade to protect prices, and Wilberforce heard that the next conference of planters was expected to agree to it unanimously. He again held off his own motion and again failed to persuade Addington to propose the suspension himself, and on 17 May the conference again decided against suspension.

A week later Addington was forced to resign by a coalition of Pitt, Grenville, and Fox. George III would not accept his enemy Fox as a minister, and Grenville stuck by Fox, so Pitt returned as an isolated Prime Minister. It looked as if a fifth session of Parliament had gone by without an abolition motion, but Wilberforce felt like a futile gesture of tenacity, so he brought his tenth full abolition bill on 30 May 1804. He repeated all the well-worn arguments, concluding with an appeal to the new MPs representing the Irish, "a brave, a generous, a benevolent people". At least one Caribbean magnate, having supported the proposed suspension of the slave trade, voted for abolition. But, more importantly, so did every single Irish MP present. To the astonishment of both sides, the motion was carried at its first reading by 124 votes to 49, and at the second by 100 to 42. Wilberforce persuaded the Irish MPs to stay a week longer than planned into the summer and on 27 June the bill was passed in the Commons by 69 votes to 33. Grenville also postponed his holiday to champion the bill in the Lords, where it passed its first reading, but then Pitt killed the bill. He told Wilberforce there was nothing to be gained from trying to rush the Lords, who would demand an enquiry, and he was not in a position to coerce them. But suddenly the abolition movement was alive again. Sharp, at sixty-nine, revived the Abolition Committee, and Stephen and Macaulay joined for the first time.

Addington had allowed the cultivation of Trinidad and Demerara to go ahead, at a cost of a thousand new slaves a month. Wilberforce pressed Pitt to stop it, and he promised an Order in Council to do so, but coping with a slim majority, a chronic ulcer, royal madness, and the threat of invasion, Pitt could not make the divisive issue of slavery a priority. Come the 1805 session, he asked Wilberforce to postpone his abolition motion, and Wilberforce, finally confident of victory after seventeen years, absolutely refused.

At the first reading in February 1805, Wilberforce's bill was unopposed, and at the second, instead of his usual detailed and impassioned speech, he said that MPs had heard it all last year and there was nothing to do but pass the motion again. But as the debate unrolled he realized he had made a terrible tactical mistake. The slavery party had prepared much better than the abolitionists, packing the house and persuading the uncommitted. Pitt kept silent and Wilberforce lost 77 to 70. "I could not sleep either on Thursday or Friday night," he told a friend, "without dreaming of scenes of depredation and cruelty on the injured shores of Africa."[13]

War in Disguise

The abolitionists forced Pitt in May 1805 to draft the Order in Council to stop slaves being brought into new British possessions by threatening to bring the matter before Parliament themselves. It turned out to be so full of loopholes that they then had to make him hold it back while Stephen and Wilberforce reworked it. It was finally issued on 15 August.

In October 1805, Stephen published *War in Disguise,* a book which drew on his experience as a St Kitts lawyer in order to help the war effort, and which seven years later started another war. One essential part of the war against Napoleon was the naval blockade that stopped enemy ships bringing supplies from their colonies. Stephen pointed out a loophole: US ships, or French ships bearing US flags, were taking cargo from the colonies, stopping for show at a US port, then going on to France. He argued that Britain should reassert the right it claimed during the Seven Years' War to stop neutral as well as enemy ships. The idea became government policy and was put into effect by two Orders in Council in January and November 1807.

War in Disguise was an influential publication, but it has also been ascribed a significance it never had. It has been repeatedly claimed and generally accepted that the book made a major contribution to the abolition of the slave trade. Cunningly, it is said, using only patriotic and economic arguments, never mentioning the slave trade and not putting his name to the book, Stephen won support for a measure whose main purpose, as far as he was concerned, was to stop the slave trade, because stopping all Atlantic trade would stop that too and because ruining enemy slave colonies would end their demand for slaves. This interpretation originated with Robert and Samuel Wilberforce's 1838 biography of their father. "Fearing if he mentioned the slave trade, that the effect of his arguments might be diminished by a suspicion of his motives," they said, "he confined himself entirely to the general question", while in truth he aimed "only at its suppression".[14] The idea was revived by Roger Anstey in his 1975 book *The Atlantic Slave Trade and British Abolition,* which said that Stephen had "a conscious, major concern to promote abolition" through the proposals. The only evidence cited for Stephen's intentions is the Wilberforce biography, but this has to be weighed against the recollections of Stephen's son George, a leading abolitionist lawyer himself. He insists the Wilberforce brothers had a

> *very erroneous impression… as to the motives for publishing this*
> *celebrated pamphlet…. It is most probable that the reverend biographers*
> *of their father never read the work; for it was long out of print, and*
> *nearly forgotten when they were children, nor is it a subject which*
> *divines, however learned, can be expected to understand.*[15]

James Stephen's sons gloried in his contribution to abolition, but none of them seem to have considered *War in Disguise* a part of it. The idea that he published anonymously to dissociate the book from abolitionism is undermined by the fact that his abolitionist tracts were then ascribed to "The author of *War in Disguise*", even before the Orders in Council were issued. The real reason he did not mention the slave trade seems to be that he was not writing about the slave trade. As for their consequences, the two Orders in Council were issued three months before and eight months after the Abolition Act. So whatever results they might have had on the slave trade it had not been abolished, their intended effect and actual effect on getting abolition passed were nil, though they may have helped enforce abolition in the years immediately after the act.

Between 1806 and 1807 Napoleon launched his Continental System, which responded to the British blockade by forbidding French allies or conquests to trade with Britain. The threat of invasion subsided when Nelson destroyed the combined French and Spanish fleet at Trafalgar in October 1805, then revived when Napoleon destroyed the combined Russian and Prussian army at Austerlitz in December. "I stand aghast at the frightful prospect," said Stephen, starting a new book, *The Dangers of the Country*. He argued that conquest was a realistic prospect and that Britain's best chance of averting it was a massive increase in the voluntary militia and the abolition of the slave trade. In similar tones, Bowles prescribed a radical moral regeneration. A number of books argued that Napoleon was the antichrist and the second coming was at hand.

The Abolition Act

Wilberforce believed it was the news of Austerlitz which killed Pitt, who died in January 1806. Ironically, considering his ardent personal desire for abolition, Pitt's death removed another major obstacle in its way, forcing George III to turn to Grenville and Fox. They assembled a cabinet which included other strong abolitionists such as Lord Henry Petty, the Chancellor of the Exchequer, as well as such committed opponents as Addington, now Viscount Sidmouth. While the government was by no means unanimous, Grenville and Fox were able to make abolition the political priority it had never been for Pitt. With proper management, carrying the motion in the Commons would be easy, but the balance in the Lords, though better, still seemed decisively against them.

James Stephen came up with two ideas to shift the balance. The first was that Wilberforce, Thornton, Grant, and Babington should offer their general support to Grenville's government if he would make abolition an official government motion. Wilberforce rejected this out of hand as both naïve and unprincipled. Stephen's other suggestion was rather more subtle. Wilberforce had already given notice of an abolition motion in the 1806 session of Parliament, but Stephen persuaded him to postpone it, suggesting that instead the government should introduce a bill to embody Pitt's Order in Council forbidding the cultivation of the new colonies – and since it prohibited the importation of slaves there they could tag onto it a ban on selling slaves to foreign colonies. In other words it would revive Wilberforce's foreign slave-trade bill, incorporated into a government measure, thus making it considerably less likely to be defeated again. It would have little direct result, the foreign trade being "all but extinguished by the war", as Wilberforce argued, but being almost the first successful abolition measure ever it might lower resistance to the full abolition bill, and would at least test the water. Wilberforce suggested the motion to Grenville on 24 March 1806, and it passed the Commons, with significant but ineffectual opposition, by May. In the Lords, it faced its usual opponents, but thanks to government sponsorship, it had a comfortable majority and Grenville concluded the debate by declaring his support for total abolition. "I felt our strength," he told Wilberforce.

Wilberforce wanted an abolition bill in the same session, but Grenville reckoned their majority in the Lords was too fragile for such haste. Instead, Fox proposed a parliamentary resolution condemning the slave trade as "contrary to the principles of justice, humanity and sound policy" and agreeing to abolition in principle, which was passed by 114 votes to 15 in the Commons, and 41 to 30 in the Lords. Wilberforce proposed a second resolution that the King be asked to negotiate multilateral abolition with other slave powers, which was passed without opposition. And Stephen proposed a law stopping any ships being brought into the slave trade for the first time, to stop the panic buying of slaves, which Fox got passed. "If it please God to spare the health of Fox…" Wilberforce told Stephen, "I hope we shall next year see the termination of all our labours." A month later Fox was struck with dropsy and he died on 13 September.[16]

An unexpected election in the summer of 1806 only strengthened their position further, as abolition proved a major issue and even Liverpool failed to re-elect one of its pro-slave trade MPs. Stephen and Wilberforce both published books in January 1807 in time for the great debate: Stephen published *The Dangers of the Country*, also issuing the section on the slave trade separately as *New Reasons for Abolishing the Slave Trade*; Wilberforce made his last major contribution with *A Letter on the Abolition of the Slave Trade Addressed to the Freeholders and Other Inhabitants of Yorkshire*, which he was lucky not to have to post as it ran to 396 pages, working through all the familiar arguments. Copies were distributed among the Lords in time for the second reading.

Grenville had two new ideas for the motion: first, to abolish the trade gradually through punitive taxation, from which the horrified Wilberforce dissuaded him; second, to take the bill to the Lords first, giving them less chance to kill it with delays, and debating it in the Commons concurrently if necessary. This was agreed and Grenville brought the bill on 2 January. Anti-abolitionists in the Lords held the bill up throughout January, and then at the second reading on 4 February tried to start another enquiry, but Grenville swept their procrastination aside. The Earl of Westmorland still insisted that, if trade could be limited by religious campaigners, then "the very freehold estates of the landholders might be sacrificed to field-preaching and popular declamation", but when the Lords divided at five o'clock in the morning, the bill passed by 100 votes to 36.

The bill was brought to the Commons by Charles Grey, the First

Lord of the Admiralty. The main debate was at the second reading on 23 February, though by now it was as much a celebration of abolition as a debate, and a celebration of Wilberforce too. The Solicitor-General compared him with Napoleon, who had reached the summit of human ambition but whose silent moments must be haunted by the suffering he had caused, while Wilberforce would go to his bed knowing that he had saved the lives of millions. MPs gave him an unprecedented salute of cheers and applause, and he sat through it in a daze of tears. The bill was passed by 283 votes to 16. He went home to Palace Yard with Thornton, Sharp, Macaulay, Grant, and Smith. "Well, Henry," grinned Wilberforce to Thornton, "what shall we abolish next?" Thornton said: "The lottery, I think."

At the committee stage, Grenville capitalized on their majority by inserting pretty stiff penalties for infringement: £100 per slave and the confiscation of ships. At the final reading in the Commons, Wilberforce declared his wish to move on to ending slavery: "I must confess, that I shall have another object after [this bill] in view, and that I look forward to a still more happy change in the state of the negroes of the West Indian islands."[17] The bill gained royal assent on 25 March 1807, and Grenville, because of the King's refusal to extend Catholic rights, relinquished office the same day.

During this last battle of the epic campaign, Thornton, playing to type, spoke for abolition but put more energy into a rather less heroic cause, cutting public expenditure. He had played a leading role on the 1804 select committee on Irish currency, whose report was a statement of his monetary theory, and was brought on to the public expenditure committee in February 1807. His brothers and city colleagues disagreed with its recommendations, but he congratulated himself on saving the state £240,000 a year.

He even parted company with the Clapham sect over the 1807 bombardment on Copenhagen. Britain attacked neutral Denmark because Napoleon had annexed half of Prussia to France and was expected to invade Denmark next and seize their fleet of sixty ships. The British bombarded Copenhagen until the Danes surrendered the fleet to them instead, destroying a third of the city and killing 2,000. The initial reaction at Clapham was condemnation, but the government explained it as unavoidable self-defence, and in the end only Thornton voted to censure the policy.

The Leader of the Commons and Chancellor of the Exchequer, Spencer Perceval, an abolitionist evangelical who had just moved to

Clapham, championed Stephen's policy of seizing neutral ships, his Order in Council in November 1807 strengthening Grenville's earlier version. Thornton broke ranks again over this, opposing the policy privately and in Parliament.

The abolition campaign transformed the standing of evangelicalism in Britain. Stopping the enslavement of 40,000 people a year was the most unambiguously good achievement of the age. It was hardly the work of evangelicals alone, but it was Wilberforce whom the public had seen carry it through years of tireless struggle, and there was no mistaking his religious imperative. He had become a moral icon, a figure attracting unique deference, the conscience of the nation. Abolition transformed Britain's self-image too, from a free people to a force for liberation; and the more British ships moved from carrying on the trade to suppressing it, the more empire was seen as being not just about gain but about giving. And all this was owned by evangelicalism. There is no evidence at all that the Clapham sect foresaw abolition having such promotional benefits for their faith, and no possibility whatsoever that they did it to win the hearts of the people. They did it because it was right, and that is what won the hearts of the people.

Slaves of the Abolitionists

Along with the legal slave trade in Britain, 1807 saw the end of the Sierra Leone Company's rule, though this was the start of the most controversial chapter in the Clapham sect's dealings with the colony. Having exhausted its capital, the company had received subsidies from the government since 1804, £14,000 a year toward civil and military costs plus £8,000 in total for fortifications. Humiliatingly, the directors had to petition Parliament for each payment. Thornton presented a petition to transfer the colony to the crown on 20 January 1807; it was passed on 29 July, and took effect on 1 January 1808.

"It remains to be seen whether fruit worthy of the expense incurred in the culture will be produced," Thornton told his children. "My own hopes are small and yet I often reflect that it may possibly please Providence to deduce some great and important consequences to the interests of the negro race from this hitherto unsuccessful project." He had lost up to £3,000 himself but believed "I am on the whole a gainer": he had become friends with Macaulay, gained extensive education, and above all "learned to feel for the African race. I hope that my children and my children's children will take up the same cause."[1]

The African Institution
With these two campaigns coming to some sort of conclusion, the African Institution was formed to take over from both and to promote the economic, commercial and social development of Africa in reparation for the slave trade. Wilberforce put the idea to Grenville two days after the Abolition Act became law, and it was established on 14 April 1807. The committee was an extraordinary assemblage: the Duke of Gloucester, the royal abolitionist, as president; fourteen lords; five bishops including the Archbishop of Canterbury; fourteen MPs including the cabinet ministers

Perceval and Canning; Thornton as treasurer, Macaulay as secretary, Wilberforce, Stephen, Babington, Grant, and Teignmouth; and members of the disbanded Abolition Committee, including Clarkson, Sharp, and the Quakers George Harrison and William Allen. This was not a committee that would have difficulty getting its views heard in Westminster.

They aimed to promote the "civilization and happiness" of the whole continent by "diffusing useful knowledge, and exciting industry among the inhabitants of Africa", ultimately allowing British entrepreneurs to establish "a legitimate and far more extended commerce, beneficial alike to the natives of Africa and to the manufacturers of Great Britain and Ireland". They would provide plants and tools to Africans, encourage British people to learn African languages, and reward those who furthered their objectives, without themselves taking part in commerce or religious mission.[2]

The key was Sierra Leone, the main British foothold in Africa. The African Institution founded a school there to teach English literacy and agriculture to locals, and Susu and Arabic to the British. They sent three of the children Macaulay had brought over to a Chelsea school for teaching practice, and then sent them back to Freetown as teachers. They offered prizes for the first significant imports of cotton wool, indigo, and rice grown in West Africa, and for the largest Sierra Leone coffee plantation. They sent fifteen tons of cotton seed to encourage Africans to cultivate it for the British market, a gin to process the results, and pamphlets explaining the procedure. Other supplies included mulberry trees for silk and a castor oil press. They asked the government to look into the debilitating taxes on African imports. They instructed Ludlam, while he remained governor, to monitor the success of abolition and to supply all possible information to help in exploration and cultivation.

Thomas Perronet Thompson

In practice, the African Institution chose the crown governor of Sierra Leone, and their choice was the 25-year-old Lieutenant Thomas Perronet Thompson. Thompson was an evangelical from a solid evangelical family: his great-grandfather (and godfather) was Vincent Perronet, an evangelical vicar and collaborator with Wesley; his father was a partner with the Sykes family and manager of the Wilberforce business in Hull, a friend of Wilberforce and Isaac Milner, and one of the new abolitionist MPs of 1807. Thomas was taught by Milner at Hull Grammar. He went from Cambridge into the navy and was briefly taken prisoner by the Spanish in the abortive attack on Buenos Aires in 1807. On his return, he sat up one night with Wilberforce discussing ideas for developing British links with Africa, and Wilberforce announced he wanted him as governor. "I should be glad to devote my life and fortune to such a cause," replied Thompson.[3]

Thornton invited Thompson to dinner, and Thompson forgot to go. He wrote a formal apology, but felt that not even repelling the French from Sierra Leone and starting two Sunday schools would exonerate him. He was appointed governor by Viscount Castlereagh, Secretary of State for the Colonies, in April 1808, to start in October. He sailed in June, with Dawes (who with Ludlam was commissioned to investigate the state of the African coast after Thompson took office), and they arrived on 21 July.

Thompson was not at all happy with the state of affairs at Sierra Leone. For one thing, the defences were poor. Wilberforce had told him they could resist six frigates, but Thompson reckoned the French could "root us up like a mushroom". He made extensive plans for improvements. Secondly, he quickly concluded that Maroons were second-class citizens compared with the Nova Scotians. He was formally introduced to leading Nova Scotians on his first day, but when two Maroon chiefs came to greet him they were turned away, so he embarrassed Ludlam by running after them and shaking their hands. Thirdly, he was disgusted by the behaviour of white officials: "The black subjects are infinitely more orderly and decent. So much for this religious colony. And while the white inhabitants are roaring with strong drink at one end the Nova Scotians are roaring out hymns at the other."[4]

Apprentices or Slaves?

But all this was nothing compared with what Thompson saw of the treatment of people released from the slave trade. After the passing of the Abolition Act, the government sent two warships to enforce it, and planned a Vice-Admiralty Court in Freetown to deal with the captives. Two ships carrying 167 slaves were seized in March 1808 and brought to Freetown. According to the act, the slaves became crown property and their deliverers were paid a bounty. But then what to do with them? The act explicitly allowed them to be conscripted, or apprenticed for up to fourteen years. So Ludlam gave the men and children to Nova Scotian farmers and British colonists, who paid twenty dollars each for apprenticeship rights. "The women were given away," Thompson said euphemistically. Thanks to the success of twenty years of struggle against the slave trade, the one place in the British Empire where African people were still legally bought and sold into forced labour was Freetown.

Thompson had argued about the arrangement with Macaulay before sailing. "He said it was ransoming," Thompson told his fiancée Nancy Barker, "and I said it was buying."[5] In fact, Macaulay had considered a voluntary apprenticeship scheme for Freetown, submitting proposals to the African Institution in June 1808 not to dispose of seized slave cargoes, but to redeem slaves held in Africa, eroding African slavery, and building a society with the benefits of European civilization. The Institution rejected the proposals, their main objection, as Macaulay foresaw, being that they would promote the African slave trade by providing a new market.

Seeing apprenticeship in action, Thompson was disgusted and outraged. Ludlam had kept some of the apprentices back to work for his government, paying them nothing but their provisions. Others had already cultivated new coffee plantations. Some escaped to neighbouring villages, where they worked for wages, and Thompson found Ludlam trying to persuade the employers to bring them back. When twenty were returned he put them in irons in Fort Thornton gaol; Ludlam considered transporting them to Goree, or even the Caribbean. When Thompson berated him, Ludlam explained that apprenticeship was authorized by the Abolition Act and the Order in Council that followed it; Thompson insisted it was slave trading and therefore illegal.

Freeing the Apprentices

Thompson was supposed to shadow Ludlam until October, but Ludlam proposed an immediate handover and Thompson leapt at it. On 31 July he emptied the gaol, and the following day proclaimed: "No person within this colony, has or can have, any claim or right to any native of Africa in consequence of any direct or indirect sale or purchase."[6] He declared all apprenticeships null and void, and made the trading and holding of slaves felonies. When the Nova Scotians protested he went from house to house, arguing that if black slavery revived none of them would be safe.

A white master, finding his eight-year-old "apprentice" unsatisfactory, burned her back repeatedly with an iron. Brought before the governor, he insisted "that he paid money for the girl and therefore she is his" and "that he has a right to do as he pleases with his own". When Thompson said buying slaves was illegal, he answered, "Lord, sir, I did not buy her, I redeemed her."[7]

A slave trader proposed to bring 300 slaves to Freetown, have Thompson apprentice them back to him, renew the term when it expired, "and by that time I think they will have pretty well worked themselves out".[8]

"These apprenticeships have after sixteen years successful struggle at last introduced actual slavery into the colony," he wrote to Nancy, and depressing as it is to say so, that is the truth of it. Reporting to Castlereagh, he said the Africans were in "a situation in no essential circumstance differing from that of slaves not only without authority, but in opposition to the order of His Majesty's Government". The agents of the Sierra Leone Company "have carried on the grossest system of prevarication and perversion... Their slaves are *apprentices*. Their sales, *indentures*. Their purchases *redemptions*." He told Wilberforce he would resign before allowing apprenticeship.[9]

Forty more rescued slaves arrived in September and the lack of accommodation, supplies, and work for them became a serious problem. Thompson housed them temporarily in the gaol buildings, and started a system whereby rescued slaves worked for wages every second week, including clearing woods for a new settlement, and on alternate weeks built themselves houses and tended their land. He found the Nova Scotians less enthusiastic about clearance work than the newcomers, so he reissued their land grants, offering extensions and better security of tenure to those who did clearance. This way he founded two new settlements, Kingston-in-Africa and Leicester, and constructed roads. For the first time a British entrepreneur bought land in Sierra Leone. Paradoxically, this champion of liberty changed the name of Freetown to Georgetown, in frustration at what he considered the Nova Scotians' "half-comprehended notions of American independence", abolishing at the same time the local currency of dollars and cents, and naming streets that had previously been numbered.

In November, seventy-eight captured slaves arrived and were immediately given paid work. "There is a perfect famine of labourers in this colony," Thompson told Castlereagh. If Sierra Leone Company agents argued that forced labour was unavoidable, he insisted, they were fools or liars; the colony needed free labour from all over Africa, which would extend British influence. "The Sierra Leone Company or its agents have been doing everything in its power to prevent the spreading of English influence or English improvement in Africa; they have been perfect volunteers in the cause of slavery."[10]

Thompson's first dispatches reached England in October 1808, along with a report from his storekeeper, Mr Smith, that Thompson had refused tribute to the local king, Firama. Firama had granted the Company land, receiving in return £60 worth of goods annually. Thompson considered him a nobody and, though Firama did in fact take his goods from the store, Thompson was furious and told Castlereagh he believed the payment should be stopped.

Castlereagh delegated all Sierra Leone affairs to the company. The directors thought it unfair, unwise, and impetuous of Thompson to have supposedly refused Firama his dues. As for the apprentices, they felt that Ludlam had been wrong to let Freetowners pay their rescuers for them, but also that Thompson was again unfair, unwise, and impetuous to void the transaction, leaving people out of pocket. Thornton replied to Thompson's dispatches, first making the point that the transaction took place after Sierra Leone became a crown colony, so Ludlam acted as a crown agent and the Sierra Leone Company had no power or responsibility, meaning Thompson was wrong to allege that they have "by means of their agents become slave traders themselves".[11] Thornton sympathized with Thompson's objections to "authorizing indented servants", as he called it, but argued that under the Abolition Act and Order in Council Ludlam was not only authorized, but required, to dispose of them in such a way, so Thompson's quarrel was with Parliament and the Privy Council, not the Sierra Leone Company. Ludlam had misjudged in the way money changed hands, he said, but since the Vice-Admiralty Court had not yet been established it was a difficult and unprecedented situation, and he deserved understanding. Thornton insisted that indenturing servants was not slavery, though it was marked with some of the same evils and could be badly abused. He hoped that Thompson would reverse his hasty actions – if he had not already done so.

Wilberforce seconded Thornton's response, warning Thompson not to jeopardize a promising career by rashness. He urged Thompson to be utterly candid with him, but not with Castlereagh or the Sierra Leone Company. He explained that the abolitionists had no control over the apprenticeship clause of the Act: "I wish I had time to go into particulars respecting the difficulties which forced us into acquiescing in the system of apprenticing."[12]

Modern readers will share that wish. Presumably the abolitionists believed that the bill would not pass the Lords without that provision, for whatever reason, and that apprenticeship was a price worth paying for the success of the bill. If the first point is true then the second certainly follows: the Abolition Act outlawed a traffic that claimed 40,000 people a year while condemning hundreds perhaps to a lesser form of slavery in Sierra Leone.

Slavery it was, though – forced labour under the threat of punishment, involuntarily entered into, and without recompense. The one difference was its maximum term of fourteen years, which means that it was only temporary slavery and not necessarily for life, though with life expectancy on Caribbean plantations being seven years that was small mitigation. Macaulay had suggested apprenticeship as an abolitionist scheme, and Sharp had ordered it for the Province of Freedom as a way for slaves to fund their redemption, but in both cases it was to be tightly regulated, voluntary, and for a maximum of five and seven years respectively. Perhaps its similarity to their own schemes helped the abolitionists reconcile themselves to it. But one of the powers of the Clapham sect in general was their political independence, and in managing Sierra Leone they were working for the government, and found it hard to see things as ideologically as usual.

Thompson was right to be outraged by apprenticeship, but wrong that it was illegal under the Abolition Act, which is precisely what authorized it – though Thornton was exaggerating to say the law required it. Practically speaking, Thompson made a serious mistake in his choice of friends and enemies. The Sierra Leone Company directors were abolitionists who accepted apprenticeship reluctantly, and had recommended Thompson as governor. If he had courted their support for suspending the system, and recompensed those who had "redeemed" slaves under Ludlam, he might have proceeded with impunity. Instead he alienated the directors from the start, denouncing them as slave traders – and appealing to Castlereagh, who had opposed abolition and took his information and advice on Sierra Leone affairs from the directors.

In December, the directors decided Thompson had to go, and Wilberforce wrote to him "that I could not but acquiesce in their unanimous reasoning and conclusion". Wilberforce complained to Thompson that he had not told him about refusing Firama's dues, an event that undermined the directors' confidence in him from the start – unfairly, since it never happened. The first communication Castlereagh had with Thompson after he left England was to dismiss him in April 1809. He had assumed the government three months before he was authorized to, said Castlereagh, "prevent[ed] prize negroes being apprenticed", failed to make Firama's regular payment, and made an offensive treaty with local chiefs. He was to come and explain himself.

Thompson went quietly and enjoyed a successful military career, becoming a general and a radical MP, and it was only in 1815 that the controversy was made public by the chief justice of Georgetown, Robert Thorpe.

Kensington

The Clapham community was broken up in December 1808 by the Wilberforces, who moved to Kensington, followed in 1809 by the Stephens. "It is the age of revolutions," lamented Hannah More. Wilberforce's new house was two and a half miles from Parliament, but still in the countryside, allowing him to sell both Broomfield and Palace Yard. This saved money, and was also supposed to cut down on visitors. Wilberforce's influence and philanthropy brought such crowds to his Palace Yard waiting-room daily that he found it hard ever to get anything done – especially as he would not ask his servants to tell callers he was "not at home" when he was. He had bought a third house outside Bath in 1799 to escape from visitors in the summer, which as Thornton predicted was pointless: "He is a man, who, were he in Norway or Siberia, would find himself infested by company."[13] It was Thornton who bought the Palace Yard house from him, so in fact Wilberforce stayed there much more often than he came home to Kensington. The Kensington house had an extra advantage, however: he bought the cottage next door as an office, which he called "The Nuisance", meaning that when he was there the servants could truthfully tell callers he was not at home.

There was another reason for the move. In a rare quiet moment at Clapham, he picked up one of his sons, who burst into tears. "He always is afraid of strangers," explained the nurse. William was shocked, and decided the time had come to be "acquainted with my own children". Though he still saw little of them during the parliamentary week, Sundays and summers were family time. He read them the *Arabian Nights* and the history of America, listened to them reciting Cowper, wrote them instructions on brotherly love, and laid himself up for a week with a cricketing injury. While Marianne Thornton learned from her earliest days that her loving father drew an absolute line between work and family time and was never to be disturbed, Wilberforce was always to be disturbed. "During the long and grave discussions that went on between him and my father and others," she said, "he was most thankful to refresh himself by throwing a ball or a bunch of flowers at me, or opening the glass door and going off with me for a race on the lawn 'to warm his feet'."[14] Not everyone at their meetings appreciated this as much as Marianne.

Hannah More's last major work was *Coelebs In Search of a Wife*, an unexpected attempt to communicate evangelical ideas about education and marriage in the form of a romantic novel. Confusing as it was for novel-hating evangelicals they of course welcomed it and, though critics were nonplussed, it was a commercial triumph. Sydney Smith mocked its puritanism in the *Edinburgh Review* as part of his concerted attack over 1808 and 1809 that included evangelical magazines, Indian missionaries, the Sunday school advocate Sarah Trimmer, and the Vice Society. Thornton dissuaded Macaulay from retaliation, arguing that the *Edinburgh Review* was not avowedly anti-evangelical and as likely to attack their High Church enemies, and it was worth keeping that way.

Macaulay went into partnership with the Babingtons' son Thomas Gisborne Babington, importing and exporting to Sierra Leone, a business which made their fortune. They were major landowners in Sierra Leone and won the African Institution's prize for the first import of rice, a silver trophy whose value Macaulay repaid to the Institution the next day. They also did well out of the recapturing of slaves: the government paid £191,100 in bounties by 1815, and Macaulay and Babington acted both as prize agents in London and as prosecutor in Georgetown.

Having been on the public expenditure committee since 1807, Henry Thornton became chairman in 1809, in which role he uncovered a scandal in the Vice Society. In 1795, John Bowles and four fellow members had been appointed commissioners to sell cargo from Dutch ships seized in the war. As no salary had been granted them, they took commission from the sales. The standard rate was 2.5 per cent of net proceeds, but they took 5 per cent of gross, ignoring instructions to consult the Privy Council over such matters, and never reported their income. They were supposed to invest all proceeds in the Bank of England, but instead kept them in private accounts, from which they were still privately drawing the interest ten years after they had finished doing any significant work. They had once been asked, by Pitt, what proceeds they could pay into the exchequer, and said they had none to spare, despite sitting on £190,000. Altogether, the commissioners gained £26,000 each.

Thornton denounced their behaviour as "highly criminal" and told Parliament that his friendship would not shield anyone from censure. The MP Samuel Whitbread, who had been on the sharp end of Bowles's tracts, denounced his hypocrisy demanding that "the severity of his punishment ought to be in proportion to the sanctity of the character he has thus falsely assumed". The Court of Exchequer told the five commissioners to repay £100,000. Those who had always disliked the Vice Society mocked it as "the society... for pilfering the public", while those who had supported it quietly stopped.[15] Lord Dartmouth, apparently forewarned, had resigned in 1808. Subscriptions fell too low to cover costs, and in 1810 the society suspended operations. The interdenominational Lord's Day Observance Society was founded to take over one part of its work. But the Vice

Society returned in 1812, smaller, without Bowles, and concentrating on blasphemy and obscenity.

Enforcing Abolition

These were years of economic misery, and a lot of blame was placed on the *War in Disguise* Orders for hurting trade. They became hugely unpopular, and in 1808 Perceval made Stephen MP for Tralee, an Irish constituency with thirteen voters, so that he could defend the Orders in Council in Parliament. Perceval became Prime Minister in 1809, with Stephen's devoted support. Not even Stephen's family considered him a great MP. He was acutely aware of his inability to garnish his speeches with classical quotations or witticisms, and had a terribly short temper. When the King of Prussia visited Parliament in 1814, his hosts were embarrassed that everyone was too well-behaved for a decent debate, so they asked Stephen's enemy Whitbread to speak knowing that Stephen would lash out, and sure enough sparks flew. Once, accused of overlooking the government's failure to enforce abolition, he replied: "I would rather be on friendly terms with a man who had strangled my infant son than support an administration guilty of slackness in suppressing the slave trade."[16] Perceval offered to make him Attorney-General, which he declined, but he agreed to be a master in chancery, using his position to start reform of chancery corruptions.

Stephen considered the Abolition Act little more than a start, requiring a lot of work to ensure it was enforced, and he was frustrated by Wilberforce's failure to drive the campaign. In particular, Wilberforce often received thirty letters a day and replied in his own hand, rambling through lengthy apologies for lateness, which provoked Stephen to send him a list of jobs, adding:

> if you, who must be the public leader, are to be only a battering-ram to be pushed forward, instead of a fore-horse in the team to pull as well as guide the rest, the cause is lost, the abolition is undone. It will sink under the weight of your daily epistles; your post privilege will be the bondage of Africa, and your covers the funereal pyre of her new-born hopes. Millions will sigh in hopeless wretchedness, that Wilberforce's correspondents may not think him uncivil or unkind.[17]

Stephen and Macaulay told the African Institution that the commercial development of West Africa that was supposed replace the slave trade was not happening because the trade had not completely stopped. The

USA had abolished its slave trade in 1807, and the Institution wanted the British government to press others to do the same, but they got nowhere. French traders were stopped by the British blockade, but after Napoleon invaded Spain and Portugal they became Britain's allies, and so could trade unhindered by her. Several slave ships were fitted out in England, were nominally sold in these allies' ports, and then traded under their flags. After the Institution alerted the Royal Navy to this – explaining why it was illegal, and what prize money was on offer in Sierra Leone – they started intercepting them. In December 1810 they stopped the supposedly Spanish *Marquis Romana*, which turned out to be the *Prince William,* carrying 109 slaves. Another Spanish slaver, the *Gallicia,* they unmasked as the *Queen Charlotte,* and its captain Giorgio Mandesilva as George Woodbine. Proving their intentions before they left England proved harder, but Macaulay caught the *Commercio de Rio* in Gravesend with 660 padlocks, 93 handcuffs, 197 shackles, 13 hundredweight of chain, one box of religious implements, and a small medicine chest. "You really deserve a statue," cried Wilberforce.

US slavers used the same ploy to a far greater extent – Sierra Leone officials said the coast was crowded with them. And at this point Stephen's Orders in Council, so far from stopping the slave trade, prevented its suppression. They gave the navy no authority to stop US ships trading under the flags of British allies, but they enraged the US government by preventing trade with Europe; the African Institution wanted a reciprocal agreement allowing the USA and UK to seize each other's slave ships, but bad feeling made it impossible.

In 1811, Stephen helped draw up a bill which William Brougham got passed, upgrading slave trading to a felony punishable by fourteen years' transportation or five years' hard labour. This proved a fearful enough deterrent to kill the British trade – George Stephen reckoned he brought the first ever prosecution under it thirty-three years later, and praised it as "the second great measure of the cause".

James Stephen realized that it left a loophole, though: it explicitly excluded transporting slaves between British colonies, under the cover of which it was easy to bring them overnight to Jamaica from Cuba, where the supply was limitless thanks to US traders. Stephen's solution was a register of all British slaves with full physical descriptions, and duplicates delivered annually to Westminster. He composed an Order in Council for Perceval in 1812 imposing the register on Trinidad. St Lucia and Mauritius voluntarily followed, and Wilberforce planned a bill extending registration to all colonies. The government was uneasy about interfering with colonial independence, however, and Perceval persuaded him to postpone it for a year.

Then on 11 May, John Bellingham, a trader ruined by the 1807 Orders in Council who had been imprisoned for debt in Russia and failed to get compensation from the government, went into the lobby of the House of Commons and shot Perceval through the heart. Whatever their effect on France, the orders had damaged Britain, and in the USA they had provoked a movement in favour of war with Britain. Brougham led a hostile enquiry into their effects, with the support of Wilberforce, Babington, and Thornton, and Stephen was cross-examining one of Brougham's witnesses, with Babington as chair, when Perceval was shot. Stephen fell ill with shock, but visited Bellingham before his execution trying unsuccessfully to persuade him to repent. At the execution, Bellingham was cheered by crowds opposed to the Orders. The new government of Lord Liverpool announced their repeal within days of its appointment, and the news was celebrated with bonfires and processions, but the USA declared war two days afterwards. Stephen was upset by the repeal, and talked of quitting Parliament, but Wilberforce talked him out of it.

Liverpool's government, with Castlereagh as Foreign Secretary and Sidmouth as Home Secretary, was thoroughly anti-abolitionist. Naturally they tried to persuade their allies to abandon their slave trade – even the plantation owners pressed for that – but they indefinitely deferred the slave registry bill. Stephen threatened to quit Parliament again, though in the 1812 election he again accepted a government pocket borough, East Grinstead, where he had hidden the pregnant Maria Rivers thirty years before.

Wilberforce also considered retiring. He found his body, voice, and memory starting to deteriorate, and his children, he said, "claim a father's heart, eye, and voice, and friendly intercourse". Babington encouraged him to go, while Thornton and Grant wanted him to stay, but he followed Stephen's advice, which was to leave Yorkshire for a less demanding pocket borough, Bramber in Sussex. Stephen argued, unsuccessfully, that if he gave up the minutiae of Parliament and only appeared for the great causes, his rationed influence would be greater than ever. He told Wilberforce, bluntly as ever, that his appearance and spirits were in decline; that apart from his memory his mind was as sharp as ever, but this might not last; and that, now he came to mention it, he had never prepared anywhere near well enough for any of his speeches.

East and West Indies

Failing to persuade any English people to go abroad as its missionaries, in 1802 the Church Missionary Society asked the Berlin Missionary Seminary for recruits, and they sent Melchior Renner and Peter Hartwig. It turned out that neither they nor the CMS could speak a word of the other's language, so they spent a year at Clapham learning English before sailing for Sierra Leone in January 1804. In their first fifteen years the society sent seventeen Germans abroad. Their first British missionaries were William Hall, a joiner, and John King, a shoemaker, who went to New Zealand in 1809 as lay evangelists. That year Scott started training their first ordinand, Thomas Norton, a former shoemaker who had taught himself Greek. The CMS also sent money to missionaries in India who were working on Bible translation. The committee made annual reports to members faithfully, but apologetically.

British mission to India was happening without the CMS. William Carey, the Baptist pioneer who came in 1793, and was yet another shoemaker, was a convert of Scott. "If I know anything of the work of God in my soul," he said, "I owe it to Mr Scott."[1] He had to raise a huge bond to pay the East India Company for inoffensive behaviour, thanks to Clapham's attempt to change the charter. He translated the Bible into six languages and parts of it into twenty-nine. Henry Martyn, the Cambridge-educated linguist, joined Carey in 1806 after hearing Simeon preach about his work. Martyn nearly went as a CMS missionary, until financial problems forced him to take a post as a company chaplain. His translations included Urdu and Persian.

The East India Company Charter

With the East India Company charter due to be renewed again in 1813, the Clapham sect were determined to use their experience and moral capital from the abolition campaign to open India for mission. One new recruit to the campaign was Charles Grant's son, Charles, a very eloquent MP for Inverness town, who in 1813 gained a minor post in Lord Liverpool's cabinet. The Grants were as concerned to keep Bengal closed to trade as they were to open it for the gospel, and his brother Robert, a lawyer, published a defence of the monopoly and a history of the company.

Clapham started working up support in 1812, when Perceval was Prime Minister, and his death was a devastating setback. When the debate started on 22 March Wilberforce reckoned that "the opinions of nine-tenths, or at least of a vast majority of the House of Commons would be against any motion which the friends of religion might make", and the same went for the government. Still, from Clapham, Kensington, the Mendips, Leicestershire, Staffordshire, and Cambridge letters and pamphlets streamed out, and meetings were called, and 837 petitions came into Parliament, more than for any previous subject. The campaigners were briefed by Claudius Buchanan, who had dropped out of Glasgow University to travel Europe as a fiddler, been converted by Newton, put through Cambridge by Thornton, and given an Indian chaplaincy thanks to Simeon. His sermon on the Battle of the Nile had so impressed the governor-general, Richard Wellesley, Lord Mornington, that the latter had it printed and put him in charge of a college for Indian languages, where Buchanan persuaded him to appoint Carey too. Back in Britain, Buchanan preached and printed popular sermons to rouse support and defend the missionaries. Grant presented his 1792 essay to the Commons, who printed it; he and Parry worked on the company directors. Pratt launched the *Missionary Register*, while the *Christian Observer* published the arguments of Wilberforce and David Brown, and reports on suttee and the journals of Baptist missionaries, demanding: "Is every form of superstition, however cruel and licentious, to be openly tolerated among the natives, while pure Christianity alone continues to labour under an interdict or proscription?" Teignmouth testified to the Commons committee, and it went badly enough for Wilberforce, Grant, Stephen, Babington, and Thornton to meet on a Sunday, and to decide to stop their proposals being included in the Lords' enquiry. Wilberforce, though Stephen at least would surely disagree, said that opening India to mission was the "greatest of all causes, for I really place it before the abolition". Wilberforce believed that the caste system was even worse slavery than the British variety, because it offered no possible escape, and that conversion to Christianity would save both souls and bodies.[2]

The nationwide pressure generated by Clapham eventually persuaded

Castlereagh: the proposed charter envisaged that a bishop and three archdeacons be provided for British India, and that the company be required to promote "useful knowledge and religious and moral improvement" in India. When he brought the proposals before the Commons on 22 June 1813, Wilberforce gave them one of the most celebrated and powerful speeches of his life, a three-hour moral bombardment of Hinduism. It utterly depraved Indian society, ruining lives. It imposed the "cruel shackles of Caste", encouraged infanticide, euthanasia, and polygamy, demanded that 10,000 widows a year be killed in the "horrible exhibitions" of suttee, and 100,000 people be sacrificed to Juggernaut. Its ceremonies were "obscene and bloody", its gods "absolute monsters of lust, injustice, wickedness and cruelty". It would be "almost morally impossible" for India not to be vastly improved by Christianity: "Our religion is sublime, pure, beneficent. Theirs is mean, licentious, and cruel." He closed with a tribute to William Carey.

Both Charles Grants spoke, a sight that thrilled Clapham as an omen for the rising generation, and the proposals were carried by 89 votes to 36. "And now", said Buchanan, "we are all likely to be disgraced. Parliament has opened the door, and who is there to go in? From the Church, not one man!"[3]

The End of Clapham

As they were glorying in this achievement, the Clapham sect started to pass away. John Venn died on 1 July 1813. His wife Kitty had died in 1803, leaving six young children, since when he had rarely been well. He had married again in 1812, but appointed his children Jane and Henry (twenty and seventeen respectively) as guardians of the younger children. "Their sorrow was beyond all control," recalled Marianne Thornton; and for herself it was "the first time I realized the fact that this is a world of sorrow". Henry told her: "This is your first experience that death has entered into the world, may you learn from it how unsafe it is to rest in it for all our happiness." Three of the Venn girls wrote very long accounts of their father's death, in accordance with the evangelical idea that a good death is the crown of a good life. He was replaced as rector by William Dealtry.

Napoleon abdicated in defeat in April 1814 and, while the victors met to negotiate peace, Clapham met to discuss what Thornton called "some dark plots... for influencing the Allied Powers in favour of the abolition of the slave trade through this earth of ours, which earth the three or four potentates now at Paris... seem to hold in their hands". They were trying to save abolition: peace would allow the French to revive and extend slave trading stopped by the war. Wilberforce wrote to the Tsar, the King of Prussia, and the French leaders, and abolitionist writings were translated into French. Macaulay went to Paris to brief and lobby Castlereagh, but returned disappointed: the treaty obliged the French to give up the slave trade, but not for five years, after they had fully restocked their colonies. Castlereagh's treaty was acclaimed in Parliament, but Wilberforce said: "I behold in his hand the death-warrant of a multitude of innocent victims, men, women, and children, whom I had fondly indulged the hope of having myself rescued from destruction." [4]

But the peace was followed by the Congress of Vienna, which redrew the map of Europe. Clapham called up the nation, and Parliament received 806 petitions in a month, containing a million signatures. "The whole nation is bent upon the subject," admitted Castlereagh, and he and the Duke of Wellington tried to secure an international convention against slave trading. Russia, Prussia, and Austria readily agreed, having no slave trade. Louis XVIII's restoration government absolutely refused: abolition combined revolutionary tenets with English imperialism, and they urgently needed to revive their colonies, as did Spain and Portugal. It was Napoleon who rescued the cause. Escaping from Elba, he seized power again in France and abolished the slave trade in a bid to gain British acquiescence. Napoleon was defeated again at Waterloo, and Louis XVIII was so dependent on allied forces that he banned the trade throughout the French dominions, though with only slight penalties.

Henry Thornton died in January 1815. His last year was darkened by serious troubles. Henry had long worried about his brother Robert's extravagance, refusing to come to the lavish fête he threw for the Queen in his Clapham orangery. In the economic turmoil of the later war years Robert lost investments that had been worth over £30,000, and his efforts to dig himself out left him £45,000 in debt, fleeing alone to France and later settling in the USA, "a fugitive, without character, without money and friendless as the most forlorn of human beings!", as Marianne Thornton senior said. Henry, shaken and distraught, tried hard to trace his brother, eventually receiving a letter from him that said little.

In June, disaster struck Henry's bank. Apparently, his partner Free had grossly overfinanced a failed business, and they lost what Free believed to be £25,000, Thornton reckoned was twice that, and turned out to be £70,000. A year before, the bank had had settled capital of £72,000. With other bad debts, including Robert's of £6,895, they were wiped out. If Free had been reckless, Thornton had failed to restrain him, having too little time for management. "My good friends Wilberforce etc etc, little know how much African meetings and Bible meetings etc etc in this respect may chance to cost." Henry fell ill in the autumn, and never recovered. His daughter Marianne wrote sixty long pages about his last hours:

> I should have rejoiced to see him in so sweet a slumber. Suddenly mama burst into tears, saying "He is sleeping in Jesus" and bending down she kissed him. "One more before it is all cold in death", she said and then Mrs Grant drew her away. I staid a little longer holding his hand.

Wilberforce and Macaulay both lost their best friend as well as an essential co-worker – "a most mysterious providence", said Wilberforce. Macaulay told Marianne senior, Henry's widow, that he had been "my polar star, my presiding, my better genius"; "What will Henry Thornton say? was with me a trying question on all occasions." Marianne fell ill the same year, and had no will to fight it. She died on 15 October, and the nine children were left in the care of Robert Inglis and his wife, who moved into Battersea Rise. Robert at twenty-nine had just retired as chairman of the East India Company, and had been a new friend of Henry Thornton's, an abolitionist but High Church, not evangelical. The Clapham sect was taken aback, but warmed to the Inglises, as did the children.[5]

In 1816 Sarah Stephen died. James swung between evangelical cheerfulness and raging grief. Wilberforce reflected: "How affecting it is, to leave the person we have known all our lives, on whom we should have been afraid to let the wind blow too roughly, to leave her in the cold ground alone!"[6] The Stephen children were starting to make their way in the world. Of four sons, three were lawyers, while William was a vicar in Buckinghamshire. Henry served in chancery; George joined the eminent solicitors Freshfields, where he dug up evidence against the Queen for the royal divorce case, surprisingly valuable experience toward the abolition campaign; James was a barrister and took on some of his father's clients when he became master in chancery. Having written a digest of colonial laws for his own amusement, James was appointed counsel to the Colonial Department by the Earl of Bathurst, reporting to him on all colonial acts, on the condition that he gave no intelligence from the office to his father. He was also on the CMS committee, and on the African Institution committee, as were his brother Henry, Tom Babington, John Thornton, and Robert Grant. Sibella Stephen married William Garratt, a barrister on the CMS committee, and Anne Stephen married the owner of the *Northampton Mercury*, Thomas Dicey. In 1814, two Clapham houses were united when James Stephen married Jane Venn; and Tom Babington married Augusta Noel, granddaughter of the Middletons who drew Hannah to evangelicalism and Wilberforce to abolition.

Tom Macaulay had his first published work commissioned at the age of fourteen an index to the 1814 *Christian Observer*. "It was wisely, but rather cruelly, judged," said More to his father, "to give him such a damper to his genius."[7] The following year, Zachary received an article defending novels from an evangelical perspective, after a recent denunciation in the magazine. He included it, perhaps for the sake of balance, though he thoroughly disapproved of novels, and it sparked off a controversy that continued in the magazine for some years. After publishing it, he discovered it was by Tom. His generation, while venerating their parents, were not going to swallow their religion whole.

Sierra Leone: Missionaries and Scandal

In Sierra Leone, Thompson was succeeded as governor by the hydrographer Captain Edward Columbine, who reintroduced apprenticeship for recaptured slaves, indenturing many to the Nova Scotians and Maroons for menial labour, though as they kept coming most were taken out to found unsupervised villages. The next governor, Lieutenant Colonel Charles Maxwell, introduced universal conscription into a strict militia, confiscating the property of any who refused, and over a hundred left Georgetown.

By 1815, the CMS had sent twenty-six men and women to Sierra Leone, and sixteen had died. Six Lutheran pastors and a teacher remained. They had produced a Bible translation, and spread beyond Georgetown starting schools, but had no success in making converts. Consulting with the new governor, Charles MacCarthy, the society decided their most promising mission field consisted of the villages of apprenticed slaves. With the Colonial Secretary, Bathurst, they divided Sierra Leone into parishes, each governed by a CMS minister. Bathurst provided for churches, schools, and two chaplains; the CMS provided teachers and started a boarding school. MacCarthy's vision was to make Sierra Leone look as much like England as possible. He shipped in weather-vanes and gothic windows for churches, and bonnets, petticoats, braces, and clothes brushes for the villagers.

Three CMS ministers, two Germans and one English, who came in 1816, had amazing success. Wilhelm Johnson, in charge of the 1,400-strong parish of Regent, was horrified by the sexual anarchy, nakedness, disease, and thieving he found there, but his prayer meetings and teaching were popular, and when he opened the church in August it sparked an evangelical eruption, with people all over the village kneeling in prayer or crying out to God for mercy on their sin. Within two years it was an orderly Christian parish of farmers, builders, carpenters and blacksmiths, with stone houses, roads, a hospital, schools, a building society, a benefit society and a local branch of the CMS, sending pennies to fund further mission.

The chief justice who dealt with recaptured slaves delivered to the Vice-Admiralty Court in Georgetown until 1813 was Robert Thorpe. Thorpe had been chief justice of Prince Edward Island in Canada, where he found himself "obliged at different times to quarrel with all orders through finding virtue in none", and was dismissed by the governor in 1807. When absent from Sierra Leone on leave, he failed to persuade the government to refund £630 he had paid a deputy, and in January 1815 he wrote to Bathurst making accusations against the governor and the African Institution. Bathurst, believing he was being blackmailed, and saying that if the charges were true Thorpe should have brought them years before, sacked him. Thorpe replied with a book called *A Letter to William Wilberforce ... Containing Remarks on the Reports of the Sierra Leone Company, and African Institution*. He charged the Sierra Leone Company with having received huge amounts of private investment and public money without ever fulfilling any of its stated aims. Trade, agriculture, civilization, Christian mission, and provision of land for former slaves: all had either failed or were never attempted. All its resources squandered, Thorpe said, the company handed the colony to the crown, took handsome remuneration for buildings there, and via the African Institution kept control of it as ever. Thorpe described Ludlam's sale of apprentices, combining them with earlier cases that Thompson uncovered of individual settlers buying slaves, to claim that the company continued deliberate extensive slave trading in Freetown. He plundered letters from Macaulay to Ludlum for incriminating or embarrassing comments, worst of all:

You somewhat misconceive our ideas in this country on the subject of African slavery. While the slave trade lasted, I certainly felt very averse to giving any direct encouragement to the purchasing of slaves, with a view to the benefit of their labour for a certain given period; but I always looked forward to the event of the abolition, as removing many objections to that system.[8]

In the original context it is clear that Macaulay was talking, however unguardedly, about his scheme to liberate local slaves through apprenticeship, but Thorpe combined it with an inaccurate account of Macaulay's African business interests to give the picture of a man for whom abolition was a cynical front for profit by any means. He implicated Wilberforce, claiming his only contribution to abolition was to appear at the last moment and take the credit for Thomas Clarkson's twenty-year campaign, calling on him to step down and leave the work to the better-intentioned Castlereagh.

It was a hugely damaging scandal. A storm of books and articles followed, many also by Thorpe. Macaulay was forced to issue a reply, which was cool and generally convincing, and the African Institution quickly published a 157-page report. The *Anti-Jacobin*'s review of the controversy, supporting Thorpe's side, spread over eight issues. As the *British Critic* noted, Thorpe marred his case by throwing in anything he could find to embarrass or discredit his opponents, including obviously wild accusations. But he also made fair criticisms of the company and the institution – which never had such influence in the Colonial Department again – and there was a case to answer for abolitionists who were prepared to use forced labour to "civilize" Africa and enrich themselves. The portrait of Macaulay as a shadowy, unprincipled profiteer was completely unfair. No one gave more to the anti-slavery cause than he did over the next twenty years, and though he made a fortune from Sierra Leone when the chance presented itself, the rest of his story proves his disregard for money. But shadowy he was, the most self-effacing abolitionist, responsible for intelligence and paperwork, not speeches or books, and now he was in the spotlight for the first time. This helped suspicion to cling to him, and he never shook it off. Throughout the 1820s "Saint Zachariah" was a *bête noire* of the influential *John Bull* magazine, which accused him of fraudulent plunder and having been sacked in Jamaica for abusing slaves.

Slave Registration and International Abolition
The African Institution had decided to delay agitation for slave registration during the Congress of Vienna, and now they hoped to get it passed with government support, but Lord Liverpool refused, preferring to encourage the colonial assemblies to arrange it themselves. Wrong-headed as it seemed to abolitionists, each successive government shared this debilitating fear of outraging the colonies. No one wanted to be the Prime Minister who caused the West Indian war of independence. Stephen finally left Parliament in protest in March 1815. Macaulay urged him to

return, but he felt his time was better spent addressing the principled public rather than unprincipled MPs. He wrote the African Institution's report calling for registration, plus *A Defence of the Bill for the Registration of Slaves* in his own name – which Macaulay gave almost half an issue of the *Christian Observer* to reviewing. Grenville persuaded Wilberforce to bring the registry bill in July, but he withdrew it because it provoked such opposition that there was no chance of getting it passed that year. In June 1816 Parliament formally requested the colonies to register slaves and improve their conditions. Barbados passed a Registry Act in 1817, and all the other islands followed, but the registration was vague, and only compulsory on three islands. "The Acts... will not be executed" complained the African Institution, "and their execution, as they stand, would be useless." The UK registry bill was still needed.[9]

Britain paid Portugal £750,000 to restrict its slave trade to sub-equatorial Africa, protecting the lands vacated by the British and French, and to transport slaves only to its own plantations. While the government negotiated abolition with Spain in 1816, Stephen published a book arguing that now the USA, Britain and France had abolished the slave trade, Britain had the right to suppress Spanish and Portuguese trade by force if necessary. On Easter Sunday slaves in Barbados revolted, burning a quarter of the sugar crop. Fifty slaves died in the fighting and 200 were executed. The slavery lobby blamed Wilberforce's registry bill for inciting them, and so abolitionists postponed it again, in case the controversy damaged the Spanish negotiations.

Negotiations continued throughout the 1817 parliamentary session, as did food riots and radical political rallies, with Wilberforce ardently supporting the government's repression – executions, suspension of Habeas Corpus, and restriction of all meetings, whether political or not. It was a measure of the rise of evangelicalism, and the failure of High Church opponents, that the government amended the seditious meetings bill specifically to exempt local Bible societies.

By the Bible Society's fifteenth year, there were 629 local societies plus a thousand smaller groups. They had distributed more than 2.5 million scriptures in Britain alone, and spent £4,000 planting societies across Europe. They had printed in 128 languages of four continents, and increased their budget by 180 times. They were condemned by the bishops of Lincoln, Chester, and Carlisle for undermining the church, while the *British Critic* exposed "*revolutionary* designs" behind their twelve regiments of 21,000 common people in Southwark.[10]

An attempted rebellion in 1817 turned out to have been instigated, not by the Bible Society, but by Lord Sidmouth's *agent provocateur*. Wilberforce opposed an enquiry, believing it would undermine faith in the government. This is why he delayed the compulsory registry bill yet again, telling Macaulay: "It would betray an ignorance of all tact to talk to them in such circumstances of the sufferings of the slaves in the West Indies." Hannah More at seventy continued her moral and political writing with ever-calcifying conservatism, and revived the Cheap Repository with a message which the *Reformists' Register* summed up as: "Do your utmost to starve with as much propriety as the most respectable amongst your neighbours."[11] When Patty died in 1819, Hannah was the last of the five sisters alive.

The Spanish agreed to slave trading restrictions similar to the Portuguese, with total abolition in three years, in return for £400,000 (2½*d*. a man throughout the empire, as Wilberforce pointed out to British objectors). Moreover, the three nations agreed to mutual rights to search and impound slave ships, giving the Royal Navy more power in suppressing the trade. The Dutch entered the same agreement and the international court for dealing with slave seizures was set up in Sierra Leone.

In 1819, Lord Liverpool's government came up with a canny measure of compromise between the abolitionists and the slavery party. It passed its own Colonial Registry Act providing for a UK register of slaves compiled from the local registers, and ruled that land sold or mortgaged in Britain – as plantations generally were – was to be valued in terms of the number of registered slaves. It was passed unanimously by Parliament, because planters were satisfied the government was not interfering directly in colonial rule, and had conceded the principle of registration in their own laws. The African Institution were glad of the act, but complained that it relied too much on the planters' willingness to keep full records and send accurate duplicates to London, and continued to press for a proper law. They never got one, but kept the issue alive, and colonists were forced through gradual adaptations to tighten up registration, making smuggling increasingly hard.

Macaulay left the *Christian Observer* in 1816, and concentrated on his thriving African trading partnership with Tom Babington. Sierra Leone had finally become a profitable colony. In 1818 it exported 160 tons of rice, 94 tons of maize, 26,000 gallons of palm oil, and 100,000 shingles, as well as timber, gold dust, silver, animal skins, elephant tusks, and beeswax, and the Macaulays, said to be worth £100,000, left Clapham for Cadogan Place, midway between the Wilberforces and Stephens in Kensington and the Babingtons in Downing Street.

Tom Macaulay started at Cambridge, sharing digs with Henry Sykes Thornton and immersing himself in a small group of friends to shelter from the "moral degradation" of the university. He told Zachary that he was not there for the academic glories expected of him, but to be equipped to fill his father's shoes. "I never had a higher ambition than that we might triumph together over the enemies of humanity." He had a romantic affair with Mary Babington which fizzled out.

Henry Venn and William Wilberforce junior were at Cambridge, though Wilberforce was removed after Venn reported his scandalous lifestyle to his father. Venn was ordained and joined the CMS committee, while his brother graduated from Haileybury College and went to India. Robert Grant was elected to Parliament, while his brother Charles became Lord Liverpool's Irish Chief Secretary, the first Tory supporter of Catholic emancipation in the post.

The older generation were reaching sixty and feeling their age. Babington left Parliament, and Wilberforce and Stephen bought country retreats. Gisborne ventured late in his publishing career into geology, and his attempt to reconcile Genesis and modern science was met with charitable bemusement. More's *Bible Rhymes* had little impact. Only Macaulay, fifty in 1818, continued at full power, and yet one last great campaign for the Clapham sect still lay ahead.

Anti-Slavery

In 1822, fifteen years after the slave trade was outlawed, the Clapham sect finally started discussing the abolition of slavery. They had been fully occupied stopping smuggling and the international trade, without which the 1807 Act would have limited effect. Ending slavery was a more difficult proposition, attacking not an activity but property, the inviolable principle of British law which it was Parliament's sacred duty to defend. It required British interference in colonial government, something to which the government had proved very reluctant to agree. Considering their fight against the trade still continued after thirty-five years, abolitionists could be forgiven for thinking that ending slavery was a dream. "Actual emancipation," as George Stephen said about the years after 1807, "was a grand concession to humanity which I firmly believe that the most sanguine abolitionist never contemplated... They deemed it visionary, and many distrusted even its practicability with safety."[1] He adds that Macaulay may have been the one exception. There was no public interest in the subject, and James Stephen said there was little hope of rousing it. Most of them believed the conditions slaves lived in had so brutalized and degraded them, and given them such cause for revenge, that freeing them en masse as they were could be disastrous – though Macaulay disagreed. And they thought the end of the slave trade would inevitably improve slaves' conditions because owners would have to keep them alive, so there was little to be gained by abolitionist interference.

But Macaulay and Stephen absorbed all information that came from the colonies, and by the 1820s it was becoming clear that nothing had changed for the slaves, and that nothing would without intervention. And although the international slave trade still continued, the government was clearly committed to ending it, which meant the Clapham sect could agitate for justice and freedom in the Caribbean without fear of hurting their slave-trade campaign.

But who would lead the campaign in Parliament? Wilberforce was increasingly weak physically, and his memory was failing. Macaulay and Stephen were not in Parliament, and were writers and thinkers, not speakers. There were prominent abolitionist MPs such as Brougham and Lushington, but they did not share the spiritual common ground that Wilberforce looked for in his successor.

The answer came in an unexpected way. When the African Institution met on 30 January 1821, one of the directors launched into a fierce diatribe against their "inactivity and ineffectiveness": they had done too little about the slave trade, had let the public lose interest in the cause, and fourteen years after the Abolition Act had done nothing at all for the slaves on the plantations. It was a shocking outburst, but afterwards he himself was shocked in turn to hear Wilberforce thank him profusely for his candour and for striking his conscience. This, with a sad disregard for the novelist's rule against introducing a major character in the closing chapters, was Thomas Fowell Buxton.

Thomas Fowell Buxton

Buxton was an evangelical MP of less than three years' standing, a partner in Fuller's brewery, and a hunter who had missed a day's shooting for the African Institution meeting. His wife and mother were Quakers, the former being Elizabeth Fry's sister, and he was related to Samuel Hoare and William Allen, leading Quaker abolitionists and directors of the institution. (Hoare had been on the original Abolition Committee.) He worked with Fry for prison reform, and campaigned to restrict the death penalty, having made himself an expert on both subjects. On 23 May 1821, Buxton seconded a motion brought by Sir James Mackintosh against the death penalty with a brilliant speech. Mackintosh called it "the most powerful appeal that he had ever had the good fortune to hear within Parliament", and it convinced Wilberforce that this was the man he had been looking for. He wrote to Buxton the next day: "For many, many years I have been longing to bring forward that great subject, the condition of the negro slaves in our Transatlantic colonies, and the best means of providing for their moral and social improvement, and ultimately for their advancement to the rank of a free peasantry."[2] He asked Buxton to join him, and to take over when he could no longer manage. Buxton worried about whether he could devote himself fully to this and his other campaigns and whether it would provoke slave uprisings. It took him eighteen months to consent, but when he did it was with the total conviction that he was on a mission from God. And so he became the last addition to the Clapham sect.

Buxton depended on Macaulay and Stephen for intelligence and advice, though he shared with them the intense application that gave them complete mastery of the subject. It was Macaulay, though, who absorbed the contents of the hugest documents with the speed and ease of a mind that knows no boredom, who became a human encyclopedia of slavery. After a busy day, George Stephen says, Macaulay would "refresh himself after dinner with a parliamentary folio that would have choked an alderman by the sight of it alone".[3] When Buxton compiled a private reference book on the subject he called it "my Macaulay". Buxton shared Stephen's passion, however, to the extent that his fervent speeches in the Commons, while thrilling for newspaper readers, annoyed MPs, who found his excitability vulgar.

The Clapham sect decided their first move should be to stop the arbitrary movement of slaves. As Buxton put it: "A man might be born on a plantation, grow up, build a house, marry a wife, and have a family; and after all, without the slightest offence committed, or even imputed, be sold by his master, and transferred from his house, wife, and family, to the most distant island in the British possession."[4] Wilberforce or Buxton was to bring a bill in 1822. But at the same time they were pressing for a new registry law and trying to overturn the tax advantages Caribbean sugar producers enjoyed over Indian producers, and they were so outmanoeuvred by colonial PR that they gave up on any further motion that year.

Stephen persuaded Wilberforce to spend the winter writing a book as the first foray of the campaign. He offered to come and stay as Wilberforce's slave-driver, "and then Mrs. Wilberforce will flog the driver every day if she thinks we do too much, (she gave me fair warning of it on Sunday,) and I shall flog myself if we do too little".[5] Wilberforce declined.

On 8 January, Wilberforce, Macaulay and Buxton held "a secret cabinet council" to plan the campaign. They agreed to work toward the end of slavery gradually but explicitly, moving in Parliament for "the abolition of the driving system, with the introduction of religious instruction and marriage, and the facilitating manumissions". They would rouse the nation as they had over the slave trade, and they would not involve the African Institution. That august body had been ideal for informing and influencing the government in international negotiations concerning the slave trade, but as George Stephen said: "When agitation became the order of the day, it was a necessary consequence that the Africa Institution and all its aristocracy should be thrown overboard."[6]

So on 31 January 1823, the Society for Mitigating and Gradually Abolishing the State of Slavery throughout the British Dominions (also known as the Anti-Slavery Society) was founded. Its vice-presidents and directors included: three Quakers from the Abolition Committee – William Dillwyn, Richard Phillips, and George Harrison – along with William Allen and Samuel Hoare junior and other relations of Buxton; the MPs Mackintosh, Brougham, Lushington, William Smith, and Marianne Thornton's brother Daniel Sykes; Thomas Clarkson; Wilberforce, Stephen, Macaulay, Babington, and Buxton; and, from the younger generation of Clapham, Tom Macaulay, Tom and George Babington, Henry Thornton, Henry Venn, and William Wilberforce. The Duke of Gloucester was president.

Wilberforce finished his manifesto, *An Appeal to the Religion, Justice, and Humanity of the Inhabitants of the British Empire in Behalf of the Negro Slaves in the West Indies*, while Clarkson produced *Thoughts on the Necessity of Improving the Condition of the Slaves in the British Colonies, with a View to Emancipation*, and the society circulated them both. It asked Stephen to finish the *magnum opus* he had started years before, a two-volume survey of colonial slavery in law and practice, the first volume of which he completed in 1824. Macaulay rather more briskly published two books: *Negro Slavery* which presented evidence from pro-slavery sources to disprove claims that conditions had improved; and *East and West India Sugar,* containing the arguments with which he had briefed Wilberforce and Buxton for the debate on duties.

Realizing it was going to be a long and demanding haul, Macaulay decided to give his whole working life to the campaign, handing over the running of Macaulay and Babington to Tom, who had proved an excellent auditor and junior partner. Macaulay told him and the Georgetown managers to make no significant changes without consulting him, and was confident he would manage. He made over the majority of the profits to Tom and, tightening their belts, the Macaulays moved to the unfashionable Great Ormond Street. It was a noble decision, but one that was to prove more costly than Macaulay realized.

The 1823 Resolutions
Buxton made the first anti-slavery motion in Parliament on 15 May 1823. Macaulay asked the Quakers to lead public agitation, and they sent the

first emancipation petition. By the day of the debate, 230 had arrived, as well as several pro-slavery petitions. Buxton, in a pungent speech, was frank about their ambitions: "nothing less than the extinction of slavery – in nothing less than the whole of the British dominions", but through gradual steps over twenty or thirty years. "It will decline; it will expire; it will, as it were, burn itself down into its socket and go out." He proposed an eleven-point plan of reform which included freeing all children immediately, attaching slaves to the soil, giving their testimony equal weight in court, allowing them to buy their freedom, providing religious instruction and sabbath rest, applying the rights and duties of marriage, and restricting managers' rights to punish and drive slaves.[7]

Responding for the government was Canning, who replaced Castlereagh as Foreign Secretary after he killed himself. (Castlereagh seems to have suffered paranoid delusions and believed he was being blackmailed after an unwitting encounter with a transvestite prostitute.) Abolitionist as Canning was, or had been, he appealed for calm and proposed milder reform. Ruling out immediate freedom for children as unhelpful and hazardous, he approved of most of Buxton's other proposals, but, instead of the eleven-point plan, he proposed a general resolution that slaves' conditions should be improved to prepare them for ultimate freedom; and, instead of making laws for all colonies, the government would impose reforms on the six crown colonies, and urge the others to follow.

After wringing from Canning an assurance that "the progeny of slaves must not be eternally slaves", Buxton withdrew his resolution, and Canning's was carried without a division. The Clapham sect felt ambivalent. Canning's proposals were horribly diluted, and relied on colonial co-operation, in which they had no confidence. On the other hand, reform was now a government measure, and passed by the Commons without any opposition, giving the government, and its drivers, a strong hand.

Bathurst, the Colonial Secretary, sent a copy of Canning's speech to each colony, and instructed the crown colony of Demerara to begin by banning the flogging of women and the use of the cart whip to drive slaves. The government was clearly in earnest, but Clapham were appalled. "I held up my hands in utter astonishment," said Macaulay. Their own proposals had aimed to improve things for the slaves without annoying their masters or provoking unrest, while this was direct interference between master and slave. The whip was "the grand badge of slavery" and removing it was like telling the slaves they were free, without considering how they and then their owners would respond. Stephen and Macaulay nearly wrote to Canning in protest, but could not bring themselves to complain about an anti-slavery measure. They were happier when on 9 July Bathurst sent the colonies a list of twenty reforms they wanted to see, which included most of Buxton's – though not freeing children – with additions such as savings banks for slaves, as well as removing the whip.

The Demerara Revolt

The results on Demerara were everything they feared. Some drivers abandonned the whip, others went out with two. Believing King George had declared them free, slaves refused to work and drivers tried to force them. On the night of 18 August 1823, 1,300 slaves revolted, capturing plantation managers, but refusing to kill anyone. One slave is reported as saying: "It is contrary to the religion we profess. We cannot give life and therefore we will not take it." Troops killed a hundred regaining control, fifty more were executed, and five sentenced to a thousand lashes.[8]

The news arrived in Britain that autumn, and seemed to destroy the anti-slavery campaign. When the 1824 parliamentary session began, the King's Speech made no mention of any further reforms of slavery, and when Buxton privately pressed Canning, he said the government was abandoning the programme. A friend of Macaulay's heard Canning's parliamentary secretary tell people that "Wilberforce, Buxton & Co." had instigated the revolt. "The slavery question looks wretchedly," said Buxton. "I begin to think that, opposed as we are by the West Indians, deserted by Government, and deemed enthusiasts by the public, we shall be able to do little or nothing. However, I rejoice that we have tried." He calculated that half a dozen MPs solidly supported them and 200 opposed them. "I much question whether there is a more unpopular individual in the House just at this moment," he said, adding of course: "For this I do not care." But he told his wife, "I cannot feel very light-hearted." Other islands claimed to have uncovered similar plots, and some unfeasibly threatened independence.[9]

On 16 March 1824, Canning reported to the Commons, and Bathurst to the Lords, on the progress of reform. Clapham expected to be attacked and scapegoated, and Stephen suggested Buxton take it in silence. Buxton replied: "'Tis odds, indeed, when valiant Warwick flies." Canning told the House he had expected slow progress, but abolitionist rhetoric and the uprising had slowed it further; nevertheless, his reforms would be imposed by Order in Council on Trinidad, the most promising of the crown colonies; others would be encouraged to imitate them voluntarily. "If I am to learn," protested Buxton, "that the engagement given as to all the colonies, is to be frittered down, at present at least, to a single island... then, I see no reason why ten centuries may not elapse, before the negroes are freed from their present state of melancholy and deplorable thraldom!"[10] Buxton had the support of 600 petitions, whatever he felt about public antipathy, but was in far too weak a position to demand a vote.

It was the colonists who saved the abolition campaign. After the uprising, Demeraran authorities arrested John Smith, an Independent minister sent by the London Missionary Society, who had annoyed planters by teaching and preaching to slaves, court-martialled him on a charge of inciting rebellion, and sentenced him to death. He died of consumption in prison.

The London Missionary Society published the minutes of the trial, without comment, and they created a storm, showing that Smith was convicted, without counsel for the crucial part, on "hearsay evidence... to the third, the fourth, aye, even to the fifth degree", as Brougham put it. The society unsuccessfully petitioned Parliament for an enquiry. In June Brougham moved for a statement condemning the mistrial and calling for reform, but Canning managed to defeat the motion by 193 votes to 146. Perhaps the most important result of the scandal was that Dissenting churches, which in England contained 10–15 per cent of the population, threw their weight into the abolition movement for the first time.

The Anti-Slavery Society held its first annual public meeting on 25 June 1824. Among other speakers, Stephen surveyed their progress, but the speaker who electrified the audience was Tom Macaulay, who proved the need for abolition from the planters' own arguments. They claimed that slaves enjoyed enviable comforts and freedoms, which they contradicted by insisting that any discussion of emancipation or amelioration in Britain incited them to revolt. They maintained that their violence against slaves was the minimum necessary to keep order, which only proved the whole system irredeemably barbarous. They defended the unconstitutional process of court-martialling Smith, saying he would have had worse dealing in a civilian court:

Sir, I have always had the happiness of living under the protection of the law of England, and therefore I am utterly unable to imagine what could be worse. But ... since the colonists solemnly assure us that a Jury of their own body not only possibly might, but necessarily must, have acted with more violence and injustice than this court martial, I certainly shall not pretend to dispute the assertion, although I am utterly at a loss to conceive the mode.

He ended to several minutes of cheers. Marianne Thornton told More that Wilberforce and Stephen forgot the decorum of the meeting chaired by royalty, "catching hold of him as he was going back to his place, and keeping him there, each shaking a hand, while the very walls seemed to be coming down with the thunders of applause".[11]

Friends and family said it must have made this the happiest day of Zachary Macaulay's life, compensating him for the continued attacks on his name. If so, he could not bring himself to tell his son. He sat throughout with his eyes glued to a piece of paper, and his only comment afterwards was to tell Tom off for folding his arms before royalty. "I think," said Tom's sister Hannah More Macaulay, "with all the love and reverence with which [he] regarded his father's memory, there mingled a shade of bitterness that he had not met quite the encouragement and appreciation from him which he received from others."[12] The disparity only increased when Tom started writing for the *Edinburgh Review* later that year, and almost immediately became a national celebrity.

"My father," says Hannah, "ever more and more engrossed in one object, gradually gave up all society, and my mother never could endure it." He went to bed at ten and rose at four to spend five hours on business, so that he could then give what for anyone else would have been a whole day to anti-slavery. Never talkative, he was now more taciturn than ever. One visitor said he came to Macaulay's office to ask him "three questions, to which Mr Macaulay replied in two monosyllables".[13]

Delays and Difficulties

The government would do nothing until they had heard how the colonies had got on, but Canning was a lot more help when it came to the slave trade, getting it reclassified in March 1824 as piracy, a capital offence. The government had made the trade a key point at the last international congress at Verona, and Canning contacted the Vatican to enlist their support. Lushington got the Slave Trade Consolidation Act passed, tightening and strengthening existing legislation, and outlawing inter-colonial transportation.

After two bouts of illness in a year, Wilberforce retired from Parliament in February 1825, asking Buxton to make the application for him. His loss demoralized the popular movement, seeming to be "ominous of its abandonment as a hopeless struggle". James Stephen junior gave up his private law practice to become permanent counsel to the Colonial Office and the Board of Trade. He quickly made himself so indispensable that a colleague said he *was* the Colonial Office and that for years "he literally ruled the colonial empire". Anonymous power was ideal for a man who combined such gifts with the most extreme shyness. He rarely went out, rarely looked people in the eye, had no mirror because he could not bear to see his face, "shy beyond all the shyness you could imagine in anyone whose soul had not been pre-existent in a wild duck".[14]

On 30 June, Macaulay launched the *Anti-Slavery Monthly Reporter*, a one-man work in which he published his research into conditions, events, and political proceedings in the colonies, reports from the Anti-Slavery Society, and his own essays. It had limited appeal, small circulation, and no entertainment value, but Macaulay constantly, reliably, and comprehensively unearthed and published all the information that could be had about the slave colonies, to equip the campaign. Much like Macaulay himself, it was dry but indispensable. The society held two general meetings in 1825 to report on the total lack of colonial reform and call for direct intervention as the only way the government could put its resolutions into effect.

Buxton planned a bill to force reform on the colonies in 1826. Parliament received 674 petitions, Buxton presenting the largest ever, with 72,000 signatures, from London. Referring to Canning's 1823 resolutions, Buxton argued:

> *Nothing could be more unequivocal than what was required from the West India colonists; nor could anything be more unequivocal than the utter refusal, on their part, to carry into execution the proposed measures for the benefit of their slaves... Either the House must renounce their pledge to the public in behalf of the negro, or at once take the question into their own hands.*[15]

Once again Canning managed to deflect them. He got his 1823 resolutions sent to the Lords, and passed there, to give them extra weight in the colonies, and Bathurst sent eight draft reform bills to the colonial assemblies, asking them to adapt them to their own situations and then pass them. Canning said that if they remained obstinate they would eventually be coerced, but they would be given a year before the subject was debated again.

Mauritius

The abolitionists made four other motions in that session, and three failed. Thomas Denman failed to get an enquiry into the executions of Jamaican slaves on trumped-up charges of conspiracy; William Smith's motion to ban colonial officials from owning slaves was thrown out without a vote; Brougham's pledge to consider how to implement Canning's resolutions in the following session was defeated 100 votes to 38.

It was Buxton who won a vote – for an enquiry into what was going on in Mauritius and the Seychelles – because he made possibly the most extraordinary revelation in the whole history of the Clapham sect's investigations into slavery. Macaulay's detective work and papers provided by the returning Mauritian commissary-general of police uncovered some strange statistics. There were two male slaves to every female in Mauritius, five to one in Seychelles. Similar ratios had existed in the Caribbean before abolition, because many more male slaves were traded than female, but in two decades the numbers had completely levelled out. The slave trade had continued in Mauritius as ever, and on a scale – there were 21,000 too many men – that implicated the colonial government. Other figures told him the same story. Returns from the Caribbean showed that slaves born there now outnumbered those from elsewhere nine to one; in the Seychelles those born there were themselves outnumbered five to one. In the ten years to 1822, sugar production in Mauritius had increased sixty-fold. Bounties had been paid for a total of 205 slaves captured *en route* to Caribbean colonies, and for 2,452 in Mauritius. The abolitionists scrutinized the governors' dispatches and complaints from their French neighbours, and talked to other Mauritian officials and naval officers. Everything confirmed that the colony was guilty of a vast criminal slave trade.

Buxton laid all this evidence before Parliament, demanded an enquiry, and got one, with Canning's consent, because of the most remarkable aspect of his accusations: Sir Robert Farquhar, governor of Mauritius from 1810 to 1817 and from 1820 to 1823 – reputed suppressor of the slave trade there, maker of abolition treaties with Madagascar and Muscat, friend of Thomas Clarkson, and honorary life governor of the African Institution – was clearly and profoundly implicated in Buxton's accusations, and as a new MP sat opposite him throughout his speech.

Macaulay made another rather different discovery in 1826. The commander of the garrison at Ascension Island, Colonel Nichols, wrote to him saying he had visited Sierra Leone and witnessed disgusting scenes of revelry and excess in the Macaulay and Babington house. Macaulay failed to get a straight answer from Tom Babington, and so summoned the Georgetown manager to bring the accounts to London. Examining them, he saw that for three years Babington had tried, against his instructions, to expand the firm into a great trade empire, and destroyed it. At least

£100,000 worth of unsaleable stock had accumulated in Georgetown, with much more on the way. Goods had been sold on credit that would never be paid. Salaries had increased up to fivefold, and jobs multiplied. Numerous far-flung factories had been built and equipped, and ships bought to travel between them. When this came to light, Tom Babington shut himself in his room pleading illness and refused to talk to Macaulay or his father. Macaulay spent several years trying to recover the business, discovering greater and greater chaos: when clients in Calcutta collapsed, Macaulay found Tom had lent them vast sums; others applied for the repayment of loans Tom had taken in Macaulay's name. Throughout, Tom refused to let Macaulay see any of his papers, pleading that the subject gave him too much anguish to think about. "His mind has been strangely thrown off its centre," said his father.[16] Macaulay dissolved their partnership in 1829, and his son Henry successfully managed the Georgetown business, winding it up about four years later, but Macaulay had lost his fortune.

Canning became Prime Minister in 1827 when Lord Liverpool died, but only lived four months himself. For the Mauritius enquiry, George Stephen travelled across Britain gathering testimonies about the slave trade from 320 people, from former governors to drummer boys, who had been there. Buxton moved to restart the enquiry early in the 1827 session, but Canning deferred it, and his motion was scheduled for May. Buxton kept working through the mass of evidence, but his health started to break down. His doctor prescribed leeches, quiet, and total abstinence from business, the last of which at least he ignored. He gradually declined until the Saturday before the debate, when going through his papers he was so overwhelmed by emotion he kept leaving the house crying, "I can't bear it!", and stopped work. He spent the Sunday morning in bed, called for the doctor, and passed out. When he woke on Wednesday he had missed the debate.

On top of the intransigence of the government and the colonies, and the lack of interest of the public, it seemed that the leader of the cause was dying. "My hopes were never lower," said James Stephen, "except in divine interposition. In that respect they were never stronger."[17] But even the strongest hopes of divine interposition could only have imagined it working through long years of attrition. It would have taken more than hope to guess that George Stephen now had in his possession the ammunition that would end the war in five years.

Deliverance to the Captives

Buxton was too ill from 1827 to 1828 to revive the Commons committee on Mauritius. In October 1827, he wrote to the new governor-general of British India, Sir William Bentinck, urging him to abolish suttee, as he himself had tried to do through Parliament in 1821. Bentinck banned suttee in 1828 and successfully suppressed it.

The slave colonies had had a year, as Canning demanded, to act on his reform resolutions and to pass the bills Bathurst sent, and the results coming back were striking. Not one of the assemblies had passed any of Bathurst's bills. As for the twenty reforms that the government had requested, some steps or gestures had been made. In the Bahamas, for example, slaves were allowed to buy their freedom, but only if they could prove they got their money honestly. Macaulay reported that, of twenty reforms required of thirteen colonies, two had stopped Sunday markets, three provided banking, Bahamas abolished the whip (never having needed it), and Grenada removed the legal onus on free black people to prove their freedom. Twenty-eight further reforms were partial or defeated the object. That left 215 cases out of 260 where nothing had been done whatsoever.

In Parliament Brougham demanded of the new Colonial Secretary, William Huskisson, whether the government was satisfied with this. Huskisson regretted progress was so slow, but said it would be unsafe to go faster. "The progress of the colonies is so slow as to be imperceptible to all human eyes, save their own," replied Brougham, insisting they could not let another session go by without taking action.[1]

But Brougham fell ill, so it did. The abolitionists' one success was that Lushington, following a Jamaican petition he had brought in the previous session, got an Order in Council issued which granted full legal rights to mixed-race people.

The Mauritius Investigation

Meanwhile, George Stephen's research into the slave trade and slavery in Mauritius had accumulated an overwhelming body of evidence. "Rocked in an abolitionist cradle" though he had been, and brought up with bloody stories of the middle passage and the plantations, he found it hard to believe what he was hearing at first, but all across Britain he heard accounts from across Mauritius throughout seventeen years, agreeing that torture was customary and early death routine. A slave was blinded by red-hot knitting needles. Another who took too long fetching water received 100 lashes and had seven teeth pulled. One was hung by his arms, beaten, had his legs coated in fat and dogs set on him, was given urine to drink, and died being sexually mutilated. A slave was sent on a day's journey without food and, because he asked for some on his return, was beaten to death with an iron bar. A slave who informed on her mistress for keeping a runaway slave had all her teeth pulled, her nose and ears cut off, and died while her breasts were being cut off. "They are not in any instance whatever treated as human beings," said one witness. Stephen summarized:

> Slaves were murdered piecemeal, roasted alive in ovens; flogged, starved, dismembered, tortured, and slaughtered. Suicide and infanticide were the daily resource of parents; mothers killed their children from humanity, and killed themselves from despair. And the decrease in the slave population was supplied by daily importations from Madagascar and the Seychelles...
>
> Since the traffic had been declared felonious in 1811, the whole slave population in the Mauritius, exceeding 60,000, had been exterminated and replaced more than once![2]

Buxton was still too weak to restart the parliamentary enquiry – his doctor said it would unquestionably kill him – but gave all these papers to Huskisson, asking him to organize it. Huskisson stalled, sending two commissioners to Mauritius to investigate instead. He was succeeded by Sir George Murray, who wrote to the colonial assemblies urging them to give slaves Sunday rest and make their evidence admissible in court.

Almost incidentally, Buxton helped to get native South Africans freed from slavery in the 1828 session. Wilberforce had raised the issue in 1822, after the London Missionary Society warned him that they were being reduced to slavery, persuading the House to pass a royal address – the best speech of his life, according to Buxton, delivered to twenty MPs. Now, when Buxton gave notice of his motion to renew that address requiring their freedom and equality, Murray told him the government would do what he wanted if he agreed not to speak. The colonial governor passed similar legislation, and an Order in Council secured native rights in January 1829.

Parliament was absorbed in 1829 by the question that had been gradually overwhelming it over recent years: Catholic political rights. The Irish Catholic Daniel O'Connell had led a mass movement, and got elected in 1828 to a seat in Parliament that the law prevented him from taking. This was the pressure that forced Wellington – having purged his government of pro-Catholics – to support Catholic emancipation, and the Act was passed on 24 March. Evangelicals generally shared popular English antipathy to Catholicism, but Thornton had supported emancipation; Wilberforce, having fiercely opposed it, was gradually won around, to the More sisters' horror; and Buxton ardently supported it, telling a friend he was forfeiting his seat in the next election by his vote. Success seemed to release Irish emancipationists from their own struggle into that of the slaves, again led by O'Connell. Macaulay reported excitedly the petitions of Irish anti-slavery societies.

With the Catholic question resolved, Buxton felt well enough to consider reviving the Mauritius enquiry, and asked Macaulay whether he should risk "inevitable death". Macaulay's reply is not recorded, but the following week Buxton told Murray he would move for an enquiry, and Brougham would move that colonial courts be required to accept slaves' evidence. Murray promised the government would arrange both the next year. It did neither.

On 1 June, the government's commissioners to Mauritius made their first report. They had met concerted opposition and obfuscation there and had access to nothing like the wealth of evidence that Buxton had amassed. And yet their conclusions were clear and inescapable: the slave trade continued as ever and conditions were barbaric. Buxton was vindicated. When he called for the report to be made available to MPs, Farquhar, unaware of its contents, protested that Buxton had never proved his allegations, and must now do so or retract them. Buxton showed the house his doctor's note, and Murray declared the enquiry would be revived to decide the question.

The Death Warrant
Zachary Macaulay, before anyone else, decided the end was in sight. That autumn he published *The Death Warrant of Negro Slavery Throughout the British Dominions*, also inserting it into the *Anti-Slavery Reporter*, declaring

imminent victory. He showed that the government was losing patience, and that slave-holders' rhetoric was increasingly desperate. The *Edinburgh* and *Westminster Review*s now actively supported abolition, while even the pro-slavery *Quarterly Review* said the colonial assemblies' "systematic opposition to every measure proposed by the King's government… appears to us to be *little short of insanity*". Ireland, said Macaulay, "has added seven millions to our ranks", the Catholic cause proving that emancipation could be won despite popular opposition 10,000 times what abolitionists faced now. "Shaking off the unimpassioned tranquility of earlier days," said George Stephen of Macaulay, "he assumed with age the ardour and fire of youth, and with an impetuosity of impatience that startled even the young, proclaimed in his *Anti-slavery Reporter* that the day was won, ere yet the battle was fought or the troops prepared for action."[3]

The Mauritius enquiry never happened because Farquhar died in February 1820. While Murray privately conceded to Buxton that his allegations were all true, he said that without Farquhar, there was no dispute to resolve, so no enquiry was needed. He announced the truth of the Mauritius slave trade parenthetically in half a sentence during a debate on irregularities in the sugar trade. As for the slave evidence bill, the government repeatedly postponed it, pleading financial constraints.

Abolitionist leaders decided that their tactic of persuasion had failed and it was time to rouse the nation to force Parliament's hand. Local anti-slavery societies had been increasingly calling for immediate abolition since 1827, led by the Quaker Elizabeth Heyrick. Her Birmingham Ladies' Society for the Relief of Negro Slaves employed a travelling lecturer in 1828 to spread this message. Buxton, robbed of the chance to get their Mauritius findings on the public record and in the newspapers, finally allowed George Stephen to do what he had long wanted, and take them directly to the people. He and a couple of friends travelled around London calling anti-slavery meetings, and telling their audiences about Mauritius. They had never spoken in public before, but quickly gained confidence as their shocked audiences seized hold of the cause, sometimes inviting them back the following day.

The Anti-Slavery Society called a public meeting to announce its new direction on 15 May 1830. So many people crammed into Freemasons' Hall, one of the largest rooms in London, that not only were more than a thousand turned away but speakers failed to reach the stage. Wilberforce chaired the meeting. Buxton made a motion expressing "unalterable determination to leave no proper and practicable means unattempted" for ending slavery. Tom Macaulay's motion expressed regret that slavery continued along with the fiscal arrangements that encouraged it. Henry Hunt the radical leader interrupted to say that English working-class conditions were worse than colonial slavery, and was booed off. The MP Charles Brownlow, seconded by Brougham, called on Parliament "to devise the best and wisest means" of ending slavery. Then came an interruption that caught the mood of the meeting. A young member of the Anti-Slavery Committee, Henry Pownall, ignoring Wilberforce's calls for order, shouted from the gallery that abolitionist leaders were still timidly fiddling with slavery after seven years, and moved an amendment demanding "that from and after the 1st of January, 1830, every child born within the King's dominions shall be free". The crowd erupted. "The shouts, the tumult of applause were such as I never heard before, and never shall hear again," said George Stephen. As Wilberforce appealed for order, Stephen and friends saved their voices until the clamour began to subside, and then started it off again. Eventually Wilberforce put a version of the amendment, Buxton supported it, and the crowd carried it.[4]

In June 1830, George IV's death caused a general election. Brougham brought the society's petition to Parliament at the butt-end of the session in July. He detailed the planters' lies, abuses, and failure to move by a hair's breadth in response to Canning's resolutions, and denounced the government's deference to their rights. Warning MPs that the country was roused, he called for a commitment to debate an anti-slavery bill soon after the election, and lost by 56 votes to 27. That month, Louis XVIII was deposed – a timely reminder to MPs, Brougham said, of the price of not listening to the people. Brougham won Wilberforce's old seat of Yorkshire, telling Macaulay slavery had been the main issue there, though nationwide it was parliamentary reform. James Stephen, in his seventies, finally published the second volume of *Slavery Delineated*, with Macaulay's revisions, six years after the first, and after an intensifying struggle against failing eyesight and memory.

The Whigs

In the new Parliament, Lord Grey's Whigs gained power over the issue of parliamentary reform. The party was naturally anti-slavery and Grey had brought the 1807 abolition bill, but they had no majority and reform was their first priority. In November, Brougham gave notice of an abolition motion, presenting 355 petitions, but then he was made Lord Chancellor, leaving the motion to Buxton. Told that Grey was willing to make the reform of slavery a government measure, Buxton replied that it was too late for that. He would not support any amelioration of slavery, but only its extinction.

As the first parliamentary reform bill staggered through the Commons – despite the celebrated oratory of Tom Macaulay – toward a defeat that would mean another election, Buxton made a motion committing the House to a debate on how to end slavery. Arguing that the most objective measure of slave conditions was the death rate, he showed, from the colonies' own registers, that (excluding manumissions) the number of slaves had fallen by 45,000 in ten years, and 100,000 since 1807. To keep up with the free black population they would have had to increase by fifty a day, but they had declined by ten a day. "If there were no other prospect for the extinction of slavery, it would be found in the rapid extinction of the negro race." It was Buxton at his most irresistible, but the debate was adjourned. Government representatives conceded for the first time that the colonies had totally failed to enact the reforms required of them, but rejected immediate abolition, offering instead a more stringent version of the 1823 orders, which they would pay colonies to adopt.[5]

James Stephen wrote to Zachary Macaulay in despair, an indulgence that drew from him the kind of scolding that Wilberforce's "busy indolence" used to draw from Stephen: "Defeat I regard not. Let us do our duty, and leave the issue to Him who ordereth all events… On whom are we to rely, under God, if the very men who are to lead battle shall utter notes of despondency and alarm? You dread failure. I have no such dread!" Macaulay wrote this between the death and funeral of his wife. He had been dangerously ill; Selina had nursed him and died as he was recovering. He was considered too ill to attend the funeral, and wrote to Stephen after giving instructions for it to his children. "Though I had called up all my calmness for the occasion," he said, "the excitement was too much for me."[6] He moved with his daughters to a small house near Russell Square, where he lived off gifts from Tom and Henry, augmented by his son John after Brougham gave him a living. Apart from his children, only one thing mattered now. The candle of Macaulay's life had burnt down to a last black wick of abolition. In July 1830, he dropped the "Monthly" from the *Anti-Slavery Reporter*, having published fifteen issues in the last twelve months, and he published twenty-one in the next.

A third member of Clapham's wealthy coterie ended up in financial disaster. Wilberforce's son William fled the country to escape arrest and left his father with £50,000 of debt. Wilberforce sold the house to which he and Barbara had retired, dismissed all but three servants, and they spent their remaining years travelling between their other sons and friends.

The Agency Committee

George Stephen told the Anti-Slavery Committee that he could rouse the country by sending bands of speakers to do nationwide what he and his friends had done in London. They rejected the idea as impractical, but several members gave him money for it, and so the Agency Committee was formed. Some of the Anti-Slavery Committee joined, but Stephen restricted their numbers, wanting his group to be more radical. It was run by him and two Quakers, Emanuel and Joseph Cooper, and advised tactically by Daniel O'Connell. They employed six agents, sending them out to lecture, start or revive local societies, influence local newspapers, and take collections, equipped with Stephen's *Slavery Delineated*, the *Anti-Slavery Reporter*, and the Baptist minister Benjamin Godwin's *Lectures on Slavery*. Many more joined them unpaid, including Pownall, Baron Nugent (a lord of the treasury), and several Baptist ministers.

To George Stephen's glee, plantation owners responded with their own travelling lecturer, who was followed around the country by Agency Committee speakers revelling in the controversies he stirred up for them. Stephen was less happy when planters sent gangs to break up anti-slavery talks, but he got them arrested and reckoned that in the long run it only served to increase audiences. In the agency's first year, the number of local societies affiliated to the Anti-Slavery Society grew from 200 to nearly 1,300.

The 1831 election gave Earl Grey a gigantic majority for reform but, when the bill was rejected by the Lords in October, Grey had Parliament prorogued, reconvening in December for a third attempt. Stephen's agents canvassed prospective voters arguing that if the reform bill gave them votes, the emancipation bill was what they should use them for.

In December the slave colonies received the Colonial Secretary Goderich's offer to buy the reform of slavery, and utterly rejected it without exception. Their attempts to stop slaves hearing his instructions only convinced them the King had ordered their release and managers were refusing to obey. In Jamaica the black Baptist lay preacher Samuel Sharpe confirmed this to his hearers, and they made a pact not to return to work after Christmas. The strike quickly turned into a revolt. While Britain was seized by reform riots, 50,000 slaves escaped and burnt 160 buildings, killing ten white people, two deliberately, and causing £800,000 worth of damage, £1 for every slave in the British Caribbean. In repressing the revolt, 400 slaves were killed. A hundred more were later executed, and more died under the whip. Soldiers, led by magistrates, destroyed thirteen Baptist churches and four Methodist. Six British Baptist missionaries and one Methodist were arrested, but avoided Smith's fate. The Baptist William Knibb, told that his life was in danger, came home and joined the Agency Committee, taking his powerful story around the country. Goderich blamed the Jamaica Assembly for the revolt, warning them "the opportunity of conceding with dignity and safety may, ere long, be irretrievably lost".[7] Buxton told a correspondent: "Our power of emancipating in one way or another is fast drawing to a close: I mean, that the negroes will take the work into their own hands."[8] Plantation owners started a poster campaign and, kicking himself for not having thought of it himself, George Stephen copied them, employing men to follow them around covering their posters with his own.

The Anti-Slavery Society's 1832 general meeting came in the "Days of May", when Grey resigned over the resistance of the Lords to the reform bill, violence broke out again and revolution was in the air. The meeting was a (metaphorically) riotous affair. The new Exeter Hall, half as big again as the Freemasons', was crammed and the street blocked by those turned away. Buxton made a shaky start by insisting controversially that the reform bill was insignificant beside the rights of slaves, but went on to give the kind of barnstorming, rabble-rousing performance that played so much better to abolitionist enthusiasts than in Parliament. "Were they, he demanded to know, all of one mind? Were they, in one word, for emancipation? For total emancipation? *(Great applause)* For emancipation with as little delay as honest necessity would allow? *(Renewed applause)* These were his doctrines, and he wanted to ascertain whether or not they were theirs. *(Loud and unanimous tokens of approval.)*"[9] A frail James Stephen chaired the meeting, correctly predicting it would be his last public act.

Buxton's Stand

Three days later, on 15 May, Grey returned to power upon the surrender of King and Lords. As the reform bill set off one more time through the Lords, Buxton moved for a select committee to consider the abolition of slavery. The government beseeched him to delay it: alienating plantation owners would risk losing the reform bill at the last moment; ministers would oppose him; and Buxton had no chance of success anyway. Buxton was in an excruciating dilemma. His conscience could not bear any more delay, and neither could his public, and yet if he forced a vote he would not only lose but force abolitionist friends on the government's side to vote against him and so risk losing their seats in the forthcoming election. With his beloved daughter and anti-slavery secretary Priscilla, he prayed "that God would give me His Spirit in that emergency", then they rode to Parliament. He told her he would make his point but could not insist on a division; but he was borne along by a compulsion that he could not explain or resist, and by the time they arrived he had decided that the slaves' sufferings must outweigh his friends'.

In his speech he demanded to know whether the government had the heart for the kind of war that a full-scale slave revolt would draw them into. Tom Macaulay supported him, while the Chancellor of the Exchequer, Viscount Althorp, proposed an amendment to negate the motion by inserting the words "and in conformity to the resolutions of this House of the 15th of May, 1823". Then the test came: during the debate Buxton reckoned a hundred MPs came to him privately and implored him not to force a vote over the amendment; one tried four times. As it concluded, the Speaker suggested the will of the House was clear without a vote. "Never shall I forget the tone in which his solitary voice replied, 'No, sir' said Priscilla."[10]

He lost by 136 votes to 90, a triumphant defeat. Althorp told Tom Macaulay: "If he can get ninety to vote with him when he is wrong, and when most of those really interested in the subject vote against him, he can command a *majority when he is right. The question is settled:* the Government see it, and they will take it up."[11] James Stephen junior, the Colonial Office counsel, had the job of writing a plan for emancipation. He proposed all slaves should be freed unconditionally and owners compensated with a loan of £15 million, while vagrancy laws and land tax would ensure they stayed and worked for wages.

The main issue in the first reformed general election in December 1832 was slavery. "The eternal 'Am I not a man and a brother?' met the eye at every corner; cartwhips, chains, and the negro, seemed stereotyped on every board." Voters "are now on their trial at the bar of the Most High!", Macaulay told them.[12] Stephen's Agency Committee demanded anti-slavery pledges from every candidate and printed lists in the newspapers of the eligible, ineligible, and doubtful, receiving 3,000 letters on the subject, not least from ineligible MPs protesting they had chaired anti-slavery meetings or knew Macaulay or had dined with Wilberforce. Macaulay disapproved of their mob tactics, though Wilberforce and Buxton totally supported them. So did Stephen's father, who died on 10 October 1832, and was buried with his mother and father and wives.

The Whigs kept a large majority, but Buxton was shocked to sit through the King's Speech on 7 February without hearing a word about ending slavery. Within minutes Brougham and Goderich told him not to schedule his own motion but leave it to them. He already had. When he rose to make the motion on 19 March, Althorp intervened, promising a government motion for full-blooded abolition in April, and Buxton agreed to wait.

Buxton's work was done, he told friends. Goderich would get the credit, but he could not care. For the first time in ages, says his son Charles, "he was able to sleep at night, and began to resume his cheerfulness of manner".[13] But then, unhappily, the enthusiastic Goderich was replaced as Colonial Secretary by Edward Stanley, and the abolition motion was delayed until 14 May.

Hearing disquieting rumours of the government's change of heart, Buxton told 330 local societies throughout the UK to send delegates, and he arranged a meeting for them with Stanley, who promised not to postpone again. On 5 May, Priscilla Buxton, having become the secretary of the London Female Anti-Slavery Society, sent a petition around women's groups across the country, expecting little response in the available time, but received a record 187,000 signatures each for the Commons and Lords. The women spent all day pasting and taping pages together until "they were like two great feather beds". Her father had to ask the Speaker about the procedure for presenting it, being unable to lift it himself, and eventually carried it with three other MPs amid laughter and cheers.

Apprenticeship and Compensation

Stanley's motion provoked other feelings. He rejected James Stephen's proposals, preferring to free immediately only children under six, apprentice others to their present owners for twelve years, let them work a quarter of each day for wages, allow them to be whipped for disobedience, though only by the decree of a magistrate, and offer slave owners a "loan" of £15 million to ease the transition. It was a mean kind of emancipation, but Buxton and Lushington decided that the solid agreement of Parliament to a government measure for abolition was too valuable to lose by trying to force radical amendments, and that defeat would inevitably lead to bloody revolt in the Caribbean. They would let it go through the second reading without a division, by which time the main point would be conceded, and then cut down the period of apprenticeship in committee. Macaulay told Wilberforce that ten years less a day since parliament first discussed the abolition of slavery "its death-blow was struck".

George Stephen was ready to fight, but Buxton persuaded him that the only issue over which to contend was the twelve years' apprenticeship. The pair led a delegation of thirty-three MPs to Stanley to negotiate a reduction, but Stanley insisted he was pledged absolutely to the plantation owners and they would not accept a day less. Petitions kept coming, bringing the total signatures to an estimated 1.5 million. Stephen called an agency meeting at Exeter Hall, and not only was it packed with campaigners, he says, but sixty-six MPs came to hear their decision – which was to accept all but the apprenticeship term – and vote accordingly. Nevertheless, Buxton was deluged with angry letters accusing him of betraying the cause.

James Stephen wrote the bill. Trying to reduce his influence, Stanley had insisted on doing it himself, failed, and gave the job to Stephen two days before the deadline, who spent the weekend dictating the 13,000 words and submitted it on the Monday.

In the committee Buxton spoke against compensation – which Stanley had increased to £20 million and which Tom Macaulay defended as a contractual obligation to colonists – but proposed no amendment on that point. Apprenticeship, however, he denounced as mere slavery and moved that the term be cut to the shortest necessary for a transition to paid labour. He lost by 158 votes to 151, but the narrowness of their win persuaded Stanley to halve the term to six years. Buxton failed to shave another four years off, but inserted a clause preventing slaves being moved without their consent, which Wellington diluted. The bill passed the Commons on 7 August, and despite Wellington's opposition had a fairly easy ride from the Lords, chastened by their last fight with Grey.

Buxton never had the chance to report back to Wilberforce on the completion of the task he had been given, as Wilberforce died on 29 July. Lodging under others' roofs as happily as in his single days, he witnessed with delight the "gospel labours" of his sons. The passing of the emancipation bill at the second reading was the last public news he heard.

Hannah More died on 7 September, aged eighty-eight. She had been confined to her room for years, and after Macaulay reported tales of the shocking behaviour of her servants she sacked them all, sold the house, and moved to Bath where she was better looked after. She left £30,000, mostly to charities and religious organizations.

Macaulay missed the passing of the bill, retreating to the country because of illness from July to September. Buxton wrote to him:

*I look back to the letter which you and I wrote to Lord Bathurst in
1823, containing our demands, twelve in number. Bad as the bill
is, it accomplishes every one of these, and a great deal more… My
sober and deliberate opinion is that you have done more towards this*

consummation than any other man. For myself, I take pleasure in acknowledging that you have been my tutor all the way through, and that I could have done nothing without you... So cheer up. [14]

Sons and Daughters

The story of the Clapham sect has a tidier ending than one has any right to expect, with Wilberforce, More, Stephen, the Anti-Slavery Society, and the legal institution of slavery all coming to an end within a year of each other. Of course the sequels go off in every direction.

Buxton devoted the rest of his life to three campaigns: the liberation of black West Indians; the rights of native South Africans; and the international slave trade. Through a parliamentary enquiry into Caribbean apprenticeship, he prevented vagrancy laws from keeping workers on their plantations, reasoning that these would have substantially preserved slavery forever. He courted bitter criticism from abolitionists for pressing this measure in preference to an early end to apprenticeship, believing it more important in the long run, but apprenticeship was ended after exactly four years in 1838, thanks to abolitionist pressure and the government's surprised gratification at the peaceful hard work of apprentices. He founded the Aborigines Protection Society in 1837 and, after another enquiry into the treatment of native people, persuaded the Colonial Secretary to dismiss the governor of the Cape and return the 7,000-square-mile Queen Adelaide Province to the Xhosa. This Colonial Secretary was Charles Grant, now Lord Glenelg, "Britain's only palindromic cabinet minister", and the Colonial Office, instead of shielding the colonies from the interference of the Saints, was itself a colony of Clapham. To fight the slave trade, Buxton organized a commercial expedition along the Niger, patronized by Prince Albert, but it was a failure, and naval suppression proved more successful.

These were personal labours of Buxton himself, rather than the Clapham sect. Macaulay's health was increasingly patchy, and he heard with strongly conflicting emotions that Tom had been appointed to the supreme council of India on a salary that would restore the fortunes of the family, and that he would take his sister Hannah when he sailed in 1834. Zachary did not expect to see them again. That year his daughter Margaret died, and Sir James Stephen warned him he was taking legal action as an executor of the straitened Wilberforce estate for debts run up by Tom Babington. Zachary moved with his daughters Fanny and Selina (an invalid) to France, where he became honorary president of the *Société Francaise pour l'Abolition de l'Esclavage*, sent proofs of the *Anti-Slavery Reporter* home monthly, and wrote books advocating French educational reform. He came home again in 1836. George Stephen paid a last visit to talk abolition and, though warned not to tire him with conversation, found that as ever "antislavery labour was his pabulum, an actual restorative under pain". He died on 13 May 1838, while Tom and Hannah were three-quarters of their way home from India.

There were institutional sequels as well as personal. The CMS was led by Henry Venn from 1841 to 1872, who saved it from financial collapse, ingratiated it with the church hierarchy and promoted the self-government of mission churches. When the *Church Mission Atlas* was printed in 1859, the society employed 227 clergy, including 47 native, and 2,367 lay workers, including 2,210 native; and had 18,433 native communicants. It had sent missionaries to Africa, India, China, the Mediterranean, Canada, and the Caribbean. When Venn died, almost all bishops were vice-presidents and the Queen was a life governor.

The Bible Society by 1834 had distributed over 8.5 million Bibles in 157 languages, and had the distinction of being denounced by the Pope. By its centenary in 1904 it had distributed 181 million Bibles with the help of 5,726 local groups in the UK and 2,230 abroad. Today Bible societies are responsible for two-thirds of languages that have the Bible.

The *Christian Observer* continued until 1874, its editors including Henry Venn and his father's erstwhile curate John Cunningham.

Then there are the genealogical sequels. The sons and daughters of Clapham permeated the British establishment. The generation of Marianne Thornton and George Stephen, including spouses, contained, as far as I have been able to trace (with overlaps): a bishop, two archdeacons, a canon, and thirteen other clergy; nine MPs; an earl, a lord, two barons, two baronets, and three knights; the governor of Bombay, along with other civil servants and lawyers; a newspaper proprietor; and the writer of the hymn "O Worship the King". Thomas Babington Macaulay was a cabinet minister, poet and the greatest English historian: his *History of England* was designed to enchant ordinary English people with the glories of their past and its progress toward the glory of England of their own time, and its first edition of 3,000 sold out in twelve days. These families were, in Noel Annan's words, the "intellectual aristocracy" of Victorian Britain.

Their own children included, among much else: the governor of South Africa, the Australian attorney-general, the editor of the *Observer*, a painter, a law professor, the director of the P&O Steam Navigation Company, a pioneer of women's university education, a bishop, the philosopher John Venn of diagram fame, the architect father of E. M. Forster, the writer of the hymn "Just as I Am", and Sir Leslie Stephen, who edited the *Dictionary of National Biography*, published Thomas Hardy in the *Cornhill*, was an apologist for agnosticism, married Thackeray's daughter Minny, and was the father of Virginia Woolf.

Forging Victorianism

The influence of the Clapham sect on Victorian Britain is hard to assess with any kind of accuracy or objectivity, but they do seem to have played a very significant part in the development of its morality; the ethos of Clapham became the spirit of the age. The earnestness and solemnity, the fervour and dogmatism, the puritanism and fastidiousness, the sense of duty and self-denial, the sexual propriety and sobriety, the philanthropy and charity, the domesticity, the sabbath-keeping, the distrust of the theatre, and the sense of a benevolent, God-given mission to the world: in all these areas, Clapham was out of key with the tone of eighteenth-century Britain, and anticipated the tone of Victorian Britain. Even in an area where Clapham was at odds with Victorianism, its pessimism about human nature, its benign achievements are one source of Victorian optimism. Similarly, like many evangelicals, Buxton was suspicious of imperialism, believing that English people were generally decent at home and villains abroad, but this very fact made him push for the paternalistic state-sponsored empire of Victorianism to protect indigenous people from unregulated colonists.

None of this is to claim that the dozen families of Clapham created Victorianism single-handed. For one thing, Clapham was not evangelicalism, and there were important evangelical concerns in which it had peripheral involvement or none. But the combined reach of Clapham's organizations, its power in Westminster, and the prominence of its achievements put it in a league of its own. Secondly, enormous social upheaval, industrialization, urbanization, the rise of the middle classes, new technology and political change at home and in Europe all combined to create a ground ready for the serious, sober, self-regulating godliness of evangelicalism, but Clapham sowed the seed, or much of it. Similarly, the story in this book has offered glances at the profound and sustained anxiety caused by revolution, war, and the threat of invasion and rebellion over the course of thirty years, which created a new mood of seriousness, but it took Clapham and their allies to channel it into evangelicalism.

There were many ways in which they contributed to this process. They supported the early Sunday school movement, which taught evangelical values to millions of children. They called up the largely symbolic but nonetheless powerful gesture of the royal anti-vice movement. Their efforts to get livings to evangelical clergy gradually but significantly increased their numbers. Simeon at Cambridge introduced the ordinands of the Church of England to evangelicalism for half a century. In Sierra Leone and India they turned the British Empire in the nation's imagination from a profiteering escapade into a mission to bring Christianity, commerce, and civilization to the world.

Then there were their writings. Hannah More's moral tirades were constant bestsellers and her stories raised more than one generation of children. Henry Thornton's family prayers were printed posthumously and became such a staple they were still bringing in royalties in E. M. Forster's day. The Religious Tract Society gave away thousands of copies of Wilberforce's *Practical View*, claiming a multitude of conversions as a result.

The influence of the Saints on Parliament was a huge contribution. Wilberforce and Thornton were unusual when they entered Parliament in that they did so for the sake of "usefulness". By the time of Victoria's accession, if not the standard reason, it was what MPs at least had to pretend to. By insisting on debating matters of justice and duty, and deciding them on principle, taking decades if necessary, and winning, they changed the moral tone of Parliament. The 1832 reform was also vital to this, but the change had started long before. Wilberforce noticed it in the 1813 Indian charter debate: "When I consider what was the state of the House of Commons twenty-five years ago, and how little it would then have borne with patience what it heard not only with patience but acceptance during the late discussions, I cannot but draw a favourable augury for the welfare of our country."[1] Then, when the Reform Act was passed, its coinciding with the culmination of the emancipation campaign meant that abolition set the tone for the new political nation.

Which brings us to their greatest contribution, the popular example of their campaign against the slave trade and slavery. Wilberforce, the friend of slaves, was the most common hero of Victorian school-books, and abolition seemed, rightly, the towering moral achievement of the age.

It was a beacon of national pride, proof of human progress, and a reason to see the British Empire as the guardian of the world's weak. In the public eye, it was the achievement of Wilberforce, and it gave the faith that drove him to it irresistible credibility.

The irony is that, as the faith of the Clapham sect won the nation, it lost many of their own children. Samuel Wilberforce was a High Church bishop. His three brothers converted to Roman Catholicism, Henry being a close friend of John Henry Newman. Tom Macaulay grew sceptical of evangelicals' literal faith in the Bible and rejected their renunciation of pleasure. Henry Sykes Thornton shocked evangelical biblical propriety by marrying Emily Dealtry, the daughter of the rector of Clapham who was, unfortunately, his dead wife's sister; it was illegal in Britain and, having failed to get the law changed, they had to marry abroad. Sir James Stephen, on the other hand, while sceptical of evangelical beliefs, took their puritanism to new levels. "He once smoked a cigar," says his son, "and found it so delicious that he never smoked again."[2] Then again, Henry Venn at the CMS and the *Christian Observer* carried on the Lord's business as usual.

Success and failure in passing on their faith to their children probably meant as much, in their way, to the Clapham sect as their more public achievements. Both were the commission of God, and the purpose of their lives. Either way they seem to have enjoyed the profound affection and gratitude of their sons and daughters.

Their wider legacy was not an unmixed blessing, the austerity of the Victorian sabbath, for example, oppressing the seventh day just as evangelical reform of working conditions lightened the burden of the other six. But there is nothing to be thrown into the balance that will outweigh Clapham's indispensable contribution to the freedom of 7 million survivors of British slavery, and the suppression of the British and European trade in 800,000 African people a year. It was costly for them. They gave it, in different ways and to different degrees, their lives, their money, their careers, their time, and their health. Few people can make a more persuasive claim to have been doing the work of God in the world.

Notes

Introduction

1. There are exceptions – what Brown said does apply pretty well to Hannah More, but not to the rest of the Clapham sect.

Chapter 1 The Thorntons

1. Thornton MSS, Cambridge University Library (CUL), Add. MS 7674/1/P/2.

2. *Recollections,* CUL, Add. MS 7674/1/P/2.

3. Henry Venn mentions Thornton's "first receiving Christ" thirty-six years before, writing in 1790, thirty-seven years after the wedding: John Venn, *The Life and a Selection from the Letters of the Late Rev. Henry Venn* (4th ed., London: John Hatchard, 1836).

4. Jonas Hanway, *Three Letters on the Subject of the Marine Society* (London, 1758), p. 12.

5. *Recollections,* CUL, Add. MS 7674/1/P/10; Lewis Bernstein Namier, *The Structure of Politics at the Accession of George III* (London: Macmillan, 1968), p. 342.

6. CUL, Add. MS 7674/1/P/9, 10.

7. Joanna Brooks (ed.),*The Collected Writings of Samson Occom, Mohegan* (Oxford and New York: Oxford University Press, 2006), p. 272.

8. Leon Burr Richardson, *History of Dartmouth College* (Hanover, NH: Dartmouth College Publications, 1932), p. 31.

9. James Dow McCallum, *Eleazar Wheelock: Founder of Dartmouth College* (Hanover, NH: Dartmouth College Publications, 1939), pp. 173–74.

10. Phillis Wheatley, *The Collected Works,* ed. John C. Shields (Oxford: Oxford University Press, 1988), p. 184.

11. *An Account of the Rise, Progress and Present State of the Society for the Discharge and Relief of Persons Imprisoned for Small Debts* (6th ed., London: "for the charity", 1783), pp. 22, 80, 82–83, 92.

12. CUL, Add. MS 7674/1/C/18.

13. Bernard Martin, *John Newton: A Biography* (London: Heinemann, 1950), p. 219; Richard Cecil (ed.), *The Works of the Rev. John Newton…: to Which are Prefixed Memoirs of His Life* (London: 1853), p. 44.

14. Josiah Bull, *John Newton of Olney and St Mary Woolnoth* (London: Religious Tract Society, 1868), pp. 301, 330.

15. John W. Grover, *Old Clapham* (London: A. Bachhoffner, 1887), p. 21; R. de M. Rudolf, "The Clapham Sect", in *Clapham and the Clapham Sect* (London: Clapham Antiquarian Society, 1927), p. 106.

16. CUL, Add. MS 7674/1/X/7, 2–3.

Chapter 2 The Venns

1. Venn, *Life and Letters,* pp. 4, 11–12.

2. Henry Venn, *Mira; or, a Memoir of Mrs Venn* (London: Religious Tract Society, 1850), p. 6; *Arminian Magazine,* 20 (1797), p. 569.

3. Venn, *Mira,* p. 6.

4. A. C. H. Seymour, *The Life and Times of Selina, Countess of Huntingdon* (2 vols, London: Seeley, Jackson, and Halliday, 1840), vol. 1, p. 430.

5. Seymour, *Selina,* vol. 1, pp. 225–26, 46, 225.

6. Peter Cunningham (ed.), *The Letters of Horace Walpole: Earl of Orford…Now First Chronologically Arranged* (8 vols, London: Richard Bentley, 1857), vol. 2, p. 158.

7. Venn, *Mira,* p. 7.

8. Venn, *Mira,* p. 7.

9. Nehemiah Curnock (ed.), *The Journal of the Rev John Wesley* (8 vols, London: Epworth Press, 1938).

10. Josiah Bull, *Memorials of the Rev. William Bull of Newport Pagnell* (2nd ed., London: James Nisbet, 1865), p. 248; John Venn, *Annals of a Clerical Family* (London: Macmillan, 1904), p. 82.

11. John Telford (ed.), *The Letters of John Wesley* (8 vols, London: Epworth Press, 1931), p. 214n (6 April, 1761).

12. Venn, *Annals,* 93.

13. Michael Hennell, *John Venn and the Clapham Sect* (London: Lutterworth Press, 1958), p. 26.

14. Seymour, *Selina,* vol. 2, p. 46.

15. Richard Whittingham, *The Works of the Rev. John Berridge… with an Enlarged Memoir of His Life* (London: Simpkin and Marshall, 1838), pp. 414, 394; Seymour, *Selina,* vol. 2, p. 47.

16. Whittingham, *Berridge,* pp. 445–46.

17. Venn, *Life and Letters,* p. 176.

Chapter 3 Henry Thornton

1. *Recollections,* CUL, Add. MS 7674/1/N, 3, 17, 19, 2.

2. *Recollections,* CUL, Add. MS 7674/1/C/3.

3. *Recollections,* CUL, Add. MS 7674/1/N 7; Henry Thornton's Diary, CUL, Add. MS 7674/1/R 3–4.

4. *Recollections,* CUL, Add. MS 7674/1/N 2, 6–7.

5. Diary, CUL, Add. MS 7674/1/R 2–3.

6. Diary, CUL, Add. MS 7674/1/R 2–3; *Recollections,* CUL, Add. MS 7674/1/N 10.

7. CUL, Add. 7674/1/X/33; *Recollections,* CUL, Add. MS 7674/1/N.

8. *Recollections,* CUL, Add. MS 7674/1/N 15.

9. *Recollections,* CUL, Add. MS 7674/1/N 17.

10. *Recollections,* CUL, Add. MS 7674/1/N 17–18.

11. *Diary and Letters of Madame d'Arblay* (7 vols, London: Hurst & Blackett, 1854), vol. 2, p. 150.

12. MS letter to Peter Free 19 November 1814, quoted in E. J. T. Acaster, "Henry Thornton – The Banker", part 1, in Mark Blaug (ed.), *Henry Thornton, Jeremy Bentham, James Lauderdale, Simonde de Sismondi.* (Cambridge: Cambridge University Press, 1991), p. 231.

13. *Recollections,* CUL, Add. MS 7674/1/P, 31.

Chapter 4 William Wilberforce

1. Robert Isaac Wilberforce and Samuel Wilberforce, *The Life of William Wilberforce* (5 vols, London: John Murray, 1838), vol. 1, p. 8.

2. Martin, *John Newton,* p. 304.

3. John S. Harford, *Recollections of William Wilberforce* (London, 1864), p. 202.

4. Wilberforce and Wilberforce, *Life of Wilberforce*, vol. 1, p. 98.

5. Wilberforce and Wilberforce, *Life of Wilberforce*, vol. 1, pp. 104, 373.

6. John Campbell (ed.), *Letters and Conversational Remarks of the Late Rev. John Newton* (London, 1811), p. 11; Robert Isaac Wilberforce and Samuel Wilberforce, *The Correspondence of William Wilberforce* (London: John Murray, 1840), p. 56.

7. Thomas Scott, *The Force of Truth: An Authentic Narrative* (London: 1779); Henry Venn, *Mistakes in Religion Exposed: An Essay on the Prophecy of Zacharias* (New York: Williams and Whiting, 1810).

8. Anne Stott, *Hannah More: The First Victorian* (Oxford: Oxford University Press, 2003), p. 86.

9. Wilberforce and Wilberforce, *Life of Wilberforce*, vol. 2, p. 235.

10. Wilberforce and Wilberforce, *Life of Wilberforce*, vol. 1, p. 107.

Chapter 5 Schooling

1. Recollections, CUL, Add. MS 7674/1/N, 7, 3, 4.

2. Wilberforce and Wilberforce, *Life of Wilberforce*, vol. 1, p. 7.

3. Clarkson MS, British Library (BL), Add. MS 41,262A/198–99.

4. William Hunter, *Plain Thoughts and Friendly Hints on the Sabbath* (2nd ed., London: J. Debrett, 1791), p. 39.

5. Sarah Trimmer, *The Oeconomy of Charity* (London: T. Longman, 1787), p. 26; *The Baptist Magazine*, 19 (1827), p. 301; Jonas Hanway, *A Comprehensive View of Sunday Schools* (London: Dodsley and Sewel, 1786), ii.; Thomas W. Laqueur, *Religion and Respectability: Sunday Schools and Working Class Culture 1780–1850* (New Haven and London: Yale University Press, 1976), p. 29.

6. Venn, *Life and Letters,* p. 447; Wilberforce and Wilberforce, *Correspondence,* p. 38.

Chapter 6 The Proclamation

1. Wilberforce and Wilberforce, *Life of Wilberforce*, vol. 1, p. 393.

2. Cunningham, *Letters of Walpole*, vol. 5, p. 485.

3. M. J. D. Roberts, *Making English Morals: Voluntary Association and Moral Reform in England, 1787–1886* (Cambridge: Cambridge University Press, 2004), p. 19.

4. *Report of the Committee of the Society for Carrying into Effect his Majesty's Proclamation against Vice and Immorality for the year 1800* (London: 1801), p. 8.

5. Robin Smith Furneaux, *William Wilberforce* (London: Hamish Hamilton, 1974), p. 54.

6. *A Letter to a Member of the Society for the Suppression of Vice* (London: J. Cawthorn, 1804), p. 33; *The Works of the Rev Sydney Smith* (3rd ed., 3 vols, London: Longman, Brown, Green, and Longmans, 1845), vol. 2, p. 337.

7. John Bowles, *A View of the Moral State of Society at the Close of the Eighteenth Century* (London: for F. & C. Rivington, 1804), vi; *Monthly Review*, 80 (1789), p. 245; Hannah More, *The Works of Hannah More* (London: H. Fisher, R. Fisher, and P. Jackson, 1834), vol. 2, p. 288.

8. Stott, *More,* p. 13.

9. Stott, *More,* p. 384.

10. *Ibid.*

11. William Roberts, *Memoirs of the Life and Correspondence of Mrs. Hannah More* (4 vols, London: R. B. Seeley and W. Burnside, 1834), vol. 1, pp. 273, 280; vol. 2, p. 387; *Monthly Review*, 5 (1791), p. 306.

Chapter 7 The Slave Trade

1. Wilberforce and Wilberforce, *Life of Wilberforce*, vol. 1, p. 145; John S. Harford, *Recollections of William Wilberforce During Nearly Thirty Years: With Brief Notices of Some of His Personal Friends and Contemporaries* (London: Longman, Green, Longman, Roberts, and Green,1864), p. 139.

2. Ford K. Brown, *Fathers of the Victorians* (2nd ed., Cambridge, 1961), pp. 108, 114.

3. E. C. P. Lascelles, *Granville Sharp and the Freedom of the Slaves in England* (London: OUP, 1928), pp. 71–72.

4. Thorkelin, *An Essay on the Slave Trade*, quoted in *The Gentleman's Magazine*, 58, p. 725.

5. Roberts, *Memoirs*, vol. 1, p. 311.

6. Wilberforce and Wilberforce, *Life of Wilberforce*, vol. 1, p. 220; *Parliamentary History*, vol. 28 (London: 1816), p. 45.

7. *Parliamentary History*, vol. 28, p. 63.

8. Wilberforce and Wilberforce, *Life of Wilberforce*, vol. 1, p. 235.

Chapter 8 Mendip Schools

1. Martha More (ed. Arthur Roberts), *Mendip Annals: Or a Narrative of the Charitable Labours of Hannah and More in Their Neighbourhood* (London: 1865), p.13; Stott, *More*, p. 105.

2. More, *Mendip Annals*, p. 20.

3. More, *Mendip Annals*, pp. 17, 15; Furneaux, *William Wilberforce*, p. 59.

4. More, *Mendip Annals*, pp. 51, 22.

5. More, *Mendip Annals*, p. 28.

6. Stott, *More*, p. 110; More, *Mendip Annals*, pp. 43, 45.

7. More, *Mendip Annals*, p. 63.

8. More, *Mendip Annals*, p. 65.

9. More, *Mendip Annals*, p. 67.

10. E. P. Thompson, *The Making of the English Working Class* (London: Pelican, 1968), pp. 414–15; Stott, *More*, p. 115.

Chapter 9 The Slave Trade Continued

1. Wilberforce and Wilberforce, *Life of Wilberforce*, vol. 1, p. 11.

2. Eliza Conybeare, *Rothley Temple in the Olden Time: Phases of English Life*, ed. Brian Verity and Terry Sheppard (Rothley: Rothley History Society, 2005), p. 9.

3. Conybeare, *Rothley Temple,* p. 10.

4. Babington MSS, Trinity College, Cambridge, 13/8, 13/74.

5. Babington MS 13/14.

6. Wilberforce and Wilberforce, *Life of Wilberforce*, p. 222.

7. Thomas Gisborne, *The Principles of Moral Philosophy Investigated and Applied to Civil Society* (2nd ed., London: B. White and Son, 1790), p. 156.

8. *Recollections*, CUL, Add. MS 7674/1/N, 38.

9. *Recollections*, CUL, Add. MS 7674/1/N, 40.

10. *Recollections*, CUL, Add. MS 7674/1/N, 40, 42.

11. *Recollections*, CUL, Add. MS 7674/1/N 39–42

12. William Jay, *The Autobiography of William Jay*, ed. G. B. Redford and J. A. James (London: Hamilton Adams, 1854), p. 43; John Telford, *Letters of John Wesley* 9 October 1786.

13. Bull, *Memorials of Bull*, pp. 156, 189.

14. *Recollections*, CUL, Add. MS 7674/1/N, 7.

15. Venn, *Life and Letters*, pp. 493, 489; *The Works of William Cowper*, ed. Robert Southey (15 vols, London: Baldwin and Cradock, 1837), vol. 10, p. 29; John Newton, *One Hundred And Twenty Nine Letters... to the Rev. William Bull of Newport Pagnell* (London: Hamilton Adams,1847), p. 245; Thomas Scott, *A Discourse... Occasioned by the Death of John Thornton* (London: J. Johnson, 1791), p. 7.

16. Wilberforce and Wilberforce, *Life of Wilberforce*, vol. 1, p. 290.

17. Thomas Clarkson, *The History of the Rise, Progress and Accomplishment of the Abolition of the Slave Trade by the British Parliament* (2 vols, London: R. Taylor and Co. for Longman, Hurst, Rees, and Orme, 1808), vol. 1, pp. 209–10.

Chapter 10 Sierra Leone: Exodus

1. Clarkson MS, BL, Add. MS 41,262A/63.

2. Prince Hoare, *Memoirs of Granville Sharp* (2 vols, London: Henry Colburn, 1820), vol. 2, pp.12–13; Clarkson MS 41,262A/153.

3. *Recollections*, CUL, Add. MS 7674/1/N 33.

4. Clarkson MS, BL, Add. MS 41,262A/34.

5. Ellen Gibson Wilson, *John Clarkson and the African Adventure* (London: Macmillan, 1980), p. 68.

6. Clarkson MS, BL, Add. MS 41,262A/168.

7. Clarkson MS, BL, Add. MS 41,262A/33, 27.

8. Clarkson MS, BL, Add. MS 41,262A/44.

9. Babington MS 13/45, 34.

10. Adam Hochschild, *Bury the Chains* (London: Macmillan, 2005), p. 264; *Gentleman's Magazine*, 64, p. 1169.

11. Wilberforce and Wilberforce, *Life of Wilberforce*, vol. 1, pp. 341–42; Newton, *One Hundred and Twenty Nine Letters*, p. 263.

12. *Parliamentary History* vol. 29, p. 1155; *The Debate on a Motion for the Abolition of the Slave Trade in the House of Commons on Monday the Second of April, 1792* (London: W. Woodfall, 1792), p. 76; Babington MS 13/44.

13. Babington MS 13/47; Wilberforce and Wilberforce, *Life of Wilberforce*, vol. 1, p. 351; Thomas Gisborne, *Remarks on Decision of the House of Commons on 2 April 1792 Respecting the Abolition of the Slave Trade* (London: J. Phillips, 1792), pp. 48–49.

14. Paul Edwards and David Dabydeen, *Black Writers in Britain, 1760–1890: An Anthology* (Edinburgh: Edinburgh University Press, 1991), pp. 99–100.

Chapter 11 Sierra Leone: The Promised Land

1. John Campbell Colquhoun, *William Wilberforce: His Friends and His Times* (London: Longmans, Green, Reader, and Dyer, 1866), p. 292.

2. Clarkson MS, BL, Add. MS 41,262A/76.

3. Clarkson MS, BL, Add. MS 41,262A/41.

4. Clarkson MS, BL, Add. MS 41,262A/145.

5. Keith Vincent Smith, "A Few Words from William Dawes and George Bass", *National Library of Australia News*, 18, no. 9 (2008), p. 7.

6. Clarkson MS, BL, Add. MS 41,262A/131, 184.

7. Anna Maria Falconbridge, *Two Voyages to Sierra Leone During the Years 1791–2–3 in a Series of Letters* (London: for the author, 1794), p. 148.

8. Clarkson MS, BL, Add. MS 41,262A/188, 161.

9. Clarkson MS, BL, Add. MS 41,262A, 173.

10. Wilson, *Clarkson*, p. 128.

11. Wilson, *Clarkson*, p. 131; BL Add. MS 41263/47.

12. Viscountess Knutsford, *Life and Letters of Zachary Macaulay* (London, Edward Arnold, 1900), p. 3.

Chapter 12 Coming to Clapham

1. Sir James Stephen, *Essays in Ecclesiastical Biography* (3rd ed., London: Longman, Brown, Green, & Longmans, 1853), p. 524; E. M. Forster, *Marianne Thornton: A Domestic Biography* (London: Edward Arnold, 1956), p. 18.

2. Hennell, *Venn,* p. 170.

3. Venn *Life and Letters,* p. 265.

4. J. W. Cunningham, *The Velvet Cushion* (London: G. Sidney for T. Cadell and W. Davies, 1814), pp. 161–62; Hennell, *Venn,* p. 43.

5. Cunningham, *Cushion,* p.165.

6. Venn, *Life and Letters,* p. 263.

7. Hennell, *Venn,* pp. 38–39.

8. Hennell, *Venn,* p. 41.

9. Venn, *Life and Letters,* p. 236.

10. Hennell, *Venn,* p. 44.

11. Hennell, *Venn,* p. 45.

12. Hennell, *Venn,* p. 62.

13. Hennell, *Venn,* p. 63–64.

14. Hennell, *Venn,* pp. 24, 77.

15. Hennell, *Venn,* pp. 77, 71, 82.

16. Venn, *Life and Letters,* p. 471.

17. This at least is what Henry Venn junior said Simeon told him: Hennell, *Venn,* p. 104.

18. Hennell, *Venn,* p. 106.

19. Henry Thornton, *An Enquiry into the Nature & Effects of the Paper Credit of Great Britain,* ed. F. A. Hayek (London: George Allen & Unwin, 1939), p. 24.

20. Acaster, *Thornton,* p. 233.

21. CUL, Add. MS 7674/1/N, 32.

22. Knutsford, *Macaulay,* p. 202; Hayek, *Enquiry,* p. 26.

23. Eugene Stock, *The History of the Church Missionary Society* (3 vols, London: CMS, 1899), vol. 1, p. 53.

24. Stock, *Church Missionary Society,* vol. 1, p. 55.

25. William Carus, *Memoir of the Rev. Charles Simeon* (Pittsburgh: 1847), p. 47.

26. Wilberforce and Wilberforce, *Life of Wilberforce,* vol. 2, pp. 26–27.

27. Wilberforce and Wilberforce, *Life of Wilberforce,* vol. 2, pp. 25, 27.

28. *Parliamentary History,* vol. 28, p. 61.

Chapter 13 Sierra Leone: New Management

1. Gibson Wilson, *Clarkson,* p. 115.

2. Simon Schama, *Rough Crossings: Britain, the Slaves and the American Revolution* (London: BBC, 2005), p. 363.

3. Clarkson MS, BL, Add. MS 41,262A/50.

4. Falconbridge, *Two Voyages*, p. 203.

5. Falconbridge, *Two Voyages*, p. 205.

6. Clarkson MS, BL, Add. MS 41263A/28.

7. Edwards and Dabydeen, *Black Writers*, p. 90.

8. Falconbridge, *Two Voyages,* pp. 222–23.

9. Clarkson MS, BL, Add. MS 41,262A/40.

10. Knutsford, *Macaulay,* pp. 43–44.

11. Falconbridge, *Two Voyages,* pp. 260–65.

Chapter 14 The Pen

1. Wilberforce and Wilberforce, *Life of Wilberforce*, vol. 2, p. 17.

2. Gisborne, *Moral Philosophy,* p. 453.

3. Wilberforce and Wilberforce, *Life of Wilberforce*, vol. 2, pp. 6, 67; Thornton MS 7674/1/N/26.

4. *Parliamentary History,* vol. 31, p.1027; R. G. Thorne, *The House of Commons 1790–1820* (5 vols, London: Secker & Warburg, 1986, vol), p. 560; Wilberforce and Wilberforce, *Life of Wilberforce*, vol. 2, p.72.

5. CUL, Add.Thornton MS 7674/1/N/26; Lascelles, *Sharp,* p. 144.

6. More, *Works,* vol. 2, pp. 287, 296, 336, 307.

7. More, *Works*, vol. 2, pp. 336–37.

8. More, *Works*, vol. 2, pp. 304, 339.

9. More, *Works*, vol. 2, pp. 221–22, 225, 227.

10. More, *Works*, vol. 2, p. 222.

11. More, *Works*, vol. 2, p. 408.

12. *Letters of Anna Seward written between the years 1784 and 1807* (6 vols, Edinburgh: George Ramsay and Company for Archibald Constable, 1811), vol. 5, p. 350.

13. Thomas Gisborne, *An Enquiry into the Duties of the Female Sex* (5th ed., London: A. Strahan for T. Cadell and W. Davies, 1801), p. 19.

14. Gisborne, *The Female Sex,* p. 22.

15. Gisborne, *The Female Sex,* p. 123.

16. Roberts, *Memoirs,* vol. 1, p. 424.

17. *Monthly Review* 22 (1797), p. 358.

18. Stott, *More,* p. 170.

19. More, *Works*, vol. 1, p. 193.

20. Jay, *Autobiography,* pp. 42–43, 379.

21. Roberts, *Memoirs*, vol. 3, pp. 5, 434; Stott, *More*, p. 174; Wilberforce and Wilberforce, *Life of Wilberforce*, vol. 5, p. 254.

Chapter 15 Sons and Lovers: Macaulay and Stephen

1. Knutsford, *Macaulay,* p. 56.

2. James Sidbury, *Becoming African in America: Race and Nation in the Early Black Atlantic* (Oxford: Oxford University Press, 2007).

3. Knutsford, *Macaulay,* pp. 65, 68.

4. James Walker, *Black Loyalists: The Search for a Promised Land in Nova Scotia and Sierra Leone 1783–1870* (Toronto: University of Toronto Press, 1992), p. 182; Knutsford, *Macaulay,* pp. 74, 77.

5. CUL, Add.Thornton MS 7674/1/R 49.

6. Sidbury, *Becoming African*, p. 111.

7. James Stephen, *The Memoirs of James Stephen,* ed. Merle M. Bevington (London: Hogarth Press, 1954), p. 52.

8. Stephen, *Memoirs,* pp. 153, 86.

9. Stephen, *Memoirs,* p. 305.

10. Knutsford, *Macaulay,* p. 100.

11. Knutsford, *Macaulay,* p. 101.

12. Stott, *More,* p. 195.

13. Knutsford, *Macaulay,* pp. 104, 107.

Chapter 16 Husbands and Wives

1. CUL, Add. MS 7674/1/P/25.

2. CUL, Add. MS 7674/1/N, 26.

3. Gisborne, *Moral Philosophy,* pp. 458–59.

4. CUL, Add. MS 7674/1/N, 49.

5. CUL, Add. MS 7674/1/N, 50.

6. *Ibid.*

7. CUL, Add. MS 7674/1/N, 53, 55; 7674/1/I/56.

8. CUL, Add. MS 7674/1/N, 58.

9. Knutsford, *Macaulay,* p. 179.

10. CUL, Add. MS 7674/1/N, 55, 59.

11. Wilberforce and Wilberforce, *Life of Wilberforce*, vol. 2, p. 225.

12. Wilberforce, *Correspondence*, vol. 1, pp. 131–32.

13. *British Critic*, 10 (1798), ii; *The Monthly Magazine*, 4 (1798), 118.

14. Furneaux, *Wilberforce,* pp. 162–63.

15. Furneaux, *Wilberforce,* p. 165.

16. Wilberforce and Wilberforce, *Life of Wilberforce*, vol. 2, p. 257.

17. Wilberforce and Wilberforce, *Life of Wilberforce*, vol. 2, pp. 256, 255.

18. Wilberforce and Wilberforce, *Life of Wilberforce*, vol. 2, pp. 238, 227.

19. Wilberforce and Wilberforce, *Life of Wilberforce*, vol. 2, pp. 260, 265.

20. Wilberforce and Wilberforce, *Life of Wilberforce*, vol. 2, pp. 265–66.

Chapter 17 Sierra Leone and Ireland

1. Knutsford, *Macaulay,* p. 154.

2. Knutsford, *Macaulay,* pp. 117, 122, 125.

3. Knutsford, *Macaulay,* pp. 134, 139.

4. Knutsford, *Macaulay,* pp. 141, 148.

5. Knutsford, *Macaulay,* pp. 157, 158.

6. Knutsford, *Macaulay,* pp.179, 203.

7. Knutsford, *Macaulay,* pp. 219–20.

8. Knutsford, *Macaulay,* p. 224.

9. Knutsford, *Macaulay,* p. 230.

Chapter 18 Church Missionary Society

1. Venn, *Life and Letters*, p. 530.
2. Hennell, *Venn*, pp. 116, 119.
3. Hennell, *Venn*, pp. 144–45.
4. Hennell, *Venn*, p. 149.
5. Stock, *Church Missionary Society*, p. 64.
6. Stock, *Church Missionary Society*, pp. 82–83.
7. *The Gentleman's Magazine*, 80 (October 1810), p. 387.
8. Edwards and Dabydeen, *Black Writers*, p. 97.
9. Wilberforce and Wilberforce, *Life of Wilberforce*, vol. 2, p. 367.
10. Leslie Stephen, *The Life of Sir James Fitzjames Stephen* (London: Smith Elder, 1895), pp. 17–18.
11. Wilberforce and Wilberforce, *Life of Wilberforce*, vol. 3, pp. 30–31.
12. James Stephen, *The Crisis of the Sugar Colonies* (London: J. Hatchard, 1802), pp. 87, 122.
13. *Monthly Mirror*, 7 (1799), p. 348; *Monthly Review*, 30 (1799), p. 411; Stott, *More*, p. 226.
14. *Anti-Jacobin*, 9 (1801), pp. 390, 394.
15. Wilberforce, *Correspondence*, vol. 2, p. 185; *Anti-Jacobin* (1808), p. 429.
16. Wilberforce and Wilberforce, *Life of Wilberforce*, vol. 2, p. 308.
17. *Christian Observer* (1805), p. 762; *Edinburgh Review* (1808), 12, no. 23, p. 181.
18. Hayek, *Enquiry*, p. 36.

Chapter 19 Vice

1. Conybeare, *Rothley Temple*, p. 13.
2. Forster, *Thornton*, p. 46.
3. Stephen, *Sugar Colonies*, p. 157.
4. Francis Place, *The Autobiography of Francis Place*, ed. Mary Thrale (Cambridge: Cambridge University Press, 1972), p. 170.
5. *Anti-Jacobin*, 2 (1799), p. 87.
6. For a start, the sardonic style is totally unlike anything Thornton could produce. Moreover the same writer, who called himself S. P., published prayers in the *Christian Observer* which later appeared in Jay's *Prayers for the Use of Families*, rather than in Thornton's *Family Prayers*. See, for example, *Prayers for the Use of Families*, p. 303, and *Christian Observer* (1804), p. 275.
7. Ben Wilson, *Decency and Disorder: The Age of Cant 1789–1837* (London: Faber & Faber, 2007), pp. 116–17.
8. Roberts, *Making English Morals*, p. 87.
9. *Christian Observer*, 2 (1803), pp. 305, 304; 4 (1805), p. 158.
10. CUL, Add. MS 7674/1/N/27.
11. Wilberforce and Wilberforce, *Life of Wilberforce*, vol. 3, p. 88.
12. John Owen, *The History of the Origin and First Ten Years of the British and Foreign Bible Society* (3 vols, New York: 1819), pp. 82n, 335; *Anti-Jacobin* (1814), 46, p. 27.
13. Wilberforce and Wilberforce, *Life of Wilberforce*, vol. 3, pp. 214–15.
14. Wilberforce and Wilberforce, *Life of Wilberforce*, vol. 3, p. 234 n.
15. George Stephen, *Anti-Slavery Recollections in a Series of Letters Addressed to Mrs Beecher Stowe* (London: Thomas Hatchard, 1854), p. 30.

16. Wilberforce and Wilberforce, *Life of Wilberforce*, p. 267.
17. *Parliamentary Debates*, vol. 9, p. 138.

Chapter 20 Slaves of the Abolitionists

1. CUL, Add. MS 7674/1/N, 33–4.
2. *Rules and Regulations of the African Institution* (London: John Hatchard, 1807), pp. 66–67.
3. Leonard G. Johnson, *General T. Perronet Thompson 1783–1869: His Military, Literary and Political Campaigns* (London: George Allen & Unwin, 1957), p. 26.
4. Johnson, *Thompson*, p. 40.
5. Johnson, *Thompson*, p. 34.
6. National Archives, Kew, CO 267/24 (*Sierra Leone Gazette*, 1 August 1808).
7. Johnson, *Thompson*, p. 40; CO 267/24 (8 August 1808).
8. Johnson, *Thompson*, p. 41.
9. CO 267/24 (8 August 1808).
10. CO 267/24 (2 November 1808).
11. CO 267/24 (20 October 1808).
12. Johnson, *Thompson*, p. 51.
13. Wilberforce and Wilberforce, *Life of Wilberforce*, vol. 2, p. 350.
14. Forster, *Thornton*, p. 34.
15. *Parliamentary Debates,* vol. 14, p. 292.
16. Stephen, *Fitzjames Stephen*, p. 22.
17. Wilberforce and Wilberforce, *Life of Wilberforce*, vol. 3, p. 487.

Chapter 21 East and West Indies

1. S. Pearce Carey, *William Carey* (rev. ed., London: Carey Press, 1934), p. 36.
2. Furneaux, *Wilberforce*, p. 323; *Christian Observer*, 12 (1813), p. 127; Wilberforce and Wilberforce, *Life of Wilberforce*, vol. 4, p. 126.
3. Stock, *Church Misisonary Society*, vol. 1, p. 104.
4. Colquhoun, *Wilberforce,* p. 327; Wilberforce and Wilberforce, *Life of Wilberforce*, vol. 4, p. 187.
5. Acaster, *Thornton*, p. 243; Forster, *Thornton*, p. 67; Knutsford, *Macaulay*, p. 320.
6. Wilberforce and Wilberforce, *Life of Wilberforce*, p. 300.
7. Edward Roberts (ed.), *Letters of Hannah More to Zachary Macaulay, Esq: Containing Notices of Lord Macaulay's Youth* (New York: R. Carter and Bro., 1860), p. 73.
8. Robert Thorpe, *A Letter to William Wilberforce: ... Containing Remarks on the Reports of the Sierra Leone Company, and African Institution* (London: F., C., & J. Rivington, 1815), p. 47.
9. African Institution, *A Review of the Colonial Slave Registration Acts* (London: Hatchard and Son, 1820), p. 121.
10. *British Critic*, 4 (1815), pp. 582–83.
11. Wilberforce and Wilberforce, *Life of Wilberforce*, vol. 4, p. 307; *The Reformists' Register*, 1, no. 11 (1817), p. 326.

Chapter 22 Anti-Slavery

1. Stephen, *Anti-Slavery Recollections*, pp. 21–22.
2. Charles Buxton, *Memoirs of Sir Thomas Fowell Buxton* (5th ed., London: John Murray, 1866), p. 126.

3. Stephen, *Anti-Slavery Recollections*, p. 51.

4. *Parliamentary Debates* (New Series), vol. 6, p. 1426.

5. Wilberforce and Wilberforce, *Life of Wilberforce*, vol. 5, p 160.

6. Stephen, *Anti-Slavery Recollections,* p. 76.

7. *Parliamentary Debates* (New Series), vol. 9, pp. 265–66, 273.

8. *Parliamentary Debates* (New Series), vol. 11, p. 1037.

9. Buxton, *Buxton*, p. 152.

10. *Parliamentary Debates* (New Series), vol. 10, p. 1114.

11. *Report of the Committee of the Society for the Mitigation and Gradual Abolition of Slavery Throughout the British Dominions* (London: for the Society, 1824); Forster, *Thornton*, p. 129.

12. G. O. Trevelyan, *The Life and Letters of Lord Macaulay* (2nd ed., London: Longmans, 1876).

13. Trevelyan, *Macaulay*; *Christian Observer* (1839), p. 806.

14. Henry Taylor, *The Autobiography of Henry Taylor, 1800–1875* (London: Longmans, Green, & Co., 1885), p. 304.

15. *Parliamentary Debates* (New Series), 14, pp. 969–71.

16. Knutsford, *Macaulay*, p. 404.

17. Knutsford, *Macaulay*, p. 439.

Chapter 23 Deliverance to the Captives

1. *Parliamentary Debates* (New Series), vol. 18, p. 979.

2. Stephen, *Anti-Slavery Recollections*, pp. 105, 107.

3. *Anti-Slavery Reporter*, 3 (1829), p. 101; Stephen, *Anti-Slavery Recollections*, p. 53.

4. Stephen, *Anti-Slavery Recollections*, p. 121.

5. *Parliamentary Debates,* vol. 3 (1831), p. 1414.

6. Knutsford, *Macaulay*, p. 461.

7. *Anti-Slavery Reporter* (1833), 5, p. 248.

8. Buxton, *Buxton*, p. 309.

9. *Anti-Slavery Reporter* (1833), 5, p. 145.

10. Buxton, *Buxton*, p. 302.

11. Buxton, *Buxton*, p. 306.

12. Stephen, *Anti-Slavery Recollections*, pp. 167–68; *Anti-Slavery Reporter* (1833), 5, p. 264.

13. Buxton, *Buxton*, p. 320.

14. Buxton, *Buxton*, p. 346.

Chapter 24 Sons and Daughters (pp. 247–251)

1. Wilberforce and Wilberforce, *Life of Wilberforce*, vol. 4, p. 125.

2. Stephen, *Fitzjames Stephen*, p. 61.

Select Bibliography

Manuscripts

Babington MSS, Trinity College Library, Cambridge.

Clarkson MSS, British Library, Add. MSS 41,262A–C.

Colonial Office, National Archives, Kew, CO 267/24.

Thornton MSS, Cambridge University Library, Add. MS 7674.

Wilberforce MSS, Bodleian College, Oxford.

Acaster, E. J. T., "Henry Thornton – The Banker", in Blaug, Mark (ed.), *Henry Thornton (1760–1815), Jeremy Bentham (1748–1832), James Lauderdale (1759–1839), Simonde de Sismondi (1773–1842)* (Cambridge: Cambridge University Press, 1991), pp. 46–61.

Ackerson, Wayne, *The African Institution (1807–1827) and the Antislavery Movement in Great Britain* (Lewiston, NY, and Lampeter: Edwin Mellen Press, 2005).

African Institution, *Rules and Regulations of the African Institution* (London: John Hatchard, 1807).

——, *Second Report of the Committee* (London: 1808).

——, *Third Report of the Committee* (London: 1809).

——, *Fourth Report of the Committee* (London: 1810).

——, *Sixth Report of the Directors* (London: 1812).

——, *Seventh Report of the Directors* (London: 1813).

——, *Eighth Report of the Directors* (London: 1814).

——, *Ninth Report of the Directors* (London: 1815).

——, *Special Report of the Directors… Respecting the Allegations Contained in a Pamphlet Entitled* A Letter to William Wilberforce, Esq. *&c. by R. Thorpe, Esq.* (London: 1815).

——, *A Review of the Colonial Slave Registration Acts* (London: Hatchard and Son, 1820).

——, *Foreign Slave Trade* (London: 1821) .

Anon., *A Letter to the Members of the Society for the Suppression of Vice.* (London, 1805).

Anon., *An Account of the Rise, Progress and Present State of the Society for the Discharge and Relief of Persons Imprisoned for Small Debts* (6th ed., London: 1783).

Anstey, Roger, *The Atlantic Slave Trade and British Abolition 1760–1810* (London: Macmillan, 1975).

Babington, Thomas, *A Practical View of Christian Education in its Early Stages* (Boston: Cummings and Hilliard, 1819).

Bebbington, David W., *The Dominance of Evangelicalism: The Age of Spurgeon and Moody* (Leicester: IVP, 2005).

Blaug, Mark (ed.), *Henry Thornton (1760–1815), Jeremy Bentham (1748–1832), James*

Lauderdale (1759–1839), Simonde de Sismondi (1773–1842) (Cambridge: Cambridge University Press, 1991).

Blodgett, Harold, *Samson Occom* (Hanover, NH: Dartmouth College Publications, 1935).

Bradley, Ian, *The Call to Seriousness: The Evangelical Impact on the Victorians* (Oxford: Lion, 2006).

Bristow, E., *Vice and Vigilance: Purity Movements in Britain Since 1700* (Dublin: Gill and Macmillan, 1977).

Brown, Ford K., *Fathers of the Victorians* (2nd ed., Cambridge: Cambridge University Press, 1961).

Bull, Josiah, *Memorials of the Rev. William Bull of Newport Pagnell* (2nd ed., London: James Nisbet, 1865).

Bull, Josiah, *John Newton of Olney and St Mary Woolnoth* (London: Religious Tract Society, 1868).

Buxton, Charles, *Memoirs of Sir Thomas Fowell Buxton* (5th ed., London: John Murray, 1866).

Carus, William, *Memoir of the Rev. Charles Simeon* (Pittsburgh: 1847).

Cecil, Richard (ed.), *The Works of the Rev. John Newton ...: to Which are Prefixed Memoirs of His Life* (London: 1853).

Clapham Antiquarian Society, *Clapham and the Clapham Sect* (London: Clapham Antiquarian Society, 1927).

Clarkson, Thomas, *The History of the Rise, Progress and Accomplishment of the Abolition of the Slave Trade by the British Parliament* (2 vols, London: Longman, Hurst, Rees, and Orme, 1808).

Colquhoun, John Campbell, *William Wilberforce: His Friends and His Times* (London: Longmans, Green, Reader, and Dyer, 1866).

Colquhoun, Patrick, *A Treatise on the Police of the Metropolis* (7th ed., London: Bye and Law for J. Mawman, 1806).

Conybeare, Eliza (ed. Brian Verity and Terry Sheppard), *Rothley Temple in the Olden Time: Phases of English Life* (Rothley: Rothley History Society, 2005).

Cowper, William (ed. Robert Southey), *The Works of William Cowper* (15 vols, London: Baldwin and Cradock, 1837).

Cunningham, J. W., *The Velvet Cushion* (London: T. Cadell and W. Davies, 1814).

Debate on a Motion for the Abolition of the Slave Trade in the House of Commons on Monday the Second of April, 1792 (London: W. Woodfall, 1792).

Edwards, Paul, and Dabydeen, David, *Black Writers in Britain, 1760–1890: An Anthology* (Edinburgh: Edinburgh University Press, 1991).

Elliot-Binns, L. E., *The Early Evangelicals* (London: Lutterworth Press, 1953).

Embrie, Ainslie Thomas, *Charles Grant and British Rule in India* (London: George Allen and Unwin, 1962).

Falconbridge, Anna Maria, *Two Voyages to Sierra Leone During the Years 1791–2–3 in a Series of Letters* (London: for the author, 1794).

Forster, E. M., *Marianne Thornton: A Domestic Biography* (London: Edward Arnold, 1956).

Furneaux, Robin Smith, *William Wilberforce* (London: Hamilton, 1974).

Fyfe, Christopher, *A History of Sierra Leone* (Oxford: Oxford University Press, 1968).

George, Claude, *The Rise of British West Africa* (London: Frank Cass, 1968).

Gisborne, Thomas, *The Principles of Moral Philosophy Investigated and Applied to Civil Society* (2nd ed., London: B. White and Son, 1790).

——, *Remarks on the Late Decision of the House of Commons Respecting the Slave Trade* (London: J. Phillips, 1792).

——, *A Familiar Survey of the Christian Religion* (3rd ed., London: for T. Cadell and W. Davies, 1801).

——, *An Enquiry into the Duties of the Female Sex* (5th ed., London: T. Cadell and W. Davies, 1801).

——, *Poems, Sacred and Moral* (3rd ed., London: for T. Cadell and W. Davies, 1803).

——, *Walks in a Forest* 3 (8th ed., London: T. Cadell and W. Davies, 1813).

——, *An Enquiry into the Duties of Men in the Higher and Middle Classes of Society in Great Britain* (7th ed., 2 vols, London: for T. Cadell, 1824).

——, *Considerations on Modern Theories of Geology* (London: T. Cadell, 1838).

Grover, John W., *Old Clapham* (London: A. Bachhoffner, 1887).

Hague, William, *William Pitt the Younger* (London: HarperCollins, 2004).

Hanway, Jonas, *A Comprehensive View of Sunday Schools* (London: Dodsley and Sewel, 1786).

Harford, John S., *Recollections of William Wilberforce During Nearly Thirty Years: With Brief Notices of Some of His Personal Friends and Contemporaries* (London: Longman, Green, Longman, Roberts, and Green, 1864).

Hennell, Michael, *John Venn and the Clapham Sect* (London: Lutterworth Press, 1958).

Hindmarsh, Bruce, *John Newton and the English Evangelical Tradition between the Conversions of Wesley and Wilberforce* (Oxford: Clarendon, 1996).

Hoare, Prince, *Memoirs of Granville Sharp* (2 vols, London: Henry Colburn, 1820).

Hochschild, Adam, *Bury the Chains* (Macmillan: London, 2005).

Hodgson, Robert, *The Life of the Right Reverend Beilby Porteus, Late Bishop of London* (2nd ed., London: Luke Hansard for T. Cadell and W. Davies, 1811).

Houghton, Walter E., *The Victorian Frame of Mind* (New Haven: Yale University Press, 1957).

Howse, Ernest Marshall, *Saints in Politics: The "Clapham Sect" and the Growth of Freedom* (London: George Allen & Unwin, 1953).

Hunter, William, *Plain Thoughts and Friendly Hints on the Sabbath* (2nd ed., London: J. Debrett, 1791).

Jackson, Gordon, *Hull in the Eighteenth Century: A Study in Economic and Social History* (London and New York: Oxford University Press, 1972).

Jackson, Thomas, *Lives of the Early Methodist Preachers* (4th ed., 6 vols, London: Wesleyan Conference Office, 1871–79).

Jay, William (ed. G. B. Redford and J. A. James), *The Autobiography of William Jay* (London: Hamilton Adams, 1854).

Johnson, Leonard G., *General T, Perronet Thompson 1783–1869: His Military, Literary and Political Campaigns* (London: George Allen and Unwin, 1957).

Keneally, Tom, *The Commonwealth of Thieves: The Story of the Founding of Australia* (London: Chatto and Windus, 2006).

Kipling, Thomas, *The Articles of the Church of England Proved Not to Be Calvinistic* (2nd ed., Cambridge: Cambridge University Press 1802).

Klein, Milton M., *An Amazing Grace: John Thornton and the Clapham Sect* (New Orleans: University Press of the South, 2004).

Knutsford, Viscountess (M. J. Holland), *Life and Letters of Zachary Macaulay* (London: Edward Arnold, 1900).

Kraphol, Robert H., and Lippy, Charles H., *The Evangelicals: A Historical, Thematic and Biographical Guide* (Connecticut: Greenwood Press, 1999).

Lambert, Sheila (ed.), *House of Commons Sessional Papers of the Eighteenth Century* (2 vols, Wilmington: Del.E: Scholarly Resources, 1975).

Laqueur, Thomas Walter, *Religion and Respectability: Sunday Schools and Working Class Culture 1780–1850* (New Haven and London: Yale University Press, 1976).

Lascelles, E. C. P., *Granville Sharp and the Freedom of the Slaves in England* (Oxford: Oxford University Press, 1928).

Lewis, Donald M. (ed.), *The Blackwell Dictionary of Evangelical Biography 1730–1860* (Oxford: Blackwell, 1995).

Macaulay, Zachary, *East and West India Sugar* (London: Lupton Relfe, 1823).

——, *Negro Slavery* (London: for Hatchard and Son, 1823).

——, *A Letter to His Royal Highness the Duke of Gloucester: President of the African Institution* (London: Ellerton and Henderson for John Hatchard, 1815).

Martin, Bernard, *John Newton: A Biography* (London: Heinemann, 1950).

Mathieson, William Law, *British Slavery & its Abolition 1823–1838* (London: Longmans and Green, 1926).

Meacham, Standish, *Henry Thornton of Clapham 1760–1815* (Cambridge, Mass.: Harvard University Press, 1964).

More, Hannah (ed. Hartford), *The Works of Hannah More* (London: H. Fisher, R. Fisher, and P. Jackson, 1834).

More, Martha (ed. Arthur Roberts), *Mendip Annals: Or a Narrative of the Charitable Labours of Hannah and More in their Neighbourhood* (London: 1865)

Morris, Henry, *Charles Grant: Director of the East India Company and Member of Parliament* (Madras: The Christian Literature Society, 1905).

Newton, John, *Cardiphonia, or, The Utterance of the Heart* (2 vols, London: for J. Buckland and J. Johnson, 1781).

——, *Thoughts on the African Slave Trade* (London: for J. Buckland and J. Johnson, 1788).

—— (ed. John Campbell), *Letters and Conversational Remarks by the Late Rev. John Newton* (London: 1811).

——, *One Hundred and Twenty Nine Letters ... to the Rev. William Bull of Newport Pagnell* (London: Hamilton Adams, 1847).

—— (ed. Josiah Bull), *Letters by the Rev. John Newton* (London: 1869).

Noll, Mark A. *The Rise of Evangelicalism* (Leicester: IVP, 2004).

Owen, John, *The History of the Origin and First Ten Years of the British and Foreign Bible Society* (3 vols, New York: 1819).

Parliamentary Debates from the Year 1803 to the Present Time (London: T. C. Hansard, 1819).

Parliamentary Debates (New Series) (London: T. C. Hansard).

Parliamentary History of England, from the Earliest Period to 1803 (London: T. C. Hansard, 1814).

Place, Francis (ed. Mary Thrale),*The Autobiography of Francis Place* (Cambridge: Cambridge University Press, 1972).

Pym, Dorothy, *Battersea Rise* (London: Jonathan Cape, 1934).

Quinlan, Maurice James,*Victorian Prelude: A History of English Manners 1700–1830* (London: Frank Cass, 1965).

Reimer, Bill, "The Spirituality of Henry Venn", *Churchman*, 114, no. 4 (2000).

Richardson, Leon Burr, *History of Dartmouth College* (2 vols, Hanover, NH: Dartmouth College Publications, 1932).

Roberts, Edward (ed.), *Letters of Hannah More to Zachary Macaulay, Esq: Containing Notices of Lord Macaulay's Youth* (New York: R. Carter and Bro., 1860).

Roberts, M. J. D., "The Vice Society and its Early Critics, 1802–1812", *The Historical Journal*, 26 (1983), pp. 159–76.

Roberts, M. J. D., *Making English Morals: Voluntary Association and Moral Reform in England, 1787–1886* (Cambridge: Cambridge University Press, 2004).

Roberts, William, *Memoirs of the Life and Correspondence of Mrs Hannah More* (4 vols, London: R. B. Seeley and W. Burnside, 1834).

Schama, Simon, *Rough Crossings: Britain, the Slaves and the American Revolution* (London: BBC, 2005).

Scott, John, *The Life of the Rev. Thomas Scott* (London: RL. B. Seeley, 1822).

Scott, Thomas, *The Force of Truth: An Authentic Narrative* (London: for G. Keith and J. Johnson, 1779).

Scott, Thomas, *A Discourse... Occasioned by the Death of John Thornton* (London: J. Johnson, 1791).

Seeley, Mary, *The Later Evangelical Fathers* (London: 1879).

Seymour, A. C. H.,*The Life and Times of Selina, Countess of Huntingdon* (2 vols, London: Seeley, Jackson, and Halliday, 1840).

Sharp, Granville (ed. J. I. Burn), *An Account of the Constitutional English Policy of Congregational Courts: And More Particularly of the Great Annual Court of the People, Called The View of Frankpledge; with Two Tracts on Colonization* (rev. ed., London: J. W. Parker, 1841).

Sidbury, James, *Becoming African in America: Race and Nation in the Early Black Atlantic* (Oxford: Oxford University Press, 2007).

Sierra Leone Company, *Substance of the Report Delivered by the Court of Directors of the Sierra Leone Company to the General Court of Proprietors on Thursday the 27th March 1794* (London: John Phillips, 1794).

Smith, Eric E. F., *Clapham Saints and Sinners* (Clapham: Clapham Press, 1987).

Smith, Sydney, *The Works of the Rev. Sydney Smith* (New York: 1862).

Society for Bettering the Condition and Increasing the Comforts of the Poor, *The Reports of the Society* (4 vols., 1798–1805).

Stephen, George, *Anti-Slavery Recollections in a Series of Letters Addressed to Mrs Beecher Stowe* (London: Thomas Hatchard,1854).

Stephen, James, *The Crisis of the Sugar Colonies* (London: J. Hatchard, 1802).

——, *War in Disguise: or the Frauds of the Neutral Flags* (3rd ed., London: J. Hatchard and J. Butterworth, 1806).

——, *Reasons for Establishing a Registry of Slaves* (London: Ellerton and Henderson, 1815).

——, *An Inquiry into the Right and Duty of Compelling Spain to Relinquish Her Slave Trade in Northern Africa* (London: J. Butterworth & Son, and J. Hatchard, 1816).

——, *Slavery of the British West India Colonies Delineated* (2 vols, London: J. Butterworth & Son, 1824–30).

——, *England Enslaved by Her Own Slave Colonies* (London: Hatchard and Son, J. & A. Arch, 1826).

—— (ed. Merle Bevington), *The Memoirs of James Stephen* (London: Hogarth Press, 1954).

Stephen, Sir James, *Essays in Ecclesiastical Biography* (3rd ed., London: Longman, Brown, Green, and Longmans, 1853).

Stephen, Leslie, *The Life of Sir James Fitzjames Stephen* (London: Smith Elder, 1895).

Stock, Eugene, *The History of the Church Missionary Society* (3 vols, London: CMS, 1899).

Stott, Anne, *Hannah More: The First Victorian* (Oxford: Oxford University Press, 2003).

Stoughton, John, *William Wilberforce* (London: Hodder and Stoughton, 1880).

Teignmouth, Baron, *Memoir of the Life and Correspondence of John Lord Teignmouth* (2 vols, London: Hatchard & Son, 1843).

Telford, John A., *Sect that Moved the World: Three Generations of Clapham Saints and Philanthropists* (London: Charles H. Kelly, 1907).

Thatcher, Benjamin Bussey, *Memoir of Phillis Wheatley: A Native African and a Slave* (Boston: 1834).

Thompson, E. P., *The Making of the English Working Class* (London: Pelican, 1968).

Thorne, R. G., *The House of Commons 1790–1820* (5 vols, London: Secker and Warburg, 1986).

Thornton, Henry, *An Enquiry into the Nature and Effects of the Paper Credit of Great Britain* (London: J. Hatchard and F. & C. Rivington, 1802).

—— (ed. Robert Inglis), *Family Prayers* (New York: 1837).

—— (ed. Hayek, F. A.), *An Enquiry into the Nature & Effects of the Paper Credit of Great Britain* (London: George Allen and Unwin, 1939).

Thorpe, Robert, *A Letter to William Wilberforce... Containing Remarks on the Reports of the Sierra Leone Company, and African Institution* (London: F., C., & J. Rivington, 1815).

Tolley, Christopher, *Domestic Biography: The Legacy of Evangelicalism in Four Nineteenth-Century Families* (Oxford: Clarendon Press, 1977).

Trevelyan, G. O., *The Life and Letters of Lord Macaulay* (2nd ed., London: Longmans, 1876).

Turner, Steve, *Amazing Grace: John Newton, Slavery and the World's Most Enduring Song* (Lion: Oxford, 2002).

Trimmer, Sarah, *The Oeconomy of Charity* (London: T. Longman, 1787).

Tyerman, Luke, *The Life of the Rev. George Whitefield* (2 vols, London: Hodder and Stoughton, 1876–77).

Venn, Henry, *The Conversion of Sinners the Greatest Charity* (London: for S. Crowder, E. & C. Dilly, and J. Matthews, 1779).

——, *Fourteen Sermons* (London: J. Townsend, E. Dilly, and T. Field, 1759).

——, *Mistakes in Religion Exposed: An essay on the prophecy of Zacharias* (New York: Williams and Whiting, 1810).

——, *The Complete Duty of Man: or, A System of Doctrinal and Practical Christianity* (New Brunswick: 1811).

——, *Mira; or, a Memoir of Mrs Venn* (London: Religious Tract Society, 1850).

Venn, John, *The Life and a Selection from the Letters of the Late Rev. Henry Venn* (4th ed., London: John Hatchard, 1836).

Venn, John, *Annals of a Clerical Family* (London: Macmillan, 1904).

Walker, James W. St. G., *Black Loyalists: The Search for a Promised Land in Nova Scotia and Sierra Leone 1783–1870* (Toronto: University of Toronto Press, 1992).

Walpole, Horace (ed. Peter Cunningham), *The Letters of Horace Walpole: Earl of Orford... Now First Chronologically Arranged* (8 vols, London: Richard Bentley, 1857).

Walvin, James, *Black Ivory: A History of British Slavery* (London: Fontana, 1993).

Walvin, James, *The Trader, the Owner, the Slave* (London: Jonathan Cape, 2007).

Warner, Oliver, *William Wilberforce* (London: Batsford, 1962).

Wesley, John, *Thoughts Upon Slavery* (London: R. Hawes, 1774).

Wheatley, Phillis (ed. John C. Shields), *The Collected Works* (Oxford: Oxford University Press, 1988).

Whitaker, Nathaniel, *A Brief Narrative of the Indian Charity School, in Lebanon* (2nd ed., London: J. & W. Oliver, 1767).

Whittingham, Richard (ed.), *The Works of the Rev. John Berridge... with an Enlarged Memoir of His Life* (London: Simpkin and Marshall, 1838).

Wilberforce, Anna Maria (ed.), *Private Papers of William Wilberforce* (London: T. Fisher Unwin, 1897).

Wilberforce, Robert Isaac, and Wilberforce, Samuel, *The Life of William Wilberforce* (5 vols, London: John Murray, 1838).

Wilberforce, Robert Isaac, and Wilberforce, Samuel, *The Correspondence of William Wilberforce* (2 vols, London: John Murray, 1840).

Wilberforce, William, *The Abolition of the Slave Trade; Addressed to the Freeholders and Other Inhabitants of Yorkshire* (London: T. Cadell and W. Davies, 1807).

——, *A Practical View of the Prevailing Religious System of Professed Christians, in the Higher and Middle Classes in this Country, Contrasted with Real Christainity* (London: 1811).

——, *An Appeal to the Religion, Justice, and Humanity of the Inhabitants of the British Empire, in Behalf of the Negro Slaves in the West Indies* (London: J. Hatchard & Son, 1823).

Wilson, Ben, *Decency and Disorder: The Age of Cant 1789–1837* (London: Faber and Faber, 2007).

Wilson, Ellen Gibson, *The Loyal Blacks* (London: Capricorn, 1976).

Wilson, Ellen Gibson, *John Clarkson and the African Adventure* (London: Macmillan, 1980).

Wolffe, John, *The Expansion of Evangelicalism* (Leicester: IVP, 2006).

Index

Printed and bound by CPI Group (UK) Ltd, Croydon, CR0 4YY

13/04/2025

14656471-0001